In the Patient's Best Interest

In the Patient's Best Interest

Women and the Politics of Medical Decisions

Sue Fisher

Rutgers University Press New Brunswick, New Jersey

Acknowledgment is made herewith for permission to reprint several
portions of this book, which have previously appeared in edited collections
or journals.

Sue Fisher, Chapter 4 is an expanded version of "Doctor-Patient
Communication: A Social and Micro-Political Performance," in *Sociology
of Health and Illness*, 6 (March 1984):1, 1–29; Chapter 3 is an expanded
version of "Institutional Authority and the Structure of Discourse,"
Discourse Processes, 7 (April–June 1984):2, 201–224; Chapter 2 is an
expanded version of "The Decision-Making Context: How Doctors and
Patients Communicate," *Linguistics and the Professions*, ed. Robert
DiPietro (Norwood, New Jersey: Ablex, 1982); and "The Negotiation of
Treatment Decisions in Doctor-Patient Communication" in *The Social
Organization of Doctor-Patient Communication*, ed. Sue Fisher and
Alexandra Dundas Todd, (Washington, D.C.: Center for Applied
Linguistics, 1983; Sue Fisher and Alexandra Dundas Todd; parts of Chapter
5 and the Appendix are drawn from "Communication and Social Context—
Toward Broader Definitions" in *The Social Organization of Doctor-Patient
Communication*, (Washington, D.C.: Center for Applied Linguistics, 1983);
and "Communication in Institutional Contexts: Social Interaction and
Social Structure," in *Discourse and Institutional Authority: Medicine,
Education and Law*, ed. Sue Fisher and Alexandra Dundas Todd,
(Norwood, New Jersey: Ablex, forthcoming). The illustration from the
cover of E. R. Novak's *Textbook of Gynecology*, 8th edition (Baltimore,
MD: Williams and Wilkins Co., 1970) is reproduced with permission
of the publisher. And the reprint of the painting by Masaccio, "Expulsion
of Adam and Eve," is reproduced with the permission of Harper & Row
Publishers.

Library of Congress Cataloging-in-Publication Data

Fisher, Sue, 1936–
    In the patient's best interest.

    Bibliography: p.
    Includes index.
        1. Gynecology—Decision making.   2. Gynecology,
Operative—Decision making.   3. Physician and patient.
I. Title.   [DNLM: 1. Decision Making.   2. Physician–
Patient Relations.   3. Women—psychology.   W 62 F536i]
RG103.7.F57   1986   362.1'98   85–30253
ISBN 0—8135–1162–3

*This book is dedicated to all
searchers in the hope that we can help each
other find a better way.*

Contents

Figures, Tables, and Illustrations

Acknowledgments

No piece of scholarly work is written in isolation and this book is no exception. Unlike research done by a solitary scholar alone in the library, at a computer terminal or a typewriter, this book is based on field work and owes a debt of gratitude to the patients and physicians who granted me permission to study their interactions. To preserve their confidentiality they shall go unnamed here; in the text, pseudonyms are used for medical institutions, physicians, and patients.

Data, while essential, is only a beginning. The intellectual heritage I brought to the project grew from my academic training and feminist commitment. As a graduate student I was introduced to medical sociology, qualitative methods, ethnomethodology, and feminism. I am indebted to many who gave support along the way: Aaron V. Cicourel, Fred Davis, Bud Mehan, Seymour Radin, Charles Lemert, Don Ploch, Irv Zola, Steve Groce, Diana Scully, Pauline Bart, Jane Prather, Pat Huckle, Bonnie Zimmerman, Joyce Oviatt, Carolyn Patton, Lynn Miller, Peggy Myers, Donna Greenberg, Bob Fisher, my sons, Mike, Jeff, and Bob Warner, and my feminist foremothers. From my earliest academic days, Bud Mehan has been a mentor and much more. From him I learned the importance of a community of scholars who were friends as well as colleagues—a community I continue to share with Alexandra Todd, Donna Eder, and my feminist study group.

The faculty and staff of Wesleyan University deserve a special thanks. Their support made the final stages of the work on the manuscript much easier than it would otherwise have been. Without the help of Irene Spinnler and Nora Molter I might still be trying to get the book ready for publication.

One of the marks of an exceptional editor is the ability to recognize potential and nurture its development. From the time this book was just taking form as an idea to the time of its completion, Marlie Wasserman has done just this. Thank you all.

1 / Whisper, Whisper, Whisper

The Scope of the Analysis

Recently, I had a routine pelvic examination and Pap smear during which a nurse-practitioner found an ovarian mass. I had been doing research on the delivery of health care to women for six years prior to this time and thought I was prepared to deal with the ways I had seen medicine practiced. I knew I would be referred to a physician who would most probably be male. I knew the medical task would be to rule out the possibility of invasive cancer. I knew what tests would be performed for diagnosis and the likelihood of surgery for treatment. My research suggested that when women are past their reproductive prime of life, as I am, the recommended surgery usually includes the removal of both the uterus and the ovaries—a total hysterectomy. Once having served their primary reproductive function, these organs are seen as potentially disease-producing and unnecessary. Therefore, even if cancer is not found, a total hysterectomy is performed as a prophylactic procedure. Finally, I knew that many, if not most, medical practitioners feel that women can be "maintained" on exogenous estrogens as well as, if not better than, they are on the estrogen their bodies produce naturally.

I was also familiar with the critique of these fairly standard beliefs and the medical practices that flow from them. I knew that if the ovarian mass was not cancerous, I neither wanted nor needed a total hysterectomy. Without cancer, I was at no greater risk of developing it than any other woman in the general population. I knew that if it was not medically necessary to remove my uterus and ovaries, I did not want healthy organs surgically removed. I knew that if I did not have a total hysterectomy, I had a greater chance of going through a natural menopause and I decreased my chances of needing to be medically "managed" with estrogen replacement therapy.

1

Feeling trepidation about the mass, but armed with information and confident about my choices, I started the medical process. As a new person in the community, I was without a doctor. The nurse-practitioner referred me to a gynecologist. My years of research did not prepare me for what followed. On my initial visit a nurse called me into an examining room, asked me to undress, gave me a paper gown to put on and told me the doctor would be with me soon. I was stunned. Was I not even to see the doctor before undressing? Was this the place to put my politics into practice? How could I present myself as a competent, knowledgeable person sitting undressed on the examining table? But I had a potentially cancerous growth, so I did as I had been told.

In a few minutes the nurse returned and said, "lie down the doctor is coming." Again I complied. The doctor entered the examining room, nodded in my direction while reading my chart and proceeded to examine me without ever having spoken to me. After the examination, I went to his consulting office and was told that indeed I had a mass and that I needed to be hospitalized for tests and surgery. No other information was offered; no choices were discussed. His plan was to put me in the hospital as soon as it was convenient for me. He would conduct the necessary tests one day and perform a total hysterectomy the next day. Even though I was stunned, I recovered sufficiently to ask if he thought the mass was malignant. He said "no" and then went on to explain that a woman my age did not need her uterus or ovaries. I would soon be going through menopause and could be managed quite successfully on estrogens.

I paid the bill and left the office a little less fearful about the mass and a lot less confident about my ability to cope during medical interactions. I knew from my previous research that the institutional authority of the doctor's role provided an interactional edge for the physician that placed the patient at a disadvantage. But I had been totally unprepared for how great that disadvantage would be for me—a well-informed professional woman. Somehow, I had assumed my research provided me with an immunity. My field of study is medical interaction. I am armed with the medical knowledge and social skill to interact with medical personnel as a competent person. Yet I fared no better than most of the patients I have studied. Perhaps I had just had a bad experience with a doctor unsophisticated in the art of communication.

I decided to inquire about other doctors in the community and was finally referred to a doctor who by reputation was both medically competent and interested in the social-psychological aspects of health care. The initial visit was better. Before I undressed for the physical examination, we sat across the desk and talked. When I was examined, the original diagnosis was confirmed. A total hysterectomy was again recommended and for the same reason: the tumor needed to come out and for a woman of my age the recommended therapy was a total hysterectomy followed by estrogen replacement.

Starting gingerly, I asked the doctor if the removal of my uterus and healthy ovary was necessary. He said that if a total hysterectomy was not performed, "I might need surgery again. *It* could come back." I asked if I were at greater risk of having to have another operation or a return of the tumor than any other woman in the community at large, and he hesitatingly said no. I then told him that I would rather run the risk of having to have surgery again than the risks associated with estrogen replacement therapy. That was a mistake. I got a lecture on how the media has done a disservice to women, frightening them about estrogen. The only statistical evidence of a relationship between estrogen and cancer shows in endometrial cancer (cancer of the lining of the uterus). Since my uterus would be removed, I had nothing to worry about. I recognized that arguing about the relative merits (or lack thereof) of estrogen replacement therapy was off the mark. We could both throw sources at each other, but in the final analysis it was my body and my right to decide. I proceeded, rather heatedly, to tell him just this. After a little further discussion, he agreed that if the mass was not cancerous, he would remove only what was medically necessary.

Three weeks later surgery was performed. The mass was not cancerous. One ovary and the tumor were removed. My uterus and the other healthy ovary were left intact and I was prepared to celebrate. But I may have won the battle at the cost of the war. Interactionally, I had prevailed, but the doctor's authority was not to be stilled so easily. I was left with an echo: "*It* could come back"; "You could need surgery again" . . . cancer . . . cancer . . . cancer . . . whisper . . . whisper . . . whisper!

Mine is a less distressing tale than most. Repeatedly, while doing research in departments of reproductive and family medicine, I saw physicians recommend treatments, and patients, usually unquestioningly, accept them. My research gave me access to behind-the-scenes information typically reserved for physicians. Hardly a week passed without some friend calling to tap into that stock of knowledge. The women who called were often well educated and articulate, yet either they did not feel that they had the information with which to make reasonable decisions, or they felt that they did not understand or could not trust the recommendations their physicians made. These feelings were exacerbated when their medical problems were related to reproduction. The women's questions were always of the same kind—How do I evaluate whether the treatment or procedure recommended is really in my best interest?

It would be easier to dismiss this question if the problem could be seen as an individual one. Individual doctors could be depicted as particularly insensitive or inept, while specific patients could be described as either too emotional to understand complex medical explanations or too dependent on authority to make independent medical decisions. While such explanations would be simpler and perhaps even plausible or more easily demonstrated empirically, they merely blame the individuals, obscure the process through which medical decisions are reached, and isolate the physician-patient relationship from the cultural, structural and institutional context in which such decision making occurs.

Medical encounters are interactions between individuals. They are also embedded in a social and political context. Physicians have medical knowledge and technical expertise that patients usually lack. By virtue of the authority vested in their professional role, physicians can and do control patients' access to and understanding of that information. In the process, they act as gatekeepers, providing options to some, denying them to others. Physicians and patients live in a common social world. A world in which their assumptions about the asymmetry of their relationship are largely shared. It is commonly held that doctors know what is best for their patients.

Patients are caught in a double bind. They have limited abilities to assess the medical knowledge and technical skill of physicians, to evaluate treatment information, or to question the need for medical procedures, yet they are dependent on their physicians' judgments. These judgments are often abstracted from the daily lives of these women and are frequently colored by traditional assumptions about appropriate roles for women in today's society (Fisher and Todd 1983; Scully 1980;

Ruzek 1978; Scully and Bart 1973). When doctors are men and their patients are women, both the asymmetry and the reciprocal nature of their relationship is heightened. In our society, the structures of the man-woman and the physician-patient relationships recapitulate and re-inforce each other, locking male physician and female patient into a dominant-subdominant relationship that may not be in the patient's best interest.

In The Patient's Best Interest grew from my own experience, from conversations with friends about their experiences, and from hundreds of hours spent in the examining rooms of two teaching hospitals. The analysis it contains was sharpened as I read analyses by feminist schol-ars of the sexual politics evident in every aspect of our lives. The truth of it was honed by my deep concern with the fabric of women's lives and therefore of necessity with the quality of medical care available to them.

Central to the Women's Movement is the belief that control over re-productive function is foundational for control over other personal, pro-fessional, and political aspects of our lives. To understand the power that medicine has over the lives of women, I spent six years doing re-search in two teaching hospitals. I examined the ways in which doctors and patients communicated to reach decisions to perform, or not to per-form, two cancer-related medical procedures: Pap smears to diagnose cervical cancer and hysterectomies to treat it. The decisions to do or not to do Pap smears were negotiated in relation to a potentially high-risk population of women for whom such procedures were mandated on medical grounds—these patients needed to have Pap smears done.[1] The decisions to do or not to do hysterectomies were negotiated in relation to a population of women with abnormal Pap smears for whom hys-terectomies were not mandated on medical grounds—although these women had abnormal Pap smears, they did not otherwise meet the stan-dard medical criteria for performing hysterectomies.[2] My goal was to see how these medical decisions were reached between the participants in the two hospital settings and to study the ways in which the decision making process reflected and sustained sociocultural factors.

This goal reflects my interests as a feminist and a sociologist—to im-prove the delivery of health care to women, while contributing to the development of sociological knowledge and to the potential quality of women's lives. These simultaneous goals stand at odds with those who argue for a value-neutral stance in academic work. Although medical decision making is the focus of this study, I also explore how the delivery of health care to women is intimately connected to the political, economic, and social struggles of our day.

Advocacy and Objectivity

While doing this research, I was in examining rooms watching hysterectomies being recommended to women when I knew such treatments were not mandated on medical grounds. I saw birth control pills being prescribed to women whose medical histories disclosed contraindications. In a population of patients who were potentially at a high risk of cervical cancer, I observed that Pap smear screens for cervical cancer were not routinely performed. And crosscutting all of my observations was an ideology that supports the authority of the medical role. I heard doctors blaming the media for inciting women to question their authority. These doctors often argued that a little knowledge was dangerous. Questioning, they said, weakened the doctor-patient relationship.

How did I make sense out of what I saw and heard? At first I was angry and silently expressed my anger alternately at both doctors and patients. Individual doctors were seen as inept and specific patients were seen as passively going along with whatever the doctors recommended. When I caught myself blaming individuals for problems my reading and experience had shown me were structural, my dilemma increased.

When I talked to patients, I found that, for the most part, they were not too emotional to understand complex medical explanations, nor were they too passive to ask for needed information. The problem was more subtle. Patients *believed* that the doctors had information and skills that they lacked; they believed, therefore, that the doctors should be the ones making the medical decisions. They believed that the doctor knew best and would act in their best interests. Their actions, then, flowed from these beliefs.

Nor were individual doctors the culprits. Many doctors seemed to share certain crucial beliefs about women and the delivery of health care. These beliefs are displayed and maintained in gynecological text books, in articles in medical journals, and perhaps most importantly, in day-to-day medical practices. My observations of these practices suggest that many doctors believe that once a woman is through reproducing, she no longer needs her uterus. They believe that the prophylactic removal of a uterus not only sterilizes a woman, but also reduces the likelihood that her uterus will become diseased. They believe that a radical mastectomy is the best treatment for breast cancer. They believe that the birth control pill is safer than an unwanted pregnancy and that a diaphragm user has to be an intelligent woman to be sufficiently motivated to have the diaphragm in place, not in the bedside drawer, during intercourse. Although this list of beliefs could be continued, perhaps the most important one is that doctors, for the most part, believe that they are the appropriate ones to be making medical decisions.[3] These beliefs and the medical practices that flow from them, rather than the ill intentions or ineptness of individual physicians, structured the medical interactions I observed.

One day, while talking with a resident, I asked him how he had chosen the specialty of reproductive oncology. He replied that he could not contract the diseases that his patients had. He did not have ovaries or a uterus that could become diseased with a malignant growth. He could be detached. Although I do not know if other practitioners chose this specialty for the same reasons, I did observe their detachment. I had no such separation. I was not a doctor and as a patient I could "catch" the same diseases and be treated in the same dehumanizing manner. I am, after all, a woman.

From my first day in the medical setting to my last, I questioned how I could be an objective bystander watching medical care being delivered to women in a manner that was distressing to me personally and politically. Over and over again, I made hard decisions in the name of doing research. I decided to be a relatively passive observer, to protect my ability to collect data. I intervened where I could, suggesting that patients ask questions and clarify their options. But for the most part, I stood quietly by, promising myself that when the data were collected, it would be worth it. Each time I compromised my feelings in the examining room, I renewed my commitment to sharing the backstage knowledge I had gained by demystifying the delivery of health care and displaying how medical decisions are accomplished in interactions, as well as how they are shaped by social and political forces.

How does this stance effect my ability to do sociology? As Krause

(1978) points out, one ultimately either accepts Weber's idea that we can have a value-free sociology or one does not. I do not. Not only do I reject the idea of a value-free sociology for myself, but I also agree with Navarro (1976) that any description of reality is already value-laden, both in the facts described as given and in their interpretation. Like Navarro, I conclude that the claim of value neutrality masks cultural values and functions in support of the status quo. The advocacy-objectivity debate is usually couched in terms of the honest use of data (Krause 1978). If all social science research is woven by means of a filter of cultural values and is in that sense necessarily political, how can it be more honest to claim neutrality while masking which side you are on. On the contrary, it seems to me that the most honest use of data comes with stating which side you are on. In so doing, the standard definition of objectivity is recast. No longer will objectivity be considered as detached from the social world or devoid of subjectivity. An alternative conception of objectivity will be substituted which, while pursuing "a maximally reliable understanding of the world" (Keller 1985), allows for the inclusion of both the social world and subjective understandings. The analysis in this book is a political as well as a sociological undertaking. It blends advocacy with objectivity, reflecting my commitment to improve the delivery of health care to women and to advance sociological understanding.

The advocacy-objectivity issue is part of a larger methodological debate. Sociology, and the other social sciences, developed in a dialogue with the natural sciences—a dialogue in which the natural sciences were dominant. Searching for legitimation, the social sciences adopted the natural sciences' paradigm. The social world was conceptualized in terms of positivist assumptions—a world of orderly causes and effects. The Durkheimian view of an external and constraining world of social facts seemed to be consistent with the natural science paradigm. This sort of world therefore seemed amenable to analysis (as the natural world was) through the application of the scientific method—a method that allowed for the discovery of an empirical relationship between cause and effect, whose rigorous use was claimed to insure objectivity.

The debate surrounding the establishment of sociology as a social science was recapitulated within sociology. From its inception as a discipline, some sociologists have argued that social action is action meaningful to the actor and therefore that it is inherently different from the objects of study in the natural sciences. Schwartz and Jacobs (1979) suggest that documenting the actor's point of view entails a paradigmatic shift away from positivist science. They contend that this shift has been supported by the Weberian concept of "verstehen" or emphatic understanding and by the Meadian notion of active actors negotiating meanings through their interactions. As alternatives to the positivist paradigm, these concepts engender different methods for gathering data and capturing meaning, as well as different epistomological assumptions about the nature of the actor and the social world.

This paradigmatic shift again raises questions about the nature of objectivity. If objectivity is not insured technically—through the rigorous application of the scientific method—and if it is not guaranteed through replication, on what does it rest? For some sociologists, objectivity is obtained by maintaining the integrity of the phenomenon under study. When research reproduces faithfully what has been seen, it redefines and reinforces a kind of ethnographic objectivity. For others, objectivity rests on certain shared cultural assumptions. When research findings "ring true," the assumption of objectivity is supported—a kind of experiencial objectivity. For still others, objectivity is increased by making the collection and analysis of data more rigorous and/or by increasing the analytic specificity for understanding how meaning and social action are accomplished—a kind of methodological objectivity (For more detailed methodological discussions, see Schwartz and Jacobs 1979; Johnson 1975; Mehan and Wood 1975; McCall and Simmons 1969; Cicourel 1964). In each case, while objectivity is connected to the social world, it remains disconnected from the researcher's subjective experience of that world—a separation I try to avoid.

While I am writing as a feminist and therefore I am advocating changes in the delivery of health care where medical practices do not seem to be in women's best interests, my advocacy is not without objectivity. It is grounded in detailed ethnographic descriptions of the medical settings I studied, rooted in my experiences as a woman in this society, and committed to methodological adequacy through the rigorous collection of data and increased analytic specificity. Data were gathered using audio and video techniques and transcribed for later analysis. A systematic analysis of the events under study—in this case medical interviews—was made and recurrent patterns of behavior were isolated, presented, and analyzed. The data were presented to display the ways in which the analyses were constructed.

I am occasionally asked how generalizable my findings are. It would be false to claim that all doctors act the same way, all or most of the time. Nor do I intend to make such a claim. Neither doctors nor patients are preprogrammed "judgmental dopes" (Garfinkel 1967) acting out organizational, structural, or cultural norms. Rather, I have identified typical patterns of behavior that cut across medical practitioners, patients, medical specialists, different kinds of training and practices, as well as geographic locations. A kind of validity for my findings is provided by the fact that two such dissimilar resident training programs did provide such similar patterns of behavior. Although the practical constraints and tasks at hand were different in each setting, in both settings, medical professionals used the authority of their role to exercise power over women patients who lacked it.

Scope of Analysis

Krause (1978) suggests that the advocacy-objectivity debate is closely tied to another issue—the scope of analysis. Traditionally, medical sociology has been characterized by several recurrent kinds of studies. There are studies that focus on treatment roles and relationships within organizational settings, and there are more political investigations of power relationships and their influences on the organization of the health care system and the delivery of medical care. There are statistical analyses of illness, mortality, and morbidity rates and of the relationships between various demographic factors and illness behavior, the availability of medical services and the patterns of medical usage. In addition, there are descriptions of the life-worlds of medical personnel and of patients. More recently, the internal dynamics of the doctor-patient relationship have been taken as a topic of study. More systematic analyses of the social production of discourse within medical contexts have been made. Whether these studies are characterized as qualitative or quantitative, as macro or micro, as being in support of the status quo or as critical of it, as being at the structural or the interactional levels of analysis, these studies share a common feature. They provide a slice of the social world that could be enriched by drawing on the others' perspectives.

At first glance, I seem to be addressing a relatively simple issue: the need to broaden and integrate the scope of analysis to increase sociological understanding. Yet the issues raised are not as simple as they seem. As Duster (1981) points out, sociology is firmly entrenched in the age of specialization—a specialization maintained by stratification. Paths to publication, status in professional hierarchies, and professional attainments in the discipline are produced or constrained by adherence to particular ideologies and practices.

In this study, I join others who are attempting to integrate two sociological perspectives traditionally seen as disparate—analyses of social structure and of social interaction (see also Knorr-Cetina and Cicourel 1981). Starting from the viewpoint that changes are needed in the delivery of health care, my first task is to display how health care is delivered to women and to discuss how the delivery of care is enacted and accomplished in the doctor-patient relationship—an empirical analysis of social interaction. Once that interaction is described, the next step requires a theoretical analysis of social structure. I try to understand why the described inequalities exist and why the system is so resistant to change by placing the empirical analysis of social interaction in a reflexive relationship with a theoretical analysis of social structure and showing how each feeds into and sustains the other.

The medical interview during which these medical decisions are negotiated does not occur in a vacuum. Health care is delivered in a context and it is within this context that I will have to make sense of it. For to ignore that context would leave us unable to address the problem of the continued existence of social inequities or to suggest remedies for them. The persistence of inequities for providers and consumers of health care and the resistance of the system to change speaks to a pattern of power and control that extends beyond the medical interview and beyond the institution of medicine to the structural arrangements of society.

This kind of analysis is not without problems. To take an example, I could describe an interaction in which a resident is persuading a poor minority woman to have a hysterectomy that, on medical grounds alone, is unnecessary. The empirical evidence would speak eloquently about inequities—e.g., inequities of class, race, and gender. To anyone who has spent any time in an outpatient clinic, there is little doubt that the practical concerns of a teaching hospital motivate residents to impose treatments on patients who are less powerful than they are for the learning experience such treatments provide. Yet, even though many sociologists have demonstrated that the structure of our medical system and of our society demands "teaching material" for residents to learn on, and provides that material in the form of poor and powerless citizens, it is difficult to directly map these structural observations onto the empirical data. It would be almost impossible to document that the structural inequalities of class, race, and/or gender *cause* unnecessary treatments. I do not intend to make such an argument.

It is not my intention to argue in a unidimensional fashion that cultural, structural, and organizational factors are the independent variables, which affect the dependent variables of the doctor-patient relationship and/or the delivery of health care. Rather the notion of causality I want to propose is more contextual, reflexive, hermeneutic, and dynamic. I want to make the claim that the doctor-patient relationship is produced and constrained in a social and political context, which, as a feature of our common sense knowledge, is illuminated and realized in the discourse between participants during medical encounters. This process reproduces the status quo. Thus social structure and social interaction are posed as context and ground in a reflexive relationship with each other.

I am not alone in suggesting that language links social interaction and social structure. For Habermas (1981) communication is constitutive of social power because human beings share an intersubjective and socially reproduced repertoire of skills for communicative interaction. And Forester (1981) claims that critical theory bridges the gap between analyses of social structure and social interaction by providing a structural phenomenology. He says:

> It is a phenomenology because it attends to the skilled and contingent social construction and negotiation of intersubjective meanings . . . ; it is structural because it attends equally to the historical stage upon which actors meet, speak, conflict, listen or engage with one another. (Forester 1981, 2)

While critical theory, as described by Habermas and others, has the potential to bridge the gap, others note that such theoretical constructs lack a theory of interaction and a solid foundation of evidence upon which to ground a careful description (see Cicourel 1975). It is argued that theoretical errors occur when social structures and the effects they have on people's lives are treated as if they had an existence attributed to them independently of people's observed behavior. To counter this theoretical separation of social structure and social interaction, attempts have been made to demonstrate empirically how social structures, particularly institutional structures, interface with the ways people behave and make sense of each others' behavior in face-to-face interactions (Mehan 1983). This shift is marked by a renewed interest in language use.

The discussion of the scope of analysis, the relationship between advocacy and objectivity and the whisper that remains for me—"*It* could come back"—all imply a relationship between language and a larger social context. The doctor's statement ("It could come back!") is an individual linguistic expression of a more macro social and political reality. And the linguistic expressions "advocacy" and "objectivity" oppose the language of social action to the language of science, obscuring the contextual relationship between them. Neither concept is what it seems. The assumption of objectivity masks a more contextual value-laden position and the assumption of advocacy blocks any possibility of objectivity. But it is in the discussion of the scope of the analysis that the critical nature of the relationship between language and context emerges most clearly. Both those who study social institutions and those who study social interactions agree that communication is the key to an analysis that links these concepts. Yet, they disagree on the relative statuses of language and of social context in this analysis—a disagreement that has a long history both in linguistics and sociology.

Language and Context

For early theoretical linguistics, the context of utterances was neither relevant nor appropriate. They focused on the structure of surface utterances, using experimental situations, texts, and more importantly, informants and introspection as sources of data. While elaborating a system of context-free linguistic rules to account for uniform linguistic behavior, they considered the use of non-linguistic materials to be inappropriate. Neither meaning nor usage were seen as researchable topics. However, there were those in the community of linguistics who felt the need to move the discipline toward a consideration of context. Without such a consideration, it was impossible to study language as it is used in everyday life. Linguists like Chomsky (1965) as well as philosophers of ordinary language such as Searle (1969), Austin (1962) and Wittgenstein (1953) contributed to the development of a perspective that sought to integrate language and context. (See the appendix for a more detailed discussion of these developments.) But it was the work of sociolinguists that most explicitly came to examine language as a form of social behavior.

In sociolinguistic research, a distinction is made between linguistic structure (form) and function—a distinction recapitulated in more recent sociological studies. The study of linguistic structure is oriented toward the problem of linguistic change and argues that to understand the forms language takes and its evolution, it is necessary to reintegrate the social context of the speech community with linguistic description (Labov 1972). Although the theoretical focus is on linguistic rules and, therefore, is not incompatible with more formal linguistic approaches, the methods and findings of this approach and these more formal approaches differ sharply.

The more functional approach is at odds with formal linguistics. The functional focus is on a more detailed, empirical, and comparative examination of the functions fulfilled by speech in particular settings— what Hymes (1974:8) refers to as "the organization of verbal means and the ends they serve." The twin concepts generated by Hymes (1962)— "communicative competence" and its methodological counterpart, an "ethnography of speaking"—are foundational to studies that examine the properties of natural language use.

While linguists and sociolinguists are not always in agreement, they do agree that language use is organized in patterned ways. Shuy's (1983) and Labov and Fanshel's (1977) research reflect this shared understanding. Because they are sociolinguists, a strong recommendation rises out of their work: to understand the relationship between language and context, researchers must undertake a systematic, empirical examination of speech and the social situations in which it unfolds. Despite this recommendation, linguistic behavior in this research tradition provides the data, while context remains an analytic resource. (See the appendix, where this research is also discussed in greater detail.) The analytic status of language and context has reemerged as an issue in sociological research as well.

Notwithstanding the early insights of George Herbert Mead on the critical role played by language in daily life, or the sociological importance attributed to language in such substantive sociological areas as face-to-face interactions, socialization, and deviance, sociologists have largely treated language as an unexamined background feature of their analysis—what Zimmerman and Pollner (1970) refer to as a "resource," rather than what they call a "topic." As Giglioli (1972) points out, even though problems broadly defined as sociological have used a language-based analysis, sociologists have not been at the forefront of this work.

Recently, conversational and discourse analysts have taken language as a topic of inquiry. Although there are important differences between these two kinds of analysis, they both developed in dialogue with a more traditional, positivistic version of Durkheimian sociology, which presents social reality as a "fact," external to and constraining upon the individual. Drawing upon theoretical perspectives that oppose the Durkheimian perspective (e.g., symbolic interaction, phenomenology, and ethnomethodology) conversational and discourse analysts present social reality as accomplished—as produced and constrained by the situated activities of participants. Even though this basic understanding is shared between them, there is little agreement on the role of context.

Conversational analysts focus on the local production of talk and highlight the ways in which the structure of this talk is socially produced. Here context is once again an analytic resource, the way it was for sociolinguists. For some discourse analysts, the focus has been shifted from the local to the situated production of discourse, and from an almost exclusive concern with the structure of discourse to a discussion of both the structure (form) and the functions such linguistic forms serve.

For example, discourse analyses have examined the language forms (structure) that characterize educational and medical settings and that function to accomplish the tasks at hand—teaching lessons and reaching medical decisions. This research has found that classroom lessons and medical interviews are social events, organized from beginning to end by medical and educational tasks—tasks shaped by the institutional setting in which they occur and the authority of those with dominant roles in the settings—teachers and doctors. Teaching and monitoring students' behavior is not the same as discussing medical problems and attempting to reach solutions about them. These different institutional realities are reflected in differences in the form (structure) and content (function) of educational and medical discourse. By examining the ways language is used to accomplish specific ends—its functions in specific institutional settings—context is elevated to a researchable topic along with language use. A fuller description of the local and situated production of discourse and a more detailed comparison of the differing forms and functions of educational and medical discourse can be found in the appendix.

A Reflexive Analysis

More recent sociological studies of language direct our attention to a series of reflexive relationships. Conversational analysts describe how utterances (discourse forms) are locally produced, collectively accomplished, and reflexively tied—a patterning of utterances into reflexively tied adjacency pairs. A greeting by one speaker calls for a return greeting by another; thus greetings are an example of a reflexively tied adjacency pair. Discourse analysts look to extend this concept of reflexivity to other areas. They illuminate how institutional settings, tasks at hand and language use are reflexively connected—a patterning of discourse that extends beyond the two-part structure of adjacency pairs, beyond a primary concern with linguistic forms, and beyond a local, collective accomplishment to embed this language production in an organizational milieu. However, the relationship between language and context that they explore does not end here. Educational and medical events take place in a social world that extends beyond specific settings.

These reflexive relationships are at the core of the analysis in this book. I examine two interrelated assumptions: first, that the spoken interactions of the medical event serve multiple functions; and second, that there is a reflexive relationship between these spoken interactions and social context, broadly defined. Picture a contextual web with communication between the participants in the medical event at its center. As they communicate, doctor and patient send and receive messages. They also simultaneously engage in speech and social acts. For example, if, while negotiating a medical decision, a patient were to say, "I agree," this speech act would accomplish the social act of agreement. Language then does more than send and receive messages. It does "work" (Searle 1969; Austin 1961). For the speech act, "I agree," to accomplish a social act of agreement, sender and receiver must engage in spoken interactions collaboratively to produce medical decisions.

This communicational work is embedded in an organizational nexus. When discourse in institutional contexts is examined as a collaboratively produced social event, organized toward a specific end, and structured, at least in part, by the task at hand, the institutional authority of the dominant actors is displayed and an analysis of the reflexive relationship between organizational context and language is made possible. Posing context and communication in a reflexive relationship suggests that context shapes the spoken interactions of the medical event and is maintained by them. The spoken interactions illuminate a context composed of the features of the specific medical setting and the organizational structure of the profession of medicine. Although illness itself may be physiological, the role of a sick person (Parsons 1951), ideas about illness (Friedson 1970) and actions taken in response to symptoms (Mechanic 1968) are all social and as such, they are related to the institutional structure of society. Doctors, not patients, have the power to legitimize illness, to make decisions about medical procedures and to recommend treatment. Doctors have an institutionally based authority that patients lack.

At this point in time, the structure of the medical profession provides a fairly stable context. The medical profession is largely autonomous. Physicians monitor the education, licensing, and conduct of their fellow practitioners, and they have a state-supported monopoly over the right to practice medicine. Features of specific medical settings are more varied. For example, bureaucratic, hospital-based settings are organized differently (Strong 1979) than smaller fee-for-service medical practices.

By moving out from a focus on interaction and by recognizing the ways events are constituted by a series of reflexive relationships, I lay the foundation for a more structural analysis. It is well within the sociological tradition to argue that structural factors are woven into the fabric of daily life, that they shape the health care delivery system and impinge on the doctor-patient relationship (Zola 1972). The institutional arrangements of the medical profession mirror the economic and political structures of society, while at the same time reinforcing them. Navarro (1976) argues that the economic, social and political factors that constitute the very fabric of society are reflected in the health care

system. The medical profession and the corporate medical establishment that markets health-related services—the pharmaceutical companies, the health insurance companies and medical supply industries as
well as proprietory hospitals and nursing homes—are big profit makers,
with powerful legislative lobbies.

The metaphor of a contextual web is clarifying conceptually. The web
stretches from the spoken interactions of participants situated within
specific medical events to the more general organizational and structural
arrangements of society. It spreads from those structural arrangements
out to the world view of the dominant culture, and then it folds back,
spiraling in upon itself, returning to the core of spoken interactions.
These reflexive relationships are both social and micropolitical (Henley
1977; Waitzkin and Stoeckle 1976). Since medical work primarily occurs during face-to-face spoken interactions and involves infinitely
practical activities performed by doctor and patient to accomplish the
task at hand, it is, in that sense, social. Medical work also reflects, helps
to sustain, and reproduces the social, economic, and political status quo
and in that sense, it is micropolitical. In the process of doing their work,
doctors have the power to control medical resources.

Language and context broadly defined provide a data base that can be
used for an analysis of the micropolitics of the medical relationship.
The spoken interactions of the medical event have the potential to display how the ways participants communicate influence the medical decisions reached, offering, at the same time, a methodological device for
making visible the ways participants accomplish the medical event. Finally, spoken interactions supply the data to build a theoretical link con-
necting social interaction with social structure.

The Research Process

My work is critical of the medical profession, and the medical professionals in charge knew that it was. Why then was I allowed not only to
study medical decision making, but also to make audio and video tapes
of residents and doctors as they diagnosed and treated patients? I suspect there are several reasons. First, attending staff physicians are
charged with teaching residents both the science and the art of medicine
and they themselves are more comfortable with the science than with the

art. Second, medical practitioners are learning to see communicational skills as being in their best interest. In recent years, doctors have paid more attention to the relationships between communication, patients' satisfaction with medical care, and patients' compliance. Third, communicational skills are seen as legal protection for doctors. Often those doctors who are sued are those who communicate poorly. The medical profession is concerned about the tremendous increase in malpractice suits and in the rapid rise in the costs of malpractice insurance. There is another reason as well. I think my commitment to improving the quality of medical care for women was both evident and consistent with the goals of a teaching hospital—teaching residents the skills to improve the quality of care they will deliver. Yet, all these interests notwithstanding, I found that my research was characterized by an almost continuous process of gaining and regaining entry, establishing and reestablishing rapport, in order for me to be able to continue to gather data.

Because I wanted to be able to describe, analyze, and come to understand the face-to-face interactions of doctors and patients, I needed to get close to the natural situations and to gain access to the participants' understandings of their situations. Because I wanted to be able to do a systematic analysis of the ways in which language is used to accomplish events like treatment decisions, I needed to capture the actual communications on audio and video tape, to save it for later analysis and to study the communication patterns that emerged.

To accomplish these goals, I spent six years examining medical decision making in two teaching hospitals, with three different organizational structures, in two very different parts of the country. The first two years were spent in the Department of Reproductive Medicine and the sub-specialty of Oncology (cancer) in an urban, west coast, teaching hospital. In this setting, outpatient care was provided through two clinical systems: the community and the faculty clinics. In the community clinic, residents provided care under the supervision of attending physicians for a largely indigent population of patients. In the faculty clinic, professors of reproductive oncology (cancer of the reproductive system) provided care primarily to patients with greater resources than those seen in the community clinic. For the most part, these patients had been referred to that department by other medical practitioners in the community. The last four years of my research were spent in the Department of Family Medicine in a teaching hospital in a rural, southeastern state. In this setting, residents provided care in a model family practice. The teaching situation was set up to model the way medicine would be practiced in a group practice. Both on the west coast and in the southeast, I spent over a year getting a feel for the setting and its participants and gaining their trust before I used mechanical means of data gathering.

In both the reproductive oncology clinics and the model family practice, gaining initial entry was facilitated by someone who already had the trust of the medical professionals in charge of the setting. In the first setting, a sociologist who acted as an advisor facilitated my entry. He introduced me to the senior reproductive gynecologist-oncologist, establishing my research credentials at the same time. Entry was not granted all at once or altruistically. The doctor in charge of the faculty clinic was concerned about two issues. He was concerned with how to make the final stages of a woman's life easier, and he was concerned about teaching residents communication skills.

My first project was to interview women who had had major surgery for invasive cancer and whose lives were in jeopardy. While this was the project that most interested the doctor, I found that I was not prepared to deal with death on a daily basis. The doctor and I renegotiated and I was granted access into the doctors' lounge in an out-patient clinic, in the Department of Reproductive Medicine—one of the clinics in the system of community clinics. Women were referred to this clinic after having had an abnormal Pap smear in a social agency in the community or in another community clinic in the hospital. These women were not facing a life-threatening situation. Pre-cancerous and cancerous lesions of the cervix are, in most cases, treatable.

Residents would greet patients in the examining rooms (at the time of my research there were no consulting offices in these clinics), take their medical histories, do physical examinations, and then return to the lounge, where they discussed their findings with an attending staff physician and made treatment recommendations. When new residents rotated onto the service, mini-lectures about diagnosing and treating precancerous and cancerous lesions of the cervix were given. While the interactions in the doctors' lounge were interesting, the real "action" for me took place in the examining rooms. I waited and watched for an opportunity to gain access to this setting. My opportunity came in an unexpected way.

I was sitting in the lounge taking notes, when a resident walked in and asked if anyone spoke Spanish. I did. Although I did not speak fluently and did not have a medical vocabulary, I could communicate. The resident asked me to come with him into the examining room and to translate. The patient was a sixteen-year-old young woman. She had been raped, had gotten pregnant and had had an abortion. The abortion disclosed a molar pregnancy—malignant cells growing wildly. It was my task to inform that young woman that she now had an additional problem—she needed to be treated for cancer. This was a discussion that would have been difficult even in English with a well-educated, articulate woman.

The young woman was terribly frightened. All thought of doing objective research left my mind. I walked over to her, held her hand, and tried to comfort her. I explained that I did not speak Spanish well, but I would try to explain her medical problem. I asked her to let me know whether she understood me. I started by asking her if she knew that she had a house inside in which babies grew (without medical Spanish that was the best I could do). She nodded yes and I continued. That house is a little bit sick and the doctor needs to treat it. From that beginning, I explained the diagnosis and treatment, translating as the doctor explained it to me. When I was finished, the patient agreed to go into the hospital for chemotherapy. I later found out that this was seen as a medical victory. The patient's mother was sure that the devil had invaded her daughter and wanted her to return to Mexico to be treated by a sorcerer.

Word of my help spread quickly and I was rewarded. The attending physician granted me entry. He gave me permission to accompany residents, at their invitations, into the examining rooms. The resident I had translated for offered me a medical reward as well. He invited me to go into the examining room with him on some of his more "interesting cases." Unfortunately, what was interesting to him was often distressing to me. For example, my first invitation was to feel a woman's ovarian tumor, while she was lying on the examining table talking about wanting to die. Without hurting the resident's feelings, I convinced him that I was interested in the routine activities that took place in the examining rooms and that I wanted to observe, not to participate.

Once I had access to the examining rooms, I thought my problems were over. Not so. Even though I had established that I was trustworthy, I was an outsider, a woman, and one interested in feminist issues. One day as I was taking notes on a routine matter, the senior attending staff physician asked what I was writing. I explained the process of taking field notes. He then asked if I was planning to do an exposé of the medical profession. I assured him that I was interested in doctor-patient communication (which in fact was the focus of my interest). He did not seem satisfied. So I handed him my notebook and allowed him to read for himself the kind of notes I had taken.

After spending a year in the community clinic staffed by residents, I was granted permission to do observations in the faculty clinic. This setting was much more like a private practice. Primarily middle-class patients were referred by other practitioners or other social agencies in the community to the senior or junior oncologist for diagnosis and treatment. All the patients who came to this clinic were treated by reproductive oncologists, rather than by residents. After three additional months, I was granted permission to tape in both the community and faculty clinics.

I am often asked if the attending physicians in this setting knew what I was really doing. As strange as it seems, the answer is yes. In the first setting, before being granted permission to tape, I wrote a paper summing up my observations of the first year. This paper was read by the senior staff physician. Similarly, one of the first steps in my gaining entry into the second setting, the model family practice clinic, was a formal presentation of my earlier work.

In many respects my entry into the model family practice training program was much easier than it had been in the reproductive oncology program. I was a new faculty member in a university that had an established relationship with the family practice training program. One of my first activities after arriving on campus was to locate a faculty member able to introduce me to the attending staff of the family medicine program. The faculty member and I found that we had interests in common and could share services. The graduate program in his department had a clinical component, which could be enriched with more instruction in research methods. In addition, their graduate students could benefit from some exposure to medical sociology. I would be offering courses both in qualitative methods and medical sociology and could include their students. They had a well-established relationship with the hospital. In fact one of their faculty members held a joint appointment. They agreed to sponsor me. It took a full year of talking informally, having lunches, attending clinical conferences, and presenting my work formally before I was granted entry. Looking back on the process, I realize that it went faster than it might have without sponsorship. Family medicine has a commitment to the social-psychological aspects of the delivery of health care and one of the attending staff physicians was especially supportive. Establishing trust in the south is a slow process. However, unlike in the west, once trust was established I was a member of the team and was not challenged to prove my trustworthiness again.

As in the west, my entry went through phases and was not altogether altruistic. After a year of lunches and informal meetings, I was invited to participate in the educational conferences for residents. From the beginning, it was understood, although not stated aloud, that we were trading services. I was filling out their program by adding to their ability to offer more education in the behavioral aspects of clinical care. They were providing a research setting for me and for my students. It was not, however until the end of my second year that I began to collect data on audio and video tape.

There were differences in the organization of the training experience in both of these settings, which also influenced my research. In this family medicine training program, as in many others in the United States, the commitment to primary care and the interest in the social and psychological dynamics of the family led to increased scrutiny of the doctor-patient relationship. Toward this end, two of the examining rooms were outfitted with video cameras and taping was considered a part of the learning experience. It would be false to claim that residents liked to be taped or that taping made no differences in the doctor-patient interaction. Residents did not like to be taped. It made them uncomfortable. Given the competition that characterizes most medical education, it was hard for them to accept that taping was a learning tool, not an evaluation device. Although doctor or patient often alluded to the taping at the beginning of the interview, they appeared to forget that the camera was rolling as the interview unfolded. The fact that they forgot presented an interesting problem for me. While the interview was being taped, I sat in another room at the video recorder monitoring the process. If there was a need for the patient to undress for a physical examination, the doctor would leave the examining room for her to do so. Not once did doctor or patient remark about the camera being on at this juncture. If I was not quick enough at the controls, the patient would stand up, drop her clothes as the doctor left the examining room and be exposed in front of the camera while donning the paper hospital gown.

The mode of training was different in these two situations as well. Residents in reproductive oncology sometimes saw patients alone, but diagnosis and treatment was directly under the supervision of the attending staff. The situation in the family practice training program was designed to model what the actual practice of family medicine would be like. Residents were not directly under the supervision of the attending staff physician; rather, attendings functioned like consultants. They were always on hand in the central lounge. Residents sought consultations only when they felt they were necessary.

By far the easiest part of the research process was the mechanical gathering of the data. In both settings, residents were told that I wanted to study doctor-patient communication and were asked to participate in the study. With patients more care was taken. The study was described to them. They were assured that their participation, or the lack of it, would in no way affect their medical care. They were informed that they could question the investigator at any time and could drop out of the study without penalty. After explaining all of this to them, they were asked to read and sign an informed consent procedure. Much to my surprise, when women were told that I wanted to study doctor-patient communication because I wanted to gather information to improve the quality of care provided to women, most women agreed to participate. Most residents agreed to participate as well. The freedom of their choices, however, was somewhat constrained. It was clear that I had the support of their professors and they were being strongly encouraged to participate.

For nine months I audio taped in the reproductive oncology, community, and faculty clinics. I, therefore, was able to collect data on the ways attending staff doctors in the faculty clinic as well as the ways residents in the community clinic communicated with patients—patients who had been referred to them because of abnormal Pap smears. In the reproductive oncology, community, and faculty clinics, I audio taped twenty-one patients as they moved through the diagnostic-treatment process.

For two months, I audio and videotaped residents' communications with women patients on their initial visits to the family practice clinic. I audio and videotaped forty-three doctor-patient encounters. In both settings (the clinics in the west and the residency training program in the southeast), I started with the patients' initial visits to the clinic. Since I wanted to tap into the ways doctor and patient negotiate a common reality, I felt I needed to catch them at the beginning of their relationship together. Yet, I realize that in some ways the selection of initial visits was arbitrary. These doctors and patients, like most people in society, share commonly held assumptions about medical encounters that influence even initial interviews. The transcripts made from these tapes and the knowledge I gleaned from them in the years I participated in both settings provide the data for the analysis that follows.

After the data were collected and the tapes transcribed, I began the analysis. For me this was a painstaking process.[4] I poured over the transcripts searching for recurrent patterns of discourse behavior. When I identified a pattern in one transcript, I checked against the others until I felt confident that I had grasped its essential function—the interactional work it performed—and made sure that these functions characterized the medical interactions under study. Then, since I planned to do a detailed analysis of specific issues and knew that in most cases it would not be possible (and would be boring if possible), to discuss each case in depth to display the persistence of the recurrent patterns, I picked a small sample to illustrate the range of patterns I had identified.

For example, in chapter 2 I discuss five cases drawn from the reproductive oncology community and faculty clinics on the west coast to document the ways language is used strategically during medical interactions to negotiate treatment decisions—in these cases, prophylactic or elective hysterectomies. With these cases, I illustrate the range of linguistic strategies used and show the medical consequences, in terms of treatment decisions, that flow from them. These five cases then stand on behalf of, exemplify, findings common to all twenty-one cases.

Using the same data base in the next chapter, the focus of the analysis shifts. While in chapter 2, the focus is on content—how language functions to accomplish the decision to do hysterectomies—in chapter 3 the analytic focus is on the structure of the discourse. As I poured over the transcripts, I discovered that they were overwhelmingly characterized by vertical and horizontal discourse structures that were both similar to and in certain ways different from the structures identified in ordinary, daily conversation and those that operate in another institutional context, e.g., elementary school classrooms. To make the argument that the patterns I found in the structure of the medical discourse reflect and sustain an institutional order, I first reviewed the findings on the structure of discourse in ordinary conversations and in classrooms and then analyzed one case in depth to illustrate the structure of the discourse during the medical interview as well as the consequences such a structure has for the delivery of health care.

In chapter 4 both the focus and the data base change. In this chapter I build upon the analysis presented in earlier chapters to construct a more general or global discussion of the medical encounter as a social event organized from beginning to end toward specific goals—in these cases, a diagnosis and the recommendation of treatment. Using the data drawn from the model family practice clinic in the south, I discuss how medical interviews are routinely organized into phases and how the discussion or lack of discussion, the in-phase or out-of-phase location of certain topics, influences the performance of an important preventive health measure—Pap smears. To demonstrate how decision making is accomplished as the phases of the interview unfold, I use all forty-three cases.

The analysis in each case blends a detailed description of the patterned forms language takes and the recurrent functions such forms serve with an examination of the social origins and social consequences of such use. To build an account of the organizational and interactional processes that undergird medical decision making, field work is combined with elements of discourse analysis and this information is arrayed against a more structural background. For example, data gathered by examining medical records, interviewing key people, and, most importantly, observing the interactions of doctors and women patients are viewed in the context of sociological descriptions of the structure of society and the shape of the health care system. In a similar way, hysterectomy trends in the United States provide the background against which decisions to perform hysterectomies are discussed and decisions not to do Pap smears are presented within the context of the practice of preventive medicine in this country. Insights not normally available are gained by combining language-based analytic strategies from a sociolinguistic tradition with an institutional analysis long associated with sociology.

The analysis is developed in increments. First, I explore how language functions in the decision making process. Highlighted by this discussion, a picture emerges of how the institutional authority of the medical relationship is reflected and reinforced in the communicational strategies through which the decision to perform a hysterectomy is reached. Then I shift the focus to examine the forms of language used during medical interviews. This discussion illuminates a view of how the asymmetry in the medical relationship structures the vertical and hierarchical organization of the discourse and influences the treatment decision reached. After treating the segments of the interview (linguistic functions and vertical and hierarchical forms), I discuss how decisions to do Pap smears are accomplished as the medical event unfolds phase by phase. In each phase, the doctor orchestrates key decisions influencing medical outcomes. The linguistically based analysis of each discussion displays the ways discourse is structured, the ways the flow of information is shaped and the ways medical decisions are produced. Collectively, these three chapters lay the groundwork for developing, in the final chapter (chapter 5), a conceptual web that accounts for these data theoretically by extending the concept of context beyond institutions to the structural and cultural arrangements of society. This research process illuminates the ways medical domination is related to the ways informational resources are distributed and the ways sexual stratification is related to the ways medical decisions are reached.

Although the data for each chapter is drawn from the transcripts and, therefore, is linguistically based, the analysis is limited neither to these tapes nor to language. It is enriched by my experience in the settings. As I analyzed the transcripts and made sense out of the data, I relied on informal conversations and chance remarks. Sights, sounds and smells once new were renewable through hundreds of pages of field notes and many hours of audio and video tapes. I could repicture doctor and patient in consulting office or examining room; I could resee facial expressions and body language; I could recapture how doctor and patient looked or dressed, where they sat or stood; I could rehear how they talked, their voices and the conversational intonations of their speech. Drawing on my experience in the setting, and on the tapes, transcripts, the field notes, I felt I knew the members in these settings and this knowledge helped to ground the analysis in ethnographic materials that extended beyond the linguistic boundaries of the transcripts.

For example, my field notes reminded me of a conversation with a doctor who told me that an unmarried, sexually active young woman was promiscuous and getting what she deserved (in this case an abnormal Pap smear). They helped me recall a conversation with another doctor. After examining a woman who had an abnormal Pap smear, the doctor and I walked into the hall and he commented that they (young women) think they are all grown up when they do it (engage in sexual intercourse) but they cry like babies when they have to pay the consequences (again the consequences were an abnormal Pap smear). Like many physicians, these doctors drew a causal inference: sexual intercourse with multiple partners at an early age caused cervical cancer.

My field notes also captured informal conversation among residents and some of the attending staff of the family practice clinic. In one instance, the topic under discussion was abortion. The few doctors in town who did abortions were named and discussed in disparaging tones. The family practice residents boasted that they would never do abortions. One of the attending physicians proclaimed that things were better before abortion was made legal. He claimed that legalizing abortion encouraged promiscuous sexual activity. Before abortion was legal, he reasoned, he had received few requests for abortions and had never had to clean up after a poorly performed illegal abortion. He went on to state that the real problem was a decline in morality. Young people were engaging in sexual relationships before they were married and young women were not responsible enough to use effective forms of birth control. He concluded that legalized abortion was not in the girl's best interest. Now they could not even get the boys to marry them! These comments, and many others like them, provide the background knowledge that grounds my presentation of data in the chapters that follow. The analysis, then, is based on linguistic data enriched by other ethnographic materials gathered over the thousands of hours I have spent in these two teaching hospitals.[5]

The purpose of this book is to explore the relationship between shared cultural knowledge (norms) and action (medical decision making) to discover how the institutional authority of the medical role is used (its patterned occurrence). It is my hope that an understanding of how such authority is used will shed light on the central questions of the book: How is health care delivered to women patients? Is care provided in the patient's best interest, and if not, what factors contribute to this situation?

2 / No More Uterus, No More Babies

How Language Functions in Medical Discourse

The scene is an examining room in a large urban teaching hospital. A resident and a patient have just discussed how to treat her medical problem and have reached the decision to treat her abnormal Pap smear with a hysterectomy. After the treatment decision has been reached, the resident presents an informed consent form for the patient to sign and says:

> Even though with this form that I have before you that the government requires you to sign, it's a request for a hysterectomy for sterilization, even though it says here that you have no problems which require a hysterectomy, and we know that you do, the hospital and the state require me to ask you to sign this so that you understand that what we're talking about is permanent sterilization with no possibilities of future pregnancies.

One might ask what kind of informed consent procedure this is? The resident, Doctor T, tells the patient what he is required to by law—that she has "no problem which requires a hysterectomy"—and then tells her to disregard that information by reminding her that "we know that you do." This small snippet of discourse displays a much larger aspect of the doctor-patient relationship: The power and authority of the medical role and how it is enacted in the decision making process.

The patient, Coleen, is in her mid-thirties, divorced, with three children. She has been referred to the clinic with an abnormal Pap smear. During the discussion about treatment options, even though she did not request sterilization, a hysterectomy is recommended as the most appropriate treatment. The grounds for this recommendation are specified as: " . . . *it* (cancer) could come back. . . ." and "for somebody your age, that's had your family, you're sure that you don't want children, I'd recommend a hysterectomy." This is a woman who is afraid that her abnormal Pap smear signals a life-threatening medical problem. The manner in which information about her condition is presented heightens the emotional impact of the abnormal Pap smear by stressing the possibility that "it" could come back. In addition, it is the resident, not the patient, who links the need for a hysterectomy with the patient's age, her prior childbearing history, her lack of desire for additional children, and sterilization.

Persuasion is often part of the doctor's job. He or she is charged with the responsibility for providing medical care that is in the patient's best interest. In the case just discussed, the resident, relying on his authority as a medical practitioner, is telling the patient what to do and implying dire consequences if she does not comply. It is not surprising that the patient agrees, signs the informed consent form and a hysterectomy not warranted on medical grounds alone is later performed. She has been socialized to believe that the doctor knows best and will act in her best interest.

Questioning the established order is part and parcel of any social movement and the women's health movement is no exception. Questions have been raised about the stratification of the health care delivery system and the roles women play in it both as providers and consumers of health care. For example, why is the health care system stratified so that the higher status, higher paid professional position of physician is predominantly occupied by white middle-class men? Why is it that as you move down in status and pay, the occupational positions become primarily occupied by women and minorities? Why is this stratification recapitulated with women workers? Why are the higher ranking nurses predominantly white and lower status aides predominantly working-class and minority women?

Critics of the medical establishment argue that racism, sexism, and class background are reflected in the stratification of health care workers and have direct consequences for the delivery of health care. American women once predominantly provided health care for each other. During the nineteenth century, the burgeoning male-dominated medical profession gained control over the treatment of women. In this transition, women lost the information and the skills needed to care for their own bodies. Perhaps even more importantly, they lost the ability to define for themselves what was normal and healthy (Rothman 1982).

As the male medical profession gained dominance, women were conceptualized as being at the mercy of their reproductive organs and of their rampant emotions—as sickly and irrational (Barker-Benfield 1976). This view, developed in the nineteenth century, is still reflected in gynecological texts and in medical practices. Increasingly, women's normal mental and physical processes have been medicalized (Reissman 1983; Todd 1983b). For example, over the last decade there has been an increase in the rates at which hysterectomies are being performed in the United States—an increase that is hard to explain on purely medical grounds. And even the most current gynecological texts counsel that if doctors spent time explaining the "facts" to patients, patients can be made to understand that the problems associated with their womanhood can be surgically managed with no adverse affects—advice reflected in the case we reviewed at the beginning of this chapter, as well as in the hysterectomy rates.

Those in the women's health movement claim that sexist assumptions combine with a male-dominated medical profession in continuing to promulgate erroneous conceptions of women and in promoting potentially damaging "cures." In this chapter, I explore the ways in which hysterectomies are often the "cure" perscribed to manage the "benign diseases" associated with women's lives.

The Background Context

When I first began doing this research, I was interested in the effects of hysterectomies on women's self-perceptions—how they felt about themselves as women. Because of the ways women are socialized, I suspected that a hysterectomy might have consequences for their sense of identity, and I wanted to see if that was so, and how such consequences varied among women. It was with this idea in mind that I began to do research in the gynecologic/oncology (cancer of the reproductive system) outpatient clinics of a major west coast teaching hospital. Women who had had prior abnormal Pap smears were referred to these clinics for diagnosis and treatment.

Since I felt that the consequences for their sense of identity might be more severe for women who elected to have a hysterectomy and less severe for women whose hysterectomies were recommended to treat cancerous or pre-cancerous lesions, I needed to understand the medical criteria for hysterectomy. Early in the research process, I began to gain this information. I sat in on the mini-lectures provided for new residents as they rotated on the service; I talked informally with the reproductive oncologists (the attending staff); I read the manual prepared for residents as well as the relevent sections of their gynecological texts. When I thought I had a good understanding of the medical criteria for diagnosing and treating abnormal Pap smears, I started to read patients' files.

On the afternoon that the coloposcope clinic (a coloposcope is a telescope-like device for magnifying and viewing the cervix) met, I came to the clinic during the lunch hour to read the files of patients scheduled for that afternoon. To test my medical understanding, I read the diagnostic laboratory work and the medical descriptions and then I tried to predict what the recommended treatment would be. I expected a high correlation to obtain between the treatments the medical criteria indicated and the treatments that were actually recommended. Much to my surprise, this was not the result. Week after week, I read patients' files and decided, based on my understanding of their medical indications, that they could be treated conservatively (by freezing or surgically removing the abnormal cells); instead, a hysterectomy was often recommended. Although the reverse also occasionally obtained, it was much less frequent. Patients for whom medical indicators suggested a hysterectomy were rarely treated more conservatively.

I went back to the experts—the residents and the attending staff— and informally discussed what I understood the decision making criteria to be. I found that my understanding of the facts was not flawed. Yet, the facts and the files were not in agreement. As the weeks passed and I poured over the files, I thought I detected a trend: older women who had had their families, poor women, minority women, women who were on welfare, women who had had multiple abortions and women who had had several children without being married seemed more likely to have hysterectomies recommended. Unfortunately, I did not consider these early impressions as data. I recorded them in my field notes and puzzled over them, but I did not keep adequate records of how many women fell into each category or what criteria were associated with each decision.

Rather, my impressions built up slowly, led to new discoveries, and eventually, to a new research focus.[1]

But when these early impressions are checked against the data on hysterectomy trends in the United States, they are largely confirmed. According to conservative estimates, 3.5 million women aged 15–44 had hysterectomies in the period 1970–1978 (Center for Disease Control 1981). Early in the decade, hysterectomy was the fourth most frequently performed operation (National Center for Health Statistics 1970). It came after tonsillectomy, hernia repair, and the removal of the gall bladder (Larned 1977). Quoting statistics from an article in the *Washington Post*, Scully (1980) reports that between 1970 and 1975, the hysterectomy rate rose 24 percent, until this surgery became the most frequently performed major operation for women of reproductive age.

In 1976 The National Center for Health Statistics estimated that 794,000 women underwent this surgery, which represented a 15 percent increase over the three prior years. In this year, an estimated ten out of every one thousand women had hysterectomies. Data collected from 1970–1978 demonstrated that on the average women were 35 years old at the time of having a hysterectomy (Center for Disease Control 1981) and that women approaching the age of menopause had the highest incidence of the concurrent removal of their ovaries. During this same time period, almost 50 percent of women aged 40–44 having an abdominal hysterectomy had their ovaries removed (Dicker et al. 1982). According to these figures, more than half of the women in the United States will have their uteruses removed before they reach 65 years of age (Scully 1980; Caress 1977, Bunker 1976) and many will have their ovaries removed as well.

This increase in the incidence of hysterectomies is consistent with an increase in the incidence of other surgeries. Scully (1980) reports findings that demonstrate that in the United States, surgery rates are growing four times faster than the population. A 1976 congressional subcommittee investigating the quality of health care in the U.S. estimated that in 1974 there were 2.4 million unnecessary surgical operations, at a high cost to the American public. The costs were more than monetary. Unnecessary surgeries caused 11,900 deaths in 1975 (United States Congress. House: Cost and Quality of Health Care 1976). The American Cancer Society estimates that in 1985, of the 52,000 new cases of invasive uterine/cervical cancer expected, 15,000 will be for cancer of the cervix and 37,000 for cancer of the endometrium (lining of the womb). Of these, 6,800 women are expected to die from cervical cancer and 2,900 from endometrial cancer. The Cancer Society claims further that the majority of these cervical cancer deaths could be prevented with regular Pap smears and gynecological examinations (American Cancer Society 1985).

Several explanations have been suggested for the increase in hysterectomy rates in the United States. The most prevalent ones are: 1) an increase in pathological conditions; 2) an improvement in diagnostic technology; 3) an increased awareness by patients; 4) a loosening of regulations regarding the performance of hysterectomies; and 5) an increase in the performance of hysterectomies for sterilization (Dicker et al. 1982). Two very different themes undergird these explanations. First, the increase in hysterectomies is related to disease. There is more pathology, there are better techniques for finding it and/or more patient awareness of it. Second, the rise in hysterectomy rates reflects an increase in the performance of elective or prophylactic procedures (e.g., sterilization and prevention). When there are more conservative measures available to treat a medical problem and a hysterectomy is chosen instead, the procedure is considered elective. By contrast, when a hysterectomy is used preventively—to avoid the potential development of future medical problems—the procedure is considered prophylactic. After all, if the uterus is removed, it can not become cancerous. When each of these rationales is examined carefully, a different picture emerges.

Increased Pathological Findings: A Rationale

In a recent issue of *Ob, Gyn News* (1983a), Dr. Neil B. Rosenstein, director, Division of Gynecologic Oncology, the Johns Hopkins University School of Medicine, said that during the last five to ten years the incidence of cervical cancer has decreased. It is during this same time period that the incidence of hysterectomy has increased. A similar discrepancy is evident in studies that examine the distribution of hysterectomies across the country. These studies indicate that with women of reproductive age, medical practice varies by geographic region. For example, women in the south have the highest rates of hysterectomies—

more than twice as high as women in the northeast (Center for Disease Control 1981); however, women in the northeast have their ovaries removed at the time of hysterectomy more often than do women in any other part of the country (Dicker et al. 1982). If increased pathology accounted for the increase in hysterectomies, it would be hard to explain why women in the northeast have both the lowest hysterectomy rate and the highest rate of concurrent ovary removal—do fewer women have more severe pathology? Similarly, it would be hard to explain the high hysterectomy rates in the south—do more women have pathology that is less severe?

There is a similar inconsistency when we explore the increase in hysterectomies across the spectrum of the female population. In addition to categories of age and sexual behavior, there are black/white, rural/urban, lower/higher social class distinctions that characterize the population at risk from cervical cancer (chapter 4 discusses those at risk in greater detail). Women from lower socio-economic ranks, rural women with long intervals since their last pregnancy, black women, women who began to have sexual intercourse at an early age and with multiple partners, and women over 35 are most at risk for cervical cancer (Richart 1980; Walton et al. 1979; Handy and Wieben 1965). While it might be argued that a rising hysterectomy rate produces a decreasing incidence of cervical cancer, for the most part, the increase in the hysterectomy rate is less evident in relation to the more at-risk groups.

For example, although hysterectomy rates have remained relatively constant for black women, the rates for white women have increased from 6.8 percent in 1970 to 9.0 percent in 1973 (Center for Disease Control 1981). The only place there is consistency between cancer and hysterectomy rates is in relation to older women. Hysterectomy rates are lowest for young women and highest for women between the ages of 35–44 (Dicker et al. 1982).[2] These inconsistencies make it hard to use increased pathology as the explanation for the increase in hysterectomy rates.

It is no easier to use improved diagnostic technology as an explanation. While there have been some modifications, the original Pap smear technique remains the predominant diagnostic measure for cervical cancer (*Ob, Gyn News* 1983a). But perhaps more importantly, as both Scully (1980) and Larned (1977) point out, the hysterectomy rate is not directly related to cancer at all. To validate her point, Scully discusses findings presented in an article in *Primary Care*. She reports that: "In

1975, The American College of Obstetricians and Gynecologists estimated that 15 percent of hysterectomies were done for cancer, 30 percent for noncancerous fibroids, 35 percent for pelvic relaxation or prolapse and 20 percent for sterilization" (Scully 1980:142).

The Case for Prophylactic and Elective Surgery

If neither increased pathology nor more effective diagnostic techniques account for the rapid rise in hysterectomy rates, relaxed medical attitudes and increased patient acceptance of such procedures are more successful as explanations. At a 1971 meeting of the American College of Obstetrics and Gynecology, a question was raised about the performance of prophylactic hysterectomies. At that time, while not all of the physicians agreed, a majority expressed their approval of the procedure (Caress 1977). The move toward elective or prophylactic surgery is consistent with the medical attitude that once reproduction is over the uterus is not only a useless organ, but a potentially disease-producing one (United States Congress. House, Quality of Surgical Care Hearing 1977; Larned 1977). This position is clearly stated in medical sources and has been widely referred to in nonmedical sources as well (Scully 1980; Schiefelbein 1980; Larned 1977; Caress 1977).

Caress quotes Dr. R. C. Wright, writing in a 1969 issue of *Obstetrics and Gynecology:* "The uterus has but one function. After the last planned pregnancy it becomes a useless symptom-producing, potentially cancer bearing organ and therefore should be removed." This attitude is perhaps best exemplified in a text popular since 1941—*Novak's Textbook of Gynecology.* In the 1970 edition, Novak agrees that after reproduction is over, the uterus is an organ of little worth. Although he does not recommend its prophylactic or elective removal, he does not criticize physicians who perform these procedures.

By the 1975 edition, his support for such procedures is more evident. He claims that while there are greater risks associated with a hysterectomy for sterilization than there are with other sterilization procedures, such "hysterectomies performed by specialists are justifiable." The implication is clear: The risks associated with hysterectomies are blamed on physicians other than gynecologists who perform this surgery. In addition to justifying the procedure, he provides the grounds to legitimize it. He states: "Menstruation is a nuisance to most women and if this can be abolished without impairing ovarian function, it would probably be a blessing not only to the woman but to her husband (Novak 1975:113).

Although the language changes in the 1981 edition, the underlying assumption remains the same: "Most hysterectomies performed by specialists are justifiable, even though the uterus shows no evidence of a pathological condition." In fact the title of the section changes from "Elective Hysterectomy" to "Hysterectomy for Benign Disease," legitimizing relaxed medical standards, while medicalizing women's normal bodily processes. Menstruation and the ability to conceive become the "benign diseases" to be treated surgically by gynecologists. Doctors are advised that if they spend time explaining "a few fundamental facts to the patient, it will be possible to make her understand that no dire consequences will occur." It is necessary for the patient to understand that "no drastic results are found after the removal of the uterus."[3]

Recently a gynecologist writing in *The American Journal of Obstetrics and Gynecology* listed several criteria commonly used by physicians as indicators for hysterectomy. These were:

> To alleviate the "drudgery of the menses"; to lower the incidence of benign uterine disease; to reduce the occurrence of malignant uterine disease; to ensure the 100 percent efficiency of a sterilization procedure; and to generally decrease the discomfort of various pelvic symptoms (Sloan 1978:602).

The author of this article asks us to consider whether similar reasons would be used with male patients to permit the elective or prophylactic removal of the prostate gland. After reminding us that such a situation is not common medical practice and would not be considered in the patient's best interest, he goes on to explore why a similar procedure for women—the prophylactic or elective hysterectomy—is commonly practiced and is consistently considered to be in the patient's best interest. He questions why women over 35 are assumed to be willing to part with menstruation and procreation and why the myth that sex is better without the uterus is being perpetuated.

His response is culture. The author claims that we live in a culture that separates mind and body. As members of this culture, doctors are able to remove a uterus that is not diseased and to believe that there will be no psychological stress for the patient. He restates the commonly held medical belief, which he feels influences medical practice, that for a woman in her late 30s or early 40s, reproduction is nearly over and the uterus is no longer needed.

The increase in hysterectomy rates are, at least partially, established by a culturally based system of beliefs and the medical practices that flow from them. The definition and performance of prophylactic and elective hysterectomies are consistent with these beliefs—to remove a woman's uterus is to prevent disease and protect life. Yet, the facts do not always support this position. As Braun and Druckman (1976) point out, life expectancy would be increased slightly if all of the women over 35 in the United States had their uteruses removed.

There are similar problems with the beliefs that support hysterectomy as an elective procedure. Such a procedure may be requested by the patient or suggested by the doctor. However, since there are other more conservative measures available to deal with such medical concerns as sterilization, pelvic discomfort, and menstrual drudgery, the hysterectomy is said to be elective—chosen by patients from among the available options. There are at least two problems with this characterization. First, we have very little data on how women actually feel about their uteruses or their menstruation and every reason to suspect that both serve important symbolic functions, for men as well as for women (Sloan 1978). Second, with doctors as the holders of medical information and technical skills—as authorities—how free is the patient's choice? When discussing regional variations in hysterectomy rates, Dicker and his colleagues (1982) concluded that differences in diagnostic styles and medical beliefs are shaped by differences in training and practice. This conclusion does not provide much room for the patients' choices. In fact we have very little data on what actually transpires between doctor and patient when they are reaching such a treatment decision. What data there are suggest that the notation in the medical file, "patient requests a hysterectomy for sterilization" often has little to do with the ways the decision is actually reached (Sloan 1978).

A Slightly Different Picture

Feminists point out that over 90 percent of all obstetrician/gynecologists are men. As men, to some extent their attitudes mirror the current views of women in society (Larned 1977). These attitudes, reflected in gyne-cological texts (Scully and Bart 1973) and reinforced in other aspects of medical training, provide the basis for residents learning to use a regular sales pitch for hysterectomies (Scully 1980). Such practices are not without precedent.

Historically, the medicalization of women's normal bodily processes went hand in hand with the development of a male medical establish-ment (Barker-Benfield 1976). During the 19th century, if women were seen as acting "inappropriately," gynecological surgery was the remedy (Reissman 1983; Todd 1983b, Ehrenreich and English 1979). Michelle Harrison (1982), writing about her experiences as a resident in obstet-rics/gynecology, argues that the situation has not changed much today and cannot be improved by just adding women to the men already re-ceiving medical educations. Sexist attitudes about women are embed-ded in the institution of medicine, are perpetuated by predominantly male professors and influence medical practices. To survive, women residents must often adopt the same attitudes and the cycle continues.

If these are the prevalent medical attitudes, it is not surprising that hysterectomy rates have risen. But attitudes do not tell the whole story. There are other contributing factors. The increase in prophylactic and elective hysterectomies coincides with a decrease in the birth rate. Since we do not normally consider birth a surgical procedure, it is often easy to forget that obstetrician/gynecologists are surgeons—surgeons who usually deliver health care on a fee-for-service basis. This point is graphically illustrated in two articles in the *New England Journal of Medicine* (Bunker 1970 and Bunker 1976; see also Scully 1980; Larned 1977). Anesthesiologist John Bunker points out that in the United States there are twice as many surgeons in proportion to the population as there are in England and Wales. There are also twice the number of sur-geries (Bunker 1970) and more than twice as many hysterectomies (Bunker 1976).

From these findings one could conclude either that Americans are sicker than the British, that the British are underinsured, or that there are other factors in the organization of the delivery of health care in the two countries that produce these differences. It is the last conclusion that Bunker reaches (see also Larned 1977). Since in Great Britain medicine is socialized, no one profits from the performance of elective or prophylactic hysterectomies. A logical extension of this position is to claim that if physicians in the United States did not have a vested financial interest in performing these procedures, we would not see as many performed. In fact, when profit is controlled, we do see a decrease in the number of hysterectomies. Scully (1980), reporting from an article in the *New York Times Magazine,* states that in a prepaid health plan, where doctors are salaried and no profit is entailed, the number of hysterectomies is four times lower than it is in a fee-for-service plan where profits are expected. In a similar vein, Schiefelbein (1980) reports that when hysterectomy rates are compared for women in prepaid health plans and for women covered by Blue Cross insurance, the insured women show twice as many hysterectomies. What remains constant across these reports is the relationship between the potential for profits and increased hysterectomy rates.

Bunker (1970) draws an additional conclusion (see also Larned 1977). The British health care delivery system is organized so that the specialist is a consultant who only sees cases referred from primary physicians after a determination has been made that the expertise of the specialist is needed. In the United States, health care is organized differently. Women are free to choose their doctors. Women who are not sick often go to a specialist—their obstetrician/gynecologist—for their routine reproduction-related care. This places the American specialist in an advantageous position for recommending elective and prophylactic procedures. It also places patients at a decided disadvantage. The patient often lacks the medical skill and technical expertise necessary to evaluate the doctor's recommendation and is without another "expert" to guide her through the medical maze.

The argument thus far is that the increase in hysterectomy rates is related to commonly held assumptions about women and reproductive surgery—assumptions learned in medical school (if not before), reinforced in the gynecological literature and sustained by the fee-for-service organization of the medical profession. If the profession of medicine is organized so that physicians profit from increased surgery rates, and if the specialists who perform these procedures simultaneously have a vested interest in performing them, and if they are furthermore the most likely persons to provide the patient's routine health care, it should not be surprising that the number of elective and prophylactic hysterectomies is increasing.

Although we have information on the numbers of hysterectomies performed annually and can extrapolate the reasons for the increased surgery rate, we still have very little information about the ways assumptions about women and institutional arrangements translate into medical practices and less information about how these practices are expressed in the medical communications that function to accomplish treatment decisions. As I pointed out in chapter 1, the spoken interactions of the medical interview serve multiple functions. Doctors and patients request and provide information, sending and receiving messages at the same time. The exchange of information is also organized to accomplish the goals of diagnosis and treatment. The participants in the medical event—doctor and patient—interact and/or communicate jointly to accomplish these goals. Yet there is evidence—increasing amounts of evidence—that this process is neither objective nor neutral. Zola (1972) argues that medicine is an institution of social control. Following this logic, doctors, as experts, have the status to redefine health and illness, to act as agents of social control, and to enforce their individual, moral, social, and political judgments using the institutional authority of their medical role.

To display the ways in which the communicational work of the medical interview is shaped by the asymmetry of the medical relationship, I present an in-depth analysis of the medical decision making process with five patients. The discussion of these cases raises several delicate issues: issues related to the status and power of the medical profession and to the rights and responsibilities involved in medical decision making. It also raises a question about the values associated with women's reproductive organs. The last is perhaps the most sensitive issue. If I am going to argue that women are pressured into having elective or prophylactic hysterectomies—surgeries that may be more consistent with doctors' rather than patients' interests—do I as a feminist place myself in a double bind? By taking exception to the dominant medical attitude that after reproduction functions are over, the uterus is dispensible, do I run the risk of elevating it to a sacred organ?

Let me make my position clear at the outset. About 800,000 hysterectomies are performed each year in the United States. Without question, when this procedure is performed by a competent physician and with "proper indications," women can benefit (Thompson and Birch 1981). However, there are strong indications that elective and prophylactic hysterectomies are overused.

The Research Context

This research was done in a west coast university teaching hospital. Because of the organization and staffing of each clinic in this setting, I have called them the faculty and the community clinics. The faculty clinic was staffed by professors of reproductive oncology. The community clinic was staffed by residents under the supervision of reproductive oncologists (staff physicians).

From the patients referred to these clinics, the research population was assembled largely for practical reasons. Because early in the research process I had decided that I was unprepared to deal with patients who had life-threatening cancer, no patients with invasive disease were part of the sample population. As a consequence, the patient population was defined as women with precancerous problems in their reproductive systems. The analysis is drawn from verbatim transcripts of audiotaped practitioner-patient communications, information gathered from medical files, and other ethnographic materials. My background knowledge grew from impromptu interviews with practitioners and was heightened by attending lectures with residents, studying the training manual prepared for them, and reading appropriate sections of their gynecological texts.

This mode of analysis was based on the assumption that neither practitioners nor patients say aloud all that contributes to their decision making. For example, patients rarely say aloud that they do not trust their medical practitioners or that they suspect them of trying to manipulate the situation. Similarly, neither staff doctors nor residents say aloud that a patient looks like a poor woman or that she talks like an uneducated woman. They do not say that the ways patients talk, look, or dress lead them to believe that the patients are not responsible and will not return for necessary follow-up care. They do not say that these factors contribute to their recommendation of a less conservative treatment. Neither doctors nor residents say aloud that a particular patient has all of the children she needs or should have because she is on welfare and cannot afford the children she already has. They do not say that hairy underarms and legs, asking too many questions, or being too quiet, acting too passively, or too aggressively, wanting children (or more children) contribute to the treatment recommended. Residents do not say aloud that they need surgical experience or that a particular patient is a good candidate for a hysterectomy (even though a hysterectomy is not absolutely necessary on medical grounds). Although these things are not said aloud, my observations in the medical setting and my conversations with the participants combined to suggest that these factors (and others like them) did shape the discourse and did contribute to the negotiation of treatment decisions.

Discourse about Pap smears provides a particularly fertile field for studying how treatment decisions are negotiated. Pap smears are preventive health measures. They are recommended for most women once a year as a screen for cervical cancer. The results of Pap smears in the middle range—classes 2, 3 and 4—represent a grey area between normal cells and invasive disease. They often indicate dysplasia, or abnormal cell changes, that, although not cancerous, may be precursors of cervical cancer.

Pap smears in the grey area give medical practitioners the widest latitude in their decision making. When a Pap smear is abnormal, the medical task is to ensure that the whole area of abnormal cells can be visualized to rule out the possibility of invasive disease. Once the extent of the lesion and the degree of abnormality have been determined, treatment decisions are based on two separate but interrelated goals: a) to protect the patient from developing more extensive disease (cancer) and b) to preserve, where possible, the patient's reproductive functions.

During my study, there were three treatment options routinely used to treat women with Pap smears in the range between normal and invasive disease: cryo-surgery (freezing), cone biopsy or conization, and hysterectomy. Cryo-surgery is an office procedure that retains a woman's reproductive capacity. Cone biopsy or conization is a hospital procedure done under an anesthetic. A thin cone-shaped slice is cored out of the endocervical canal and examined. Cone biopsies can be either diagnostic or therapeutic. If the upper limits of the cone sample are free of abnormal cells, then this diagnostic procedure becomes an effective therapeutic one. It threatens, but does not terminate, reproductive capacity and has been demonstrated to be as effective in treating dysplasia as hysterectomy is. Hysterectomy is the surgical removal of the uterus.

The manual prepared for residents further stipulates the way treatment decisions are to be made. It says that when the limits of the lesion are seen and there is no evidence of invasive disease, treatment should be based on the patient's wish. If she wishes to retain her reproductive capacity, conservative measures like cryo-surgery may be utilized. If she requests sterilization, hysterectomy is the treatment of choice. According to the manual, hysterectomies are only indicated when conservative techniques fail, when there is evidence of invasive disease, or when patients request hysterectomy for sterilization.

These seem to be rather clear criteria for medical decision making. Yet, based on my observation, actual treatment decisions are not as clear as they seem. I found that women with abnormal Pap smears referred to the community clinic were more likely to be treated nonconservatively—to receive hysterectomies—than were women treated in the faculty clinic. On purely medical grounds, it is hard to explain why no patients in the faculty clinic received hysterectomies. Or, even though there was no evidence of invasive disease, why seven out of thirteen women in the community clinic were given hysterectomies.

Given the parameters just outlined, we could speculate that perhaps the women in the community clinic requested hysterectomies for sterilization. However, I was in the examining room while treatment decisions were being reached and during the two years of my research, these patients never requested sterilization.

To study the decision making process, I identified communicational patterns that held true across both settings (the faculty and community clinics) and among providers of medical care (residents and reproductive oncologists). As I studied these patterns, I noticed a dominant theme and an exception. In the dominant theme, practitioners had and used quite a wide latitude in recommending treatments, and patients, usually unquestioningly, accepted the treatment recommended. Although patients could and did ask questions, they rarely questioned the information presented or challenged the treatment recommended. In the exceptional theme, however, patients asked questions challenging the treatment recommended.

To disply both themes, I explored the ways doctors and patients communicated to negotiate treatment decisions. In this discussion, although I point out some differences in the ways information is presented by residents and attending staff, in each case, the health care providers discussed for the most part, are representative of the medical population I studied; however, the patients I discussed have been chosen to represent a small subset of the larger sample—a subset selected because it best exemplified the strategies patients used to influence the decision making process. First, I discuss the strategies providers and patients used to exchange information. Since both doctor and patient ask and answer questions, at first glance, this seems to be a relatively equitable exchange. On closer examination, however, the authority of the medical role and the influence such authority has in the decision making process emerges clearly. Doctors, as medical experts, control patients' access to information—a control illuminated by the ways medical information is presented and questions are answered.

An analysis of the patterns of practitioner-patient communication through which treatment decisions are negotiated provides information not available when only the criteria underlying medical decision making are considered. These criteria are, in many ways, external and constraining "social facts," which produce and inhibit the decision making process. Yet, treatment decisions are affected by participants' interactional activities and, as such, they are socially produced. An analysis of the strategic use of language in medical interviews displays the ways treatment decisions are accomplished within a contextual framework. Such an analysis illuminates how physicians have an institutionally based authority that patients lack—a power manifested and reflected in how practitioners answer questions and present information. Although patients do not have the same kind of authority, they have the potential to question the information provided and the treatment recommended—a potential with important consequences. When patients use this potential, they can and do redirect talk about treatment options and affect the way the treatment decision is reached.

The Communicational Context

In analyzing how language is used strategically over the course of the medical interview to accomplish treatment decisions, I do not intend to characterize the field of medicine as a whole or to praise or criticize particular medical practitioners. Rather, it is my intention to demonstrate that medical practitioners and patients have different practical concerns and differential access to power, which differently organizes how they exchange information. This organization has consequences in terms of the decisions reached.

Patients enter medical interactions from a position of relative weakness. For example, they have an abnormal Pap smear and feel threatened by the possibility of a cancer-related medical problem. They enter unfamiliar surroundings in which all of the other participants seem to share a common language. This language is, for the most part, unintelligible and frightening to them.

Medical practitioners, on the other hand, are in their "home court" in the medical setting. They understand and have some control over the workings of the hospital and of the clinic bureaucracies. Medical jargon is their professional lexicon. They have knowledge and skills that are usually mysterious to patients. It is from this position of relative strength that practitioners greet patients and the medical interview begins.

Medical practitioners, in addition, are very busy. Their time is budgeted—some for this patient and some for the next. For them, the diagnostic/treatment process is a general concern. Their focus is on how, within certain parameters, best to treat a specific medical problem. The patient is one among many with similar problems.

For residents, the diagnostic/treatment process includes an additional concern. They need surgical experience if they are to become competent practitioners. This creates a dual focus for them: 1) providing adequate medical care; and 2) maximizing the opportunities for surgery.

In addition, medical practitioners are not as able, as I was, to separate themselves from death. The relationships between abnormal Pap smears, cancer, and the kind of deaths most cancers cause may contribute to the practitioners' treatment recommendations. This may be especially true when they treat lower-class, minority women, who have a reputation for being immature, irresponsible, and unlikely to return for the necessary follow-up care.

The practical concerns and the access to power are not the same for patients as for doctors. Patients are not interested in making a diagnosis, they cannot recommend treatments, they do not need surgical experience and, usually, they have not faced death on a daily basis. Their time is not measured into equal increments to be divided among a maximum number of treatment interviews. For patients, the focus is on the meaning of their own medical problems and how they will affect their everyday lives. Their time is measured as time away from school, job, or family; time until they find out the results of the laboratory tests or the treatments to be recommended; time as a bomb ticking away precious moments before the suspected cancer explodes and takes over their lives. Patients are interested in finding out what their abnormal Pap smears mean, whether they indicate cancer, and what needs to be done about that. They are afraid of the unknown, worried about the possibility of having cancer, and fearful that their lives, reproductive capacities, and value as women may be at risk.

Both the medical practitioner and the patient have knowledge that is necessary for the decision making process of the other. To gain access to this knowledge, they exchange information organized around topics by requesting and providing information to each other. During the exchange, language functions strategically to move the decision making process closer to a treatment decision. On some occasions, requests for information function as "questioning" strategies. Both practitioner and patient request specific information from each other and provide access to less specific information. For example the question, "What did A. tell you about your Pap smear?" is a request for specific information. It is also a way to gain more subtle information about the woman's competence as a patient.

Both medical practitioners and patients use questioning strategies. They are used by medical practitioners during talk about reproduction to gain access to information that only patients can supply. Patients use questioning strategies during talk about treatment options to gather information about the necessity of a recommended treatment. And in each case, the ways they are used influences the decision making process. When used by residents and staff physicians, questioning strategies are used differently. Staff physicians are more likely to use questions in ways that provide a slot for patients to display their competence, and residents are less likely to provide such a slot. In a similar way, patients can ask questions in ways that elicit information essential to their decision-making process or in ways that do not elicit such information.

On other occasions, information is provided in ways that function as "presentational" and "persuasional" strategies. Both of these strategies are negotiating mechanisms. They provide information while suggesting or specifying the ways the information should be understood.

Presentational strategies are "soft sells." They provide information while suggesting the way patients should make sense out of it. For example, a practitioner might say, "We usually treat this by freezing."

This presentation provides the patient with information about a treatment option, while at the same time suggesting that it is the "usual" or "normal" way to treat her condition.

Persuasional strategies are harder sells. They provide information while specifying the way it should be understood. For example, a practitioner might say, "What you should do if you don't want any more children is have a hysterectomy. No more uterus, no more cancer, no more babies, no more birth control, and no more periods." This presentation provides the patient with information about what treatment she should have, while at the same time specifying why she should have it (no more uterus, no more cancer, etc.).

Only medical practitioners use presentation and persuasional strategies. They are used when talking about cancer and treatment options to provide information about what treatment decision the patient should make. And, again, the strategies are used differently by residents and staff physicians. Residents are more likely than staff physicians to use a harder sell.

Questioning, presentational, and persuasional strategies are the interactional mechanisms by which treatment decisions are accomplished. They are the strategies that provide the information necessary for negotiating treatment decisions.

Physicians' Questioning Strategies

Questioning strategies provide a slot for patients to display their competence.[4] Susan, for example, was diagnosed and treated in the faculty clinic. She was a twenty-one-year-old Anglo woman, a student at a local university, had never married, and had been pregnant once and had an abortion. She was referred to Doctor M., the junior oncologist in the faculty clinic, by a woman's health care specialist.[5] A routine Pap smear taken in this clinic was returned with the notation that it contained abnormal cells, and because of the professional relationship between the woman's health care specialist and the new doctor in the hospital (the junior staff oncologist), she was referred to the faculty clinic.

On her first visit, the doctor twice requested information in a way that functioned strategically. He said, "Now did A. explain to you the abnormal, what this abnormal Pap smear business is?"

The patient answered, "She (the women's health care specialist) explained that the cells looked abnormal . . . the cells are in a dysplastic condition."

The doctor continued by asking, "Dysplasia, what's your understanding of that?"

To which she responded, "Well, what's anyone's understanding of it? They're abnormal and you don't know why and they don't know if it leads to cancer."

In both of these requests for information, Susan responded by providing the information requested, and in so doing, presented herself as a competent young woman.

In the next case, the patient did not display herself as competent. The patient, Bertha, was a thirty-year-old Anglo woman. She had been married once, divorced, been pregnant once, and had given the child up for adoption. She was referred by the same women's health care specialist to the same clinic (the faculty clinic) and was seen by the same doctor, who asked questions similar to those he had asked Susan.

During the interview, the doctor asked, "Do you know that the Pap smear, do you understand what the Pap smear means? What it does?"

The patient responded by saying, "Uhm, A. explained a little, but I'm not sure of the possibilities. I don't even know what all those are, but she told me not to worry yet."

Bertha's response neither provided the information requested nor made her appear competent. To be sure that Bertha had the necessary information to understand her medical problem and to reach a decision, the doctor followed up this exchange by providing her with information about her Pap smear and about the diagnostic and therapeutic procedures used to manage it.

In the third example, the patient was referred to the community clinic, where she was diagnosed and treated, by Doctor S., a resident. As they talked, no slot was provided for her to display her competence. Marta, a twenty-three-year-old Mexican-American woman was married and the mother of three small children. She had been referred by the Primary Care Clinic, where a post-partum checkup and routine Pap smear had disclosed abnormal cells. At the time of her visit to the community clinic, she was pregnant with an unwanted pregnancy, which later led to an abortion. Although this was her first abortion, it was not her first birth control failure. Given these factors and the previous findings, it is not surprising that the resident in this case recommended a hysterectomy. What is more surprising is that she did not end up having one. She is the only woman in the sample population with several children who was treated with cryo-surgery (freezing).

The bureaucratic organization of the outpatient clinic system contributed to Marta's treatment. At the community clinic, Doctor S. advised Marta not to have a tubal ligation. Instead, he recommended a hysterectomy to treat her medical problem and for sterilization. When the patient was referred to another clinic for abortion counseling, that clinic encouraged her to have a tubal ligation for sterilization. Through the second clinic, Marta had an abortion and a tubal ligation. When she returned to the community clinic, there were no longer any medical grounds upon which a hysterectomy could be justified, and so she was treated with cryo-surgery.

The exchange of information in Marta's case took place in a different way from the exchanges in Susan's and Bertha's cases. Susan and Bertha were treated by Doctor M., the junior oncologist in the faculty clinic. In each case, he asked questions that functioned strategically. These questions provided a slot into which the patients could respond—displaying their competence in the process.

Marta, on the other hand, was treated by Doctor S., a resident in the community clinic. Doctor S. did not use questions in a strategic manner. Thus, Marta did not have an opportunity to display herself as a competent patient. When the resident questioned her, he asked only very specific questions about her birth control practices. Because she had come to the clinic with an unwanted pregnancy, it was quite clear that Marta had not been an effective user of birth control. It is interesting to speculate on the reasons why the resident did not use more general questions, which might have allowed Marta to display her competence. I suspect that he had already judged her to be incompetent on grounds that are not displayed in the verbal communications between them. These assumptions of his structured the exchanges of information that followed and influenced his recommendation of a hysterectomy.

Patients' Questioning Strategies

Some patients also ask questions. They ask them in response to information provided by medical professionals during discussions of treatment options. When asked by patients, questions have the potential to change the direction of the treatment decision, as shown in the following examples.

When Bertha returned to the faculty clinic to discuss the results of her tests and make a treatment decision, she asked a question during a discussion of treatment options. On her previous visit, Bertha had provided the information that she did not want to have any more children. Doctor M. responded by recommending a hysterectomy as a permanent method of sterilization and to treat her abnormal Pap smear.

On the second visit, their exchange opened with a discussion that reviewed what had transpired on the previous visit and during a previous phone conversation. The doctor reminded Bertha that he had recommended a hysterectomy, and Bertha asked a question that redirected the talk about treatment options and in fact affected the final treatment. She said, "Have a hysterectomy and that, I'm that, if there's an alternative. I'm terrified of operations." Doctor M. responded, "Uh, okay, well, there certainly is an alternative, yeah, we can treat this by just freezing it here in the office and that usually will take care of it about 90 percent of the time." The discussion of options and the treatment performed were redirected because the patient raised a question. She was treated with cryo-surgery.

The next patient, Carmen, was also diagnosed and treated by Doctor M. She was referred to the faculty clinic from a social agency staffed by native Spanish-speaking workers. Carmen was a forty-two-year-old, bilingual, Mexican-American woman. She was married and had three children. Her diagnosis and treatment were related to her being a poor, bilingual, Mexican-American woman and to my participation both as a researcher and translator. (The need for translation with a bilingual woman will become clearer.)

The patient had a medical problem for which she had gone to her private physician. He had recommended surgery, but she did not have the money to pay for it. In her search for less expensive medical care, a friend referred her to the outreach clinic staffed by native Spanish speakers. At the clinic, Carmen received advice about how to apply for MediCal (The California equivalent of medicaid) and was referred to Doctor M.

When the doctor and patient met to discuss her treatment options, he informed her that the extent of her lesion had not yet been visualized, told her that she needed to have a conization biopsy as the next diagnostic step, and talked about a hysterectomy. Carmen was concerned about how she would pay for hospital care and was confused by the letter she had received from MediCal. She asked the doctor to clarify the letter and he was unable to do so (which does not speak well for MediCal's style of communication).

To provide the information that Carmen requested, the doctor called the billing office. While he was on the phone, Carmen turned to me and asked, in Spanish, if the doctor had said he was going to take out her uterus. I explained, in Spanish, the difference between conization biopsy and hysterectomy and confirmed that the doctor had been talking about removing her uterus. She asked if that would be necessary and I suggested that she ask the doctor.

Two things particularly struck me about our exchange. First, because Carmen spoke English so well, both the doctor and I had assumed that she understood it equally well. She did not. After reviewing the transcript, I was not surprised. When talking about treatments, the doctor used several words interchangeably: womb, uterus, cervix and hysterectomy. I was also struck by the consequences of our exchange. At the next opportunity, which occurred during a discussion of treatment options, the patient requested information, changed the direction of the discussion of options, and this had consequences for the treatment performed.

While talking about how long the patient would have to be in the hospital, Doctor M. explained that the longer stay was because they would be taking out her uterus. The patient then asked, "Is that necessary?" The doctor responded, "Well, it isn't absolutely necessary; it may or may not be. . . ." For most of the remaining exchanges of information, the doctor worked to move the patient toward a treatment decision of hysterectomy. In each such instance, the patient responded by asking if it was necessary or by saying that, if it was not necessary, she did not want it. She was treated with a conization biopsy.

Another patient, Colleen, was diagnosed and treated in the community clinic by Dr. T., a resident. Although Colleen asked questions, she did not change the direction of the discussion of options or the treatment performed. Colleen, a thirty-two-year-old Anglo woman, had been married, divorced, pregnant five times, and had three children. Although she was an American citizen, she had married and lived most of her adult life in Ireland. Her children still lived there with their father.

When she returned to the community clinic to discuss her treatment options, Doctor T. told her that the extent of the lesion had not been visualized, asked her if she wanted more children, and recommended a conization biopsy followed by a hysterectomy.

During the discussion of these treatment options and in response to information that the resident was presenting, Colleen made a request for information, a request that functioned strategically. She said, "Well, for this way now would you say, for instance, you're talking about there could be surgery, if, uhh, there is an advancement of cancer there, a sign of cancer. Well, also the fact that you asked me did I want any more children, there's another way of doing it too, but it also means that it could travel, is that it, the cancer could spread, say for instance, if I don't have a hysterectomy, is that the idea?"

Doctor T. responded, "Well, if you have cancer, then it has to be treated because it can spread, right." The talk about treatment options did not change the direction of the discussion of options or the treatment performed. Colleen was treated with a vaginal hysterectomy.

The communication in this case between the resident and the patient is different from those that took place with the two prior patients (Bertha and Carmen). Colleen is the only patient who added information to the "facts" provided by the medical practitioner. She added the notion that cancer could spread if it were not treated with a hysterectomy. It was this information that the resident picked up and used to justify his treatment recommendation. It might be argued that Colleen asked her question in the way that she did in order to influence the direction of the treatment decision—to make a stronger case for a hysterectomy. However, the question she asked is not as clear or as strong as those used by the other two patients. She did not directly confront the resident by asking if there were alternatives or if a hysterectomy was necessary. In addition, she asked two questions during the same utterance. The resident avoided discussing alternatives entirely. And he answered only part of the second question. He did not address the question of whether the abnormal cells would spread if she did not have a hysterectomy. Instead he answered a hypothetical question that she had not really asked. He answered the question, "If it is cancer, would it spread without a hysterectomy?" He did not tell her that if she did not have cancer, there were other treatment alternatives.

In Bertha's, Carmen's and Colleen's cases, the medical providers (Doctor M., a reproductive oncologist and Doctor T., a resident) did present information that provided a slot into which the patients could request information that functioned strategically. In each case, the medical professional's response to the question was different. In addition, the medical professionals themselves elicited information from patients differently. With Bertha, Doctor M. asked questions to request specific information and to provide a slot for her to display her competence. In response, she neither provided the information he asked for nor displayed her competence. In the cases of Carmen and Colleen, neither the reproductive oncologist (Doctor M.) nor the resident (Doctor T.) asked questions. Neither patient was given an opportunity to display her understanding of her medical problem or her competence as a patient.

It is interesting to speculate on the reasons why Carmen and Colleen were not given the opportunity to display their competence, as Bertha was; or why neither Carmen or Bertha were treated by a hysterectomy, and Colleen was. On closer inspection, Carmen shares features in common with both Bertha and Colleen. Although Carmen and Bertha were both treated in the faculty clinic by the same reproductive oncologist, their referral patterns had been quite different. Bertha had been referred to the clinic by a woman's health care specialist with whom she had a long-standing relationship. This relationship provided an outside advocate, who could hold the medical practitioner in the hospital accountable. Neither Carmen nor Colleen had an outside advocate. Carmen had been referred from an outreach clinic staffed by native Spanish-speakers, and Colleen had been referred from within the system of community clinics. In these cases, neither the interest of the referring medical practitioner nor the organization of the bureaucracy provided the kind of support Bertha had developed with the woman's health care specialist.

It seems reasonable to speculate that both the reproductive oncologist and the resident judged Carmen and Colleen to be less powerful than Bertha, on grounds that are not immediately evident from their verbal communications. These judgments then structured the exchange of information between practitioner and patient and had a determining impact on the treatment decision reached. Although in each case the medical practitioner did provide a slot for the patient to request information that functioned strategically, he responded to the questions that the patients inserted into these slots differently.

At first glance, then, it would be reasonable to assume that Carmen and Colleen, denied the opportunities to display their competence, lacking an outside advocate and having been perceived as not powerful, would be treated with hysterectomies, and Bertha would not be. My observations suggest two reasons why these were not the outcomes. First, Carmen was treated in the faculty clinic by a reproductive oncologist— a staff physician, and Colleen was treated in the community clinic by a resident. The reproductive oncologists who are staff physicians do not have the same "need" to perform hysterectomies as do residents, who must have surgical experience to become fully qualified as doctors. Second, Carmen used a strong questioning strategy and kept returning to it each time the doctor suggested a hysterectomy. Colleen used a weaker questioning strategy and did not return to it, even when her questions were not really answered. Thus, Colleen's impact on the decision making process was weaker, and she was treated with a hysterectomy.

Physicians' Presentational and Persuasional Strategies

Although both medical practitioners and patients can ask questions, doctors do so during exchanges of general information and to gather the details of their patients' reproductive histories and their desires for children (or more children). Patients, by contrast, ask questions during discussions about treatment options. When patients ask questions, there are differences in the ways medical practitioners present information to them about cancer and treatment options. They use presentational and persuasional strategies to provide patients with the information necessary to reach treatment decisions and ways of understanding or making sense out of that information.

In each of the previous three cases, the medical professional's response to the patient's questions provided specific information and also suggested how that information should be understood. In Bertha's case, Doctor M. responded by saying, "There certainly is an alternative . . ." and by providing the information that cryo-surgery is an alternative that is 90 percent effective. He both provided specific information and by the tone of his presentation made the choice of cryo-surgery perfectly acceptable.

In Carmen's case, Doctor M. responded by saying, "Well, it isn't absolutely necessary . . ." The statement that "it isn't absolutely necessary" frames the medical information in such a way as to suggest a preference: although a hysterectomy is not absolutely necessary, it certainly is preferable.

In Colleen's case, Doctor T., a resident, avoided directly answering the patient's question. By answering only a small part of what was asked, he suggested that the answer to the whole was contained within the part; that is, that a hysterectomy was a necessary procedure.

In each case, the medical practitioners suggest the ways information should be understood. In the next case, information is presented by the resident in a way that does more than suggest how to make sense out of it. Persuasional strategies are used to specify the grounds upon which the patient's understanding is to be based. In presenting the options to Marta, the resident, Doctor S., said:

> What I was going to tell you is that there are two ways this can be treated. Okay? One is for dysplasia that we could do a hysterectomy and just remove the uterus. That means no more babies in the future and so you know, as a form of contraception also, okay? The second is to freeze the cervix and then follow you with the understanding that that should cure it, but that you need to be followed in the future and that you could have children in the future if that's what your plans include.

Doctor S. presented information about a hysterectomy as a means to have no more babies and as a method of contraception. To a woman who is pregnant and doesn't want to be and who has had repeated birth control failures, this is a particularly persuasive presentation. He continued by saying that she could be treated by freezing the cervix, but then she could still have children and would have to be followed up. Again, a very persuasive presentation. This is a poor woman who does not want more children and does not have either the time or the money to return to the hospital for frequent follow-ups in the case. In addition, the resident presented the hysterectomy option first, and then presented cryosurgery as an option. This order suggested that the less conservative treatment (hysterectomy) was somehow the preferable one. Later on in the exchange, the resident summed up his position using another persuasional strategy. He said, "Absent uterus, no periods, no cancer, no babies"—a straight reflection of what he had learned in medical school and continues to read in gynecological texts and journals.

These findings should not be too surprising. They mirror the ways women have been socialized to accept the authority of others—particularly more dominant male others. They are consistent with the traditional view that a woman's primary value is as a wife and mother. If women reject marriage or motherhood, if they do not want children or more children, if they are near the end of their reproductive years, or if they cannot manage reproduction without financial assistance from the State, then they no longer need their uteruses.

These findings also reflect the structure of medical education. Residents need surgical experience to become qualified physicians. Obstetrics/gynecology is a surgical specialty. It follows, then, that residents in this specialty need surgical experience. Since their inception, hospital-based training programs have relied on poor, relatively powerless patients as "training material." Therefore, it should come as no surprise that in this study, patients with few resources who were treated in the community clinic staffed by residents received elective or prophylactic hysterectomies, while patients with more resources who were treated in the faculty clinic by reproductive oncologists received no such procedures. While the number of patients involved is small, the findings are suggestive. Not only is the attending staff not motivated by profit or the need for surgical experience, but their patients are often referred to them by their colleagues in the community—colleagues who could hold them accountable.

These findings also illuminate an alliance between the legislative process and the American Medical Association—an alliance rooted in economics and maintained by powerful legislative lobbies. The medical profession has a vested interest in protecting its status as the only legally authorized group to practice medicine. As the only game in town, medical "experts" control the delivery of health care. The autonomy of the medical profession, insured by means of legislative and legal processes, is reflected in the self-education and self-policing of its members, in the continued resistance of the profession to a national health insurance schema or to socialized medicine, and in the minimal impact of consumers on health care policies or practices.

In each of the cases we have discussed, the institutional authority of the doctors' role—their power—is amplified by the ways doctors translate their medical attitudes and individual judgments into communicational strategies and medical practices. Their authority is equally evident in the ways language is used—its functions—over the course of the medical interview, in the ways doctors are able to manipulate the decision making process and in the decisions reached. In the next chapter, I examine how the asymmetry in the medical relationship shapes the very structure of medical discourse.

3 / What Brings You In Today?

The Structure of Medical Discourse

If one could telescope a medical interaction into a few utterances, it might look like this:

1. Doctor: What brings you in today?

2. Patient: I have an ear ache.

3. Doctor: Let's take a look at that ear.

4. Doctor: Uhm.

5. Patient: What I was going to ask you was//

6. Doctor: //How long has the ear been bothering you?

7. Patient: About two days—since I went swimming in very cold water.

8. Doctor: Well, ok, it looks like swimmers ear all right. I'll just give you a prescription for some drops. Use them three times a day for five days and call me if you have any problems.

Even though the above medical dialogue is hypothetical, it can be illustrative. At first glance it appears to be an innocent medical encounter—one that would be familiar to most of us. Because of an ear ache, a patient seeks the medical advice of an "expert." Once the patient is in the examining room, the doctor enters and asks what the presenting complaint is, talks with the patient for a while, does a physical examination, reaches a diagnosis, prescribes a treatment, and the patient leaves. Although such encounters are familiar, they are not innocent. Obscured in their familiarity is a language pattern: during medical encounters, language use is structured by the authority of the medical role.

This institutional authority is revealed in the structure of the discourse. It is the doctor who opens and closes the interaction (lines 1 and 8). It is the doctor who asks most of the questions and initiates most of the topics (lines 1, 3, 6 and 8). After looking in the patient's ear, it is the doctor who utters the ubiquitous "Uhm" (line 4). When the patient begins a question, the doctor interrupts(//) and it is the doctor's line of questioning that prevails (lines 5 and 6). The issue here is not that the patient has no power or that the doctor always has all of the power. Patients can seek second opinions or change doctors. They can and do ask questions, interrupt, change topics and claim and/or maintain the floor. Doctors' styles of communication can and do vary—some being more dominant and others more egalitarian. It is the institutional authority of the medical role and the control it gives to medical practitioners that does not change.

In the last chapter, I explored how this institutional authority is evident in the ways language is used in a medical interview—the functions language serves in the negotiation of treatment decisions. In this chapter, I examine how the relationship's asymmetry shapes the structure of the discourse—its form—and has consequences in terms of the delivery of care. I want to highlight the reciprocity between language forms and functions—a reciprocity grounded in the organization of the setting. Again, my position is not just that patients should be allowed to have more control—should ask more questions or initiate more topics. Rather, by illustrating the ways language is used and the ends accomplished by its uses, I can develop a picture of the ways medical interactions mirror and contribute to power relationships within as well as outside of the institution of medicine.

If, as I have claimed, the medical relationship is characterized by an institutionally based authority, which shapes the discourse structure and has consequences for the delivery of health care to women, then a close analysis should reveal how this authority is reflected in medical discourse and influences the delivery of care. To provide this kind of an in-depth analysis, the range of material must, of necessity, be limited. My analysis in this chapter is limited to one of the cases I discussed in the last chapter—the case of Susan and Doctor M., the junior oncologist in the faculty clinic on the west coast. After identifying communicational patterns and comparing them across transcripts, I chose this case for two reasons: First, while all of the transcripts shared an essential discourse structure, this transcript contained an especially clear example of the kind of talk that only occurred on some occasions and not on others. Second, the doctor-patient interaction was especially interesting.

Although Dr. M. was the junior oncologist in the clinic, he was in his forties. By his own description, after many years as a practicing obstetrician-gynecologist, he burnt out. In informal conversations, he told me that women's changing attitudes, the increasing criticisms of his profession, and the irregular hours all contributed to his decision to do a residency in oncology (cancer). He was also a practicing Catholic and a "family man." After having had several children, he and his wife had recently adopted a son. These background features of his life are part of the context of this case.

The patient, Susan, also comes to the medical interaction from a particular life context. She is young (twenty-one years old), scared, and evidences a strong desire to be an informed, active participant in her own health care. When I interviewed her, she admitted that her attitude was rooted in her recent experiences and supported by her relationship with a women's health care specialist.

Susan was the adopted daughter of a Catholic family and a student at a local Catholic college. During the year preceding the discovery of an abnormal Pap smear, she met and fell in love with another student. Even though they were in love, they lacked the resources to marry and continue their educations. They talked about living together and decided against it. They talked about birth control and becoming sexually involved and decided in favor of both. However, this was an easier decision for them to make than to implement. They put off getting information about birth control, drifted into a sexual relationship, and Susan got pregnant. Her pregnancy took her to the neighborhood clinic where she established a relationship with a women's health care specialist, made an agonizing decision and had an abortion. A routine Pap smear done at this clinic disclosed abnormal cells on her cervix and she was referred to the junior oncologist at the faculty clinic. She brought her guilt about having had unprotected sexual relations and an abortion as well as her fear about the abnormal Pap smear into the doctor's office with her. She also entered the doctor's office armed with information and determined to be in charge of her life and her health care—no more drifting for her.

If I mean to argue, as I do, that institutional authority, not individuals, is at the focus of this analysis, then why should I provide this information about an individual doctor and patient? The interactions between this doctor and patient were characterized by a struggle—a struggle that provided an especially clear picture of how the institutional authority of the medical role influences the structure of medical discourse and has consequences for the delivery of health care. Drawing upon research on the structure of everyday conversations and of educational discourse, I explore the ways medical decision making is organized sequentially (horizontally) and vertically. By examining the structure of medical interactions (their communicational form) and drawing comparisons across institutions as well as between everyday conversations and institutional discourse, we can see how these interactions are at one and the same time social and political performances. Language provides information, molds the decision making process, and influences medical outcomes, while at the same time reflecting and sustaining institutional authority.

Sequential Organization

Patients with abnormal Pap smears come to the doctor concerned about their health. They bring with them information that doctors need—information about their past medical histories and the demographic and social characteristics of their lives. Doctors, too, come into medical interactions with a "stock of knowledge" (Schutz 1962), both medical and social. They know, or know how to determine, what abnormal Pap smears mean and what treatments are available. In order to ascertain which treatment to recommend, they need information about the patient's past history and current life style.[1] The discourse is structured by the need to reach a decision about how to treat an abnormal Pap smear.

Although both doctors and patients bring their knowledge and personal concerns into the examining room, it is the doctor who is the recognized authority—an authority reflected in the forms of his[2] opening initiation. These forms are: information requested and information provided. Doctors provide information about what the abnormal Pap smear means and about the kinds of treatments that are available. They also request information about patients' past medical histories and about the demographic and social features of patients' lives—especially about their reproductive histories and desires.

These forms of discourse serve more than one function. They are related to the tasks of getting and giving information and, in addition, they shape the structure of the reply. The form of the opening initiation creates the possibility of different types of responses. When doctors request information, the expected reaction is that the patient's response will contain that information. When doctors provide information, there is more latitude for the patients' responses. The patient may request or provide additional information (see figure 3.1).

For example, if the doctor provides information by saying, "You have a precancerous condition," the patient has conversational options. She can request additional information by saying, "Am I going to die?" or "How serious is it?" She can also provide additional information by saying, "My mother died of cancer," or "I've had abnormal cells before." However, if the doctor requests information by saying, "How old are

Figure 3.1. The Sequential Organization of the Initiation/Response Act

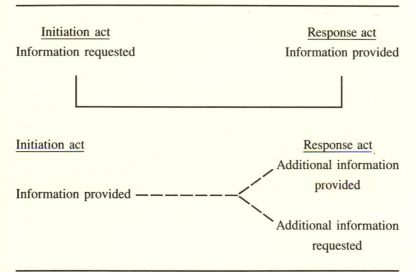

key: broken line = options

you?" a specific conversational expectation is set up, namely, for the patient to respond with her age.

In normal conversation there is balanced participation among all conversational partners (Shuy 1983). Conversational partners each ask questions, initiate topics, and they interrupt each other about equally. This equality is also evident in studies that have found that ordinary conversations are usually characterized by a symmetrical discourse structure—the adjacency pair. For example, in an ordinary conversation, if a greeting is initiated by one conversational partner, it is followed by a greeting (see figure 3.2). If this response is not forthcoming, its absence is noticeable. The first greeting calls for the second and the second reinforces the appropriateness of the first (Sacks, Schegloff, and Jefferson 1974; Schegloff and Sacks 1973).

In ordinary conversations, this symmetry is disrupted when one conversational partner has more status and power than the other. For example, Zimmerman and West (1975) find that when men are talking with men or women with women, interruptions are about equally distributed across the conversing pair. But when men and women talk with

Figure 3.2. Adjacency Pairs

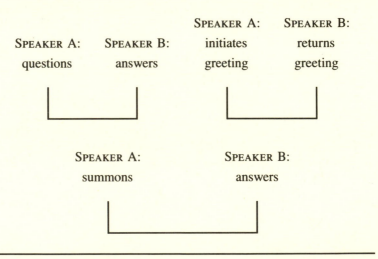

SOURCE: Sacks *et al.* (1974)

each other, men do most of the interrupting. Zimmerman and West conclude that this finding reflects the higher status of men in society. Imbalances have been found to affect other forms of discourse as well: touching, gazing, smiling, certain specific forms of address, the choice and development of topics of conversation, the allocation of speaking turns and the words chosen (Eakins and Eakins 1978; Thorne and Henley 1975).

At first glance, the structure of the initiation/response acts of a medical discussion is much like the structure of an ordinary conversation. Just as conversational partners in normal conversations can request and provide information, so too can doctors and patients. But whereas in normal conversation there exists an expectation of balanced participation, in medical discourse the doctor is largely in control—a control that is evident whether he is requesting or providing information. This control becomes even more apparent when the three-part sequential structure found to characterize institutional discourse is examined.

When discourse within educational settings is considered, the findings suggest that both task and discourse structures are different from those found in ordinary conversations. Mehan (1979) found that classroom lessons have a three-part sequential structure (see figure 3.3). If the teacher initiates a question and a student provides a correct response, an evaluation marks the completion of the sequence. For example:

> T: What is two plus two? S: Four. T: Good.

But classroom discourse is not limited to adjacency relationships. If the reply called for is not immediately forthcoming, the teacher may prompt or repeat the elicitation until a satisfactory reply is provided. The completion of these "extended sequences" is also marked by an evaluation (see figure 3.3). For example:

> T: What is two plus two? S: Five. T: Almost.
> T: Who knows what two plus two is? Many: Four. T: Good.

The elaborated structures of classroom discourse illuminate the ways in which educational discourse is organized differently from ordinary

Figure 3.3. The Organization of Horizontal Interactional Sequences

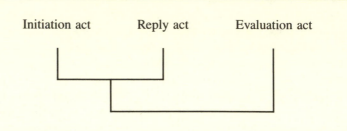

Initiation act   Reply act   Evaluation act

SOURCE: Mehan (1979)

conversation. It is a truism that conversational partners—be they teachers and students or co-conversationalists in an ordinary conversation—jointly accomplish events. Forms of discourse also illustrate how the institution within which the discourse occurs, the authority of the institution's dominant actors, and the functions that the language they use serve to influence the forms that discourse takes. These factors are evident in the almost ubiquitous presence of evaluation acts as the third pair-part in classroom discourse and in the almost total absence of similar behavior on the part of students. Teachers, not students, usually select and initiate topics of discourse, claim and maintain access to the floor, and do the evaluations that reflect and sustain their role as the judges of the students' academic and social accomplishments. During classroom lessons, language use functions to accomplish educational goals—a function that is reflected in the forms of discourse used. This reciprocity between language function and form is another manifestation of the ways discourse is structured by an institutional context.

Medical interviews occur in a different context than classroom lessons and are oriented toward different tasks. Teachers in classroom situations often ask students questions for which they know the answers and they then evaluate their responses. These "known information questions" (Mehan 1979; Griffin and Humphrey 1978) are responsible in part for the presence of evaluation acts as the third-pair-part of lesson discourse. This kind of question is not usually asked in medical interactions. Doctors do not ask patients questions for which an answer is already known. Rather, doctor and patient each have information that the other needs in order to reach a diagnosis and/or decide upon a treatment. It is this task that is reflected in the sequential structure of medical discourse.

Although medical interviews are different in crucial ways from classroom lessons, they are also similar to them in important ways. Both are social events oriented toward specific ends—teaching lessons and reaching medical decisions, respectively. The institutions of medicine and of education lend their dominant actors—doctors and teachers—authority. The asymmetry that exists in medical and in educational relationships springs from this institutionally based authority and the concomitant desire to maintain it. This authority shapes medical and educational discourse in the process.

Institutional Authority and Sequential Organization of Medical Discourse

During medical interviews, a speech act initiated by one party is followed by a response by the other, which on some occasions is followed by a comment act (see figure 3.4). This sequential organization of discourse into initiation, response, and comment acts (IRC) is influenced by the exchange of information on the basis of which treatment decisions will be made and is more similar to the three-part sequence that characterizes classroom discourse than it is to the two-part adjacency pair that characterizes everyday conversation. Just as teachers are more dominant than students in classroom interactions, doctors are more dominant than patients during medical interactions. Patients describe

Figure 3.4. Sequential Organization

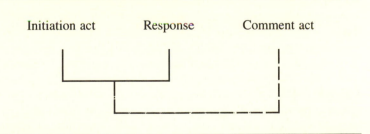

Initiation act   Response   Comment act

SOURCE: Fisher (1984)

symptoms and ask for clarification about their medical problems, but it is doctors who make a diagnosis and recommend a treatment. Patients react. They can agree, disagree, or negotiate.

The need for the information on which treatment decisions will be based also structures third-pair-part comment acts. These acts take four discourse forms, each of which serves a different function: corrections, comments on the interaction, back channel utterances, and overlaps. Unlike evaluations, which are only performed by teachers, occur after and comment upon the correctness of the response, and signal the completion of the sequence, comment acts are performed by both doctor and patient, occur across the flow of the IRC sequence, and may or may not mark the completion of the sequence.

Corrections. Corrections are the response most like evaluations. They are performed by the person in authority and basically serve a teaching function. They are an attempt to get the facts straight by filling in an appropriate medical term or correcting a mistaken impression. In the following example, about midway through Susan's response, she stumbled over the pronunciation of a piece of equipment—the colposcope—and Doctor M. corrected her. (The double slash mark // is used to help the reader follow the speech. It indicates a change of speaker.)

Initiation	*Response*	*Comment*
D. Somehow they got the impression that you were going to have a conization biopsy of your cervix. That what you told your mother?	P. No, when I talked to her yesterday, she got upset, but when I told her that you were just going to look at it today colpo// and, uhm if a biopsy was necessary, it was just a small pinch from the tissue of the cervix. She got upset, but I told her it would be okay.	D. //Colposcope

Doctor M. and Susan are discussing her mother's concern over her medical care. Doctor M. asks what Susan has told her mother. From the tone of the question, it seems he is accusing her of alarming her mother.

In the course of her answer, Susan displays a good understanding of her medical problem, but is unclear about the name of the piece of equipment that will be used to magnify her cervix. When she stumbles after the first syllable, Doctor M. fills in the correct pronunciation. The correction is much like one a teacher would make. Although Susan's speech is disrupted (and, uhm), she continues her presentation without acknowledging the correction.

In terms of my data, this example represents an unusual interaction. I did not see patients interrupt doctors often. And in the context of the medical relationship, this seemed to make sense. The dominant partner—the doctor—was more likely to interrupt the less dominant partner—the patient. This observation was consistent with findings that in casual conversations, interruptions are shared relatively equally, unless one partner is more dominant—a finding that is supported by West's (1984) research in medical settings. She finds that doctors more frequently interrupt patients, unless the doctor is a "lady." Shuy (1983) disagrees. While he suggests that in medical interactions, patients more often interrupt doctors, he goes on to argue that dominance is usually displayed, not in the interruption, but in who keeps the floor afterwards. With either interpretation, this quoted interaction is unusual. The patient interrupted and kept the floor. Does this mean she is the dominant speaker? I think not, and an analysis of the rest of the transcript confirms my opinion. Alternatively, she may just be dominant in this exchange. I think there is another explanation—one that maintains what we know to be the dominant interactional position of the doctor. Perhaps the doctor's goal was just to correct the pronunciation of the term colposcope. Perhaps he had no intention of reclaiming the floor at this time. Of course, there is no way to determine whether this was or was not the case. Other interactions, however, suggest that although this was an unusually dominant patient, when the doctor wanted the floor, he could and did claim it and get it.

Comments. Comments on the interaction are made by both physicians and patients. They display that the hearer is following the interaction, has additional information to add, or is competing for control. In the examples that follow, Doctor M. adds information, as does Susan, and doctor and patient appear to argue about the information exchanged.

Initiation	*Response*	*Comment*
1. D. Oh, you came from A.	P. Yes.	D. Good old A.
2. P. A cauteri . . . a cauterization?	D. Uh, we normally would freeze it.	P. Yeah, that's what I mean.
3. P. Well just because cause these cells// can turn cancerous, they can.	D. They can become cancerous, but they aren't now.	D. //It isn't.

The first two examples are rather clear-cut. In the first example, the doctor's comment on the interaction, "Good old A.", takes the form of an assessment of A. It could be functioning to provide information and/ or to end a sequence while holding the floor. In the second, the patient uses the comment act to provide the information that by the term cauterize she meant freeze—she corrects the doctor's correction.

The third example is less clear-cut and more interesting. Doctor and patient are discussing whether the dysplastic cells on the patient's cervix are likely to turn cancerous. The patient says, ". . . just because these cells" and the doctor interrupts with, "It isn't." The patient thus goes on to finish her statement and the doctor responds. Taken out of context, the doctor's interruption (//) "It isn't" has little meaning. But in context, it appears to be part of the patient's ongoing challenge about the nature of her medical problem and the likelihood that it could become more serious. The patient's statement links her abnormal cells with cancer. The doctor responds by providing the information that the abnormal cells are not cancer. The patient goes on without acknowledging in words that she has heard him; although she seems to add extra stress, perhaps as a response, with the emphasis on "they can"—meaning that they can turn cancerous. The doctor's remarks continue his half of the argument, "They can become cancerous, but they aren't now."

In a final example, the doctor is responding to the patient's question about how a cone biopsy is performed. The patient asks, "Does that cut through you on the outside?" The answer is a prolonged one. During it, the patient twice makes comments on the interaction.

Response	*Comment*
D. No, it's a cone through the vagina. The problem with the cone is that it ends in some complications,	

Uh, about 10 percent of the patients develop bleeding, uh after they go home and have to be readmitted
to stop the bleeding, and, uh// sometimes you get in-   P. //infections probably
fections and infertility. It's about 10 percent. So we
don't like to do cones. We try to get around them at
all costs. In young women we usually can, so, it
used to be that we didn't have a colposcope and
everybody had to have a cone. If you had an abnormal Pap smear you had to have a cone because we
didn't know where the bad place was, so we just had
to take out the whole suspicious area. But the col-
poscope is really, uh, eliminated most of the cones.   P. Yea, good thing.

Both of these comments expand on the information the doctor is
providing. The first occurs while the doctor is hesitating in formulating
his response. The juncture created by this hesitation ". . . uh, and,
uh . . ." provides a slot for the patient's comment. Her statement "infections probably" expands on the doctor's presentation, and indicates
that she has been paying close attention and has anticipated the problem
to be discussed. The doctor continues, recycling her comment and link-
ing it with infertility. These seem to be problems of such different mag-
nitudes that I wonder whether infections would have been part of the
doctor's discussion if they had not been brought up by the patient.

The second comment on the interaction occurs at the end of the doctor's response. Then Susan again expands upon the doctor's presentation
and shows that she has been paying attention. She says, "Yeah, good
thing," indicating agreement that cone biopsies are hazardous. This
comment, like the doctor's earlier "Good old A." and like teachers'
evaluations, marks the end of a sequence. However, unlike the doctor's
comment or the teacher's evaluation, it does not hold the floor for the
patient. The doctor takes the floor and changes the topic.

These interactions are somewhat uncharacteristic. The patient
wrestles with the doctor for control. She expands on the information he
is presenting, challenges his medical knowledge, and at least implicitly
suggests that he is not telling her the whole medical story. This power
battle is marked in the discourse in several ways. It is evident in the
patient's expansions and in the doctor's interruptions. It is apparent when
the doctor interrupts and corrects the patient (example 3) and when the
patient corrects the doctor's correction (example 2). More characteristic

discourse structures are also evident in these snippets of discourse. After each comment act, the doctor maintains or reclaims the floor to continue the topic under discussion or to initiate a new one.

Back Channel. Back channel comments (Duncan 1972) are much like comments on the interaction, except that they take the form of "clucking noises" (Uh, um, hum) and do not usually mark the end of sequences. If you can imagine communication between the doctor and the patient taking place in the foreground or main channel, then these comments take place in the background or back channel. In everyday conversations, back channel comments are used to indicate that the hearer is listening and understands the preceding "chunk" of information. In the following example, Doctor M. is again trying to convince Susan that she does not need to be as concerned as she is about cancer. Several times during his presentation of information, she makes back channel comments.

Response	*Comment*
D. Well we do know quite a bit about dysplasia[3]//	P. //Yeah
Yeah, we know quite a bit about it and, uh, we know	
that, uh, dysplasia can become cancerous// It can	P. //Uh hum
become cancerous. We don't know how long it takes	
but we think it usually takes several years, between	
five and ten years//depending on the degree of dys-	P. //Uh hum
plasia//but in some people it may take six months.	P. //Uh hum
We don't know. So that's one thing we don't know	
about it, but we do know that it can become cancer.	
However, it also can regress to normal. It can also	
become normal.	

This is an important discussion for the patient. She has indicated her concern about the possibility of developing cancer as well as her distrust of the medical information the doctor is providing. Her back channel comments may indicate that she is paying close attention and understands or agrees with what is being said. Often in casual conversations, back channel comments are used in this manner. Or the patient's "yeah" and "uh-hum" may be what linguists call lax tokens. As Shuy (1983) points out, the meaning of these tokens changes when they are used during medical discourse. During a medical interview, yes or no would be strong responses. "Yeah," "uh-hum," or "huh-uh" are weaker responses—lax tokens—and may indicate uncertainty. But whatever their meaning, the doctor's interactional dominance is marked in the discourse. Although not acknowledged in words, these back channel comments structure his presentation of information. The doctor either recycles the utterance immediately preceding the back channel comment, or continues as if he has not heard it.

Overlaps. Overlaps, or simultaneous speech, are similar to back channel comments except that they occur in the foreground or main channel. By occurring in this channel, they represent a struggle for the floor. In the following example, Doctor M. and Susan continue to discuss the relationship between her problem and the likelihood that it will become more serious. Susan asks:

Initiation	*Response*	*Comment*
P. What's to prevent me from going through this all again?	D. All we know is that// if we cure it by freezing your cervix . . .	P. //Yeah, didn't know

There is a struggle for the floor going on here. The patient requests information from the doctor and while he is trying to provide it, she interrupts him, challenging the information he has just given. From the tone of the previous discourse, it seems that she is about to draw attention to what is not known about dysplasia and to challenge his statement that the medical profession understands the relationship between freezing and cancer. The doctor continues to talk over her overlap and maintains the floor. Although this patient is uncharacteristically dominant— she challenges the authority of the medical provider—the institutional authority of the doctor remains undiminished and is marked in the discourse. The patient interrupts the doctor's presentation of information and talks while he is talking—she overlaps her talk with his. But the doctor overrides this interruption without acknowledging it and continues as if he has not been interrupted.

Summary. I started this chapter by claiming that the institution of medicine lends its dominant actors authority—an authority that shapes the structure (form) of medical discourse and has consequences for the delivery of care. I argued that although doctors' styles can vary and patients can have input into the decision making process, the asymmetry of the medical relationship remains constant. The institutional authority of the medical role and the control it provides for the physician does not change. To make this point, I analyzed the sequential structures of discourse during a medical interview between an attending staff physician, Doctor M., and Susan, a rather atypical patient—one who fights to maintain control in the medical situation. Both the battle for control and the doctor's dominance were evident in their discourse.

The structure of doctor-patient discourse into a three-part sequence with comment acts reflects the differences in the relationship between co-conversationalists in natural, daily contexts and between participants in institutional contexts. One of the ways to understand these differences is in terms of the asymmetry of the relationship between participants. In daily contexts, conversationalists may or may not be equal; however, their equality or their lack of equality is not a critical feature of the interaction. Whereas in the contexts of the classroom or the examining room, teachers and doctors have and use more authority than students and patients. This lack of equality is mirrored in and is a critical feature of the discourse. For example, although both doctors and teachers have institutionally based authority, their primary tasks are different. The similarities in their roles and the differences in their tasks are reflected in the differences in their discourse. Both share a sequential three-part discourse structure; however, this structure serves different functions and takes different forms.

All four forms of the comment act (correction, comments on the interaction, back channel, and overlap) reflect the asymmetry of the doctor-patient relationship and show how that asymmetry is enacted in the ongoing interactions between them. Corrections are the most like evaluations. In them, doctors, the persons with authority, correct patients' pronunciation of medical terms, correct their understandings of their medical problems, and have the last word on the definition of the problem in terms of cancer. All of the other comment acts share one feature with corrections (and for that matter with evaluations). They display the authority of the doctor. Comments on the interaction do several kinds of interactional work for both doctor and patient. They can signal the completion of a sequence. They can be used to hold the floor. And they can be used to add to or reinforce information. However they are used, the doctor either maintains or regains control of the floor in order to begin a new sequence.

Similarly, back channel and overlap comments reflect the asymmetry of the doctor-patient relationship. During medical interviews, doctors have greater access to the floor than patients. Therefore it is logical that it is patients, not doctors, who most often use back channel utterances or overlapping speech. These forms of discourse provide access to the floor for patients. However, when patients make back channel comments, doctors maintain control of the floor in the main doctor-patient channel of communication. They either recycle their talk and keep going or they ignore the back channel comments and proceed as if they have not occurred. This control can be seen in overlaps as well. When the patient overlaps, the doctor maintains control of the floor. He either repeats her utterance or talks over it. When the doctor overlaps, the patient loses control of the floor.

The Hierarchical Organization of the Medical Interview

Medical interviews, like classroom lessons, are organized hierarchically. They have an overall discourse structure shaped, at least in part, by the task at hand. Using this same transcript as an example, I now want to discuss the ways in which medical discourse is assembled into larger hierarchical units—units larger than the previously discussed IRC sequences. I show how the exchange of information between Doctor M. and Susan occurs in sets of utterances organized around topics. These topically oriented sets, like the sequential organization already discussed, are influenced by the practical concerns of the participants, are negotiated as doctor and patient communicate, and are shaped by the asymmetry of the medical relationship.

The medical task entails two concerns—to protect patients from developing a more extensive cancer and preserve their reproductive capacities.[4] The patients, too, have concerns. They are concerned about their diagnoses and about what treatment options they have. The negotiation of the doctors' and the patients' concerns structures the exchange of information necessary to make a diagnosis and reach a treatment decision. The necessary topics include discussions about the patient's history and future plans as a reproductive being, about cancer, and about treatment options.

Doctor and patient also discuss topics that, although not directly oriented toward treatment decisions, contribute general information and lend themselves to the decision making process. The discussion about what the patient told her mother about her abnormal Pap smear and its treatment is an example of this kind of general talk.

Doctor and patient discuss additional topics that are not necessarily involved in reaching a treatment decision. In this case, they talked about the patient's morality. This "morality talk" occurs in some doctor-patient interviews and not others. It is situationally specific or occasioned.[5] An example occurs in this interview when the patient challenges the origin of her abnormal Pap smear and the doctor responds by talking about morality.

The medical interview, then, is composed of necessary, occasioned, and general topically organized sets of discourse about disease (e.g., cancer), treatment options, reproduction, morality, and general information. These topical sets are established in one of the two kinds of initiation acts discussed earlier: information provided or information requested.[6] Once established, topics stay in force until a new topic emerges or until the topic is changed by one of the participants. The categories of occasioned, general, and necessary topics come clearer in the analysis of the transcript that follows, as the production of topics is discussed.

Once Susan has been ushered into the consulting office, Doctor M. initiates the medical interview with a discussion about the concern expressed by her mother. This general discourse is not directly oriented toward a treatment decision; however, since doctor and patient are engaged in an ongoing process of sizing each other up, this opening set, like all of the others, contributes bits of information upon which basis treatment decisions will later be made.

Doctor M. begins the exchange by saying, "Uh, your mother's doctor called me yesterday." Susan says, "Did she?" The doctor continues by requesting information from the patient about her understanding of her abnormal Pap smear. The answer to this request provides general information about what the patient knows and what additional information she needs, while shedding light on her competence as a patient. The doctor continues, "You have an abnormal Pap smear?" The patient responds by saying "yes"; and the discussion moves on until she mentions cancer in her response.

Cancer is a necessary topic of discussion. Discussion on this topic continues until the patient asks a question, which the doctor answers by explaining the available treatment options, and in this way another necessary topic is initiated. These necessary topics provide the patient with information about cancer and treatment options and are oriented toward a treatment decision.

The discussion about cancer begins with the doctor's initiation. He says, "The important thing is that it's not cancer." And the patient responds by saying, "It's not cancer now." A few sequences later, in response to a question from the patient, the discussion about treatment options begins. The patient says, "They don't, you don't know the extent of it from my Pap smear." The doctor responds by saying:

> That's correct. We don't know the extent. That's why we do a colposcopic examination with the colposcope, which is like a microscope; we can usually see the extent of where these cells are coming from. Sometimes it is so small you can barely see it. Uh, just a little tiny microscopic area, and if that's the case, by just biopsying you often times cure it because you remove the whole area the abnormal cells are coming from. If it is more extensive, then we might have to do something else to treat it.

Several IRC sequences later the doctor changes the topic and requests information from the patient about her reproductive history. This exchange about reproduction provides the doctor with information about the patient as a reproductive being; it is necessary and oriented toward a treatment decision. He says, "Yeah, so how old are you?" and the patient responds by saying, "twenty-one."

The medical interview moves toward the physical examination with another exchange initiated by the doctor. The doctor requests additional information from the patient. This information is occasioned and is not specifically oriented toward a treatment decision. He says, "Okay, do you have any questions that you want to ask me?" The patient responds, "Uhm." Although "Uhm" is not a response, it may function to hold the floor.[7] The doctor, however, invited the patient's questions, and the patient's "uhm" neither asks a question nor says that she does not have any to ask.[8] The doctor initiates again, "You seem upset." With tears noticeably running down Susan's cheeks, she says, "I am."[9] Several sequences later after discussing what is upsetting her, she asks, "What's going to prevent me from going through all of this again?" and the doctor responds:

> All we know is that if we cure it by freezing the cervix, uh, it doesn't seem to come back very often. Maybe less than 10 percent of the time. But you have to look at it. It's a very common problem, all right. And, uh, it's becoming

more common because, I think, the sexual attitudes of our population are changing and so you have to look at it as, uh, like a person who has arthritis or psoriasis or some other problem, uh, it's a medical problem. It's a medical problem. It's not cancer. It can be treated and it can be cured and it can be followed closely and, uh, if you look at it from that standpoint, it's just like (pause). Unfortunately, this whole dysplasia business, uh, abnormal Pap smears, has got the label of cancer attached to it.

The doctor uses the patient's concern about what is happening to her to initiate a discussion of morality. The discourse continues with the doctor making a connection between intercourse and cancer by saying, ". . . we almost never see it in virgins" and "you usually don't see it in, for instance, tribes or monogamous situations where women have intercourse with only one person."

Morality is discussed on one other occasion in this interview. Earlier in the interview the patient challenges the doctor's medical knowledge about abnormal Pap smears and mentions cancer (a topic usually reserved for introduction by medical professionals). At this time, the doctor says, "Dysplastic, what is your understanding of that?" (challenging her in return). The patient responds, "Well, what's anyone's understanding of it. They're abnormal and you don't know why, and they don't know if it leads to cancer." The patient mentions cancer and the doctor reclaims the topic by stating that the dysplasia she has now is not cancer. The patient offers another challenge to his knowledge and in response he raises the issue of morality. The patient says, "Well, do they know why the cells, they don't know why the cells grow this way, dysplastic, do they?" He responds:

No they don't. There are many theories. One of them is related to herpes infections. Another is that it's related to intercourse but nobody has been able to identify a specific etiology. All we know is that it almost never occurs in nuns. So, uh, but if you have dysplasia, we can usually see it with the colposcope.

The doctor's response to this challenge to his authority is a moral pronouncement. He says that dysplasia may be caused by herpes, or be related to intercourse and that nuns do not get it. The assumption here is that there is a direct causal relationship between intercourse (herpes is sexually transmitted and nuns are presumably virgins) and dysplasia. At the conclusion of this chapter, these assumptions are discussed further.

For now it is sufficient to say that this relationship is not as clear as it is made to seem here. More to the point, the patient has asked a series of questions that challenge the doctor's medical knowledge. She has pointed out that the doctor does not know where the abnormal cells come from or what will prevent them from coming back. In one of these early challenges, the patient mentions cancer—a topic usually reserved for physicians—and the doctor responds by changing the topic to morality.

The second episode of morality talk, which we have discussed earlier, occurs toward the end of the medical interview and is in response to the doctor's question about what's bothering the patient. In this instance the doctor explains that dysplasia only returns in about 10 percent of the cases and is a common problem associated with changing sexual attitudes (this point will be discussed in more detail later). Both of these discussions of morality rely on the medical assumption that abnormal Pap smears are related to early intercourse with multiple partners. Both of them appear to blame the patient for causing her medical problem with her inappropriate sexual behavior. And both of them occur after a challenge to the doctor's authority.

By bringing up a topic (cancer) normally reserved for doctors and by challenging the doctor's medical knowledge about this topic, the patient is behaving inappropriately. She is breaching the taken-for-granted assumption that medical professionals present information about cancer and treatment options and patients present information about their social, medical, and reproductive histories. The doctor responds by reasserting his authority. At the challenge to his status as the medical expert, he first reclaims the floor by talking about cancer and morality and later, when the patient questions how, given all of the unknowns, the doctor can assure her that her abnormal Pap smear will not return, he again uses morality talk.[10]

Interactional Authority and the Control Over Topic and Floor

Medical interviews are assembled through the production of topics, and both the medical interview and the production of topics are influenced by the practical concerns of the participants, negotiated as they communicate, and structured by the asymmetry of their relationship. It is another truism to state that all conversations have topics. Yet, while true, very little data exists on how the production of topics is influenced by the setting in which a conversation takes place. A detailed examination of the production of topics during one medical interview, when compared with the assembly of topics in more ordinary conversations and in educational discourse, provides some of the missing data. Such an analysis allows us to notice patterns in the ways topics are introduced, responded to, and/or changed.

As Shuy (1983) points out, in ordinary conversation one conversational partner does not ask all, or even most, of the questions, or initiate all, or most, of the topics. In both educational and medical discourse, that structure changes. In classrooms and medical settings, teachers and doctors take a more dominant position. They ask most of the questions and initiate most of the topics. In fact, Shuy claims that in these settings discourse is organized more like an interview than a conversation.

The response to topics is also different within institutional settings. In ordinary conversations, conversational partners can "expand" on a topic, "amend it," or "argue" with it. In the case of medical interviews, the expectations are more rigid. Patients are expected to answer questions and to provide the information asked for. They can request clarifications, interrupt or express uncertainty, but they are not expected to expand, amend, or disagree with the topic under discussion (Shuy 1983).

Even though Susan is unusually assertive, Doctor M.'s authority and his control of the medical situation is not diminished. For example, when the patient expanded on the information the doctor presented, doctor and patient wrestled for control and the doctor won (see the last example under the heading comments on the interaction). When the patient tried to introduce a topic normally reserved for doctors (cancer) or to amend and argue with the medical information the doctor was presenting, a battle for the floor ensued—a battle that resulted in a switch of topics to morality talk. Not only does the doctor retain control, but negotiations such as theirs illuminate the way medical authority is reflected in and shapes the discourse, while also having consequences for the delivery of health care.

In the medical interview just discussed, there are two exchanges about general information, one each about cancer, treatment options, and reproduction, and two about morality, totaling seven topically oriented sets (see table 3.1). Both general information sets are introduced by the doctor. Since general information is not a topic engendered by

The Negotiation of Asymmetry: Topically Oriented Sets

Speaker	Initiation Act	Language Function	Speaker	Response Act	Researcher's Comments
D	Uh, your mother's doctor called me yesterday.	IP*			The doctor establishes the topically oriented set about general information.
D	Oh, You came from A?	IR*			The doctor establishes the second instance of general information talk.
D	Dysplastic, what's your understanding of that?	IR	P	Well, what's anyone's understanding of it. They are abnormal and they don't know if it leads to cancer.//	The patient's mention of cancer here generated, in the next initiation, the topically oriented set about cancer.
P	Well, do they know why the cells grow this way dysplastic, do they?	IR	D	No, they don't. There are many theories.	In response to the patient's challenge, the doctor does morality talk.
P	Ok, well, uh, a Pap smear. They just, it's just a little scrape from inside of your uterus,	IR			In response to the patient's question, the doctor starts to talk about treatment options.
D	Yeah, so how old are you?	IR			With this question, the doctor initiates reproduction talk.
D	Ok. Do you have any questions you want to ask me before we examine you?	IR	P	Uhm	With this question, a discussion is begun that produces the last instance of morality talks.
D	You seem to be upset?	IR	P	I am ((crying))	
P	What's to prevent me going through this all again?	IR	D	. . . It's a very common problem, all right, and uh, it's becoming	The challenge, which the doctor created space for with his prior two questions, generated the second instance of morality talk.

*IP = Information provided
*IR = Information requested

either the doctor's or the patient's concerns, the doctor's initiation of it may reflect his desire to put the patient at ease, but whatever it reflects, it is indicative of the asymmetry in the medical relationship—the patient did not seem to have a similar license to initiate non-medical topics. The discourse about reproduction and the second discussion of morality are more in line with medical tasks and concerns. The doctor needs information about the patient's reproductive history and desires. If the medical task is to protect women's reproduction, it is consistent for doctors to initiate this topic. Similarly, if the doctor believes that sexual behavior is linked to the increasing rate of abnormal Pap smears found in young women, then it is also logical that he should use his authority to initiate the morality topic as well.

But Doctor M. does not initiate all of the topics. He did not initiate discourse about treatment options, or the first discussion of morality, and the subject of cancer is discussed after the patient brings it up. Susan is primarily concerned with what her Pap smear means and how it can be treated. It is not surprising, then, that she introduces the topic of treatment options. There are two topics that need a little closer scrutiny: the topic of cancer and the first discussion of morality.

While talking about the patient's understanding of her medical problem and in response to a doctor initiation, the patient mentions cancer. The doctor immediately interrupts her, takes control of the floor, and in his next turn discusses cancer. Technically, since the patient mentions cancer in response to a question and the doctor takes control of it, introducing it in his next initiation act, it can be seen as his topic. The discussion of morality that follows the discussion of cancer is similar. The patient asks a challenging question. The doctor responds to the challenge by discussing morality. So, technically, this discussion of morality is introduced by the patient. However, putting the technicalities aside, and accepting for the moment that the discourse about cancer and morality reflects the disruption caused by the patient's challenges to the doctor's authority, both these topics speak clearly to the asymmetry in the doctor-patient relationship.

The practical concerns of Doctor M. and Susan and the asymmetry in their relationship is also reflected in the IRC sequences within each topically oriented set (see table 3.2). At first glance, the doctor and patient seem to initiate about an equal number of initiation/response/comment sequences. The doctor initiates twenty-three sequences and the patient

Table 3.2.
The Negotiation of Asymmetry: Initiation Acts

Topic	Doctor Initiation	Patient Initiation
General information	6	4
Cancer	4	0
Treatment option	1	7
Reproduction	6	0
Morality	6	9
Total	23	20

initiates twenty; however, when the initiations are broken down by topic, some interesting differences appear. Looking at the discussion of general information, the doctor initiated six IRC sequences and the patient initiated four. The greater number of doctor initiated sequences suggests more control of the floor and, therefore, is indicative of the authority relations between doctor and patient. Not only does the doctor establish the topic in each case, but he also initiates most of the IRC sequences. If the form of the initiations is considered, all of the patient's initiations request information, as do all of the doctor's. In each case, these requests for information are part of a general sizing-up process— a process that functions differently for doctor and patient. When the doctor requests information of a general kind, the assumption is that he needs the information and the patient provides it. When the patient requests information, the same assumption is not operating. Not only does the doctor decide what the patient needs to know, but he also evaluates the appropriateness of her request. As we have seen, requests for information that challenged his authority generated discussions of morality.

While cancer is a topic that is important to both the doctor and the patient, it is also a topic that the doctor controls. He has more information about it. Susan needs this information to understand her medical problem and to reach a treatment decision. This situation is reflected in the initiation acts involving this topic. Doctor M. initiates all four sequences about cancer and each sequence takes a form that provides information. The doctor not only has the medical knowledge that the patient lacks, but he also has information based on his clinical experience about what the patient needs to know in order to reach a treatment decision—again, the doctor is in control. While his technical knowledge, clinical experience, and his familiarity with the medical setting are at the root of his authority, the way this authority is used is critical to the decision making process.

Treatment options are a central concern for Susan, but again Doctor M. has control over the information she needs. She wants to know what her diagnosis means and how her medical problem can be treated. Underlying this concern is her knowledge that a Pap smear is a test for cancer and that cancer is a killer. This concern is reflected in the initiations concerning treatment options. The topic is initiated by the patient and she initiated seven out of the eight sequences within this category. Each of her initiations takes a form that requests information. Most of the information about treatment options is provided by the doctor in response to the patient's questions. The only exception is the doctor's single initiation. This initiation takes a form that provides information and occurs after the patient uses the comment act, but does not hold the floor with it (see the previous discussion of comments on the interaction, example 2). While for doctors, being the initiator is indicative of power, for patients, this is not the case. Even though the patient initiates almost all of the sequences about treatment options, the doctor's power is not diminished. The patient asks questions, but the doctor has the information she needs, and since he is providing the information, he can control what information she receives.

Reproduction is one of two main organizing concerns for doctors. Not only does Doctor M. take responsibility for protecting the patient from developing cancer, but he also takes responsibility for preserving her reproductive capacity, when he sees this as desirable. In order to balance these responsibilities, he needs information. Susan is a young woman, who can still use her uterus for its intended purpose—reproduction. She is not on welfare. She has not had multiple abortions or given a child up for adoption. And she wants to get married and have children in the future. The doctor's need for information can be seen in their discourse. He initiates the topic of reproduction as well as each of the sequences within the category. All six of these initiations take a form that requests information. The doctor's power as well as his concern is reflected in these sequences. He does not tell the patient why he is asking questions or what he will do with the information once he has it.

The talk about morality perhaps most clearly reflects the doctor's concerns. The doctor is a reproductive oncologist. Every day he treats women dying from cancer of the reproductive system. If he believes, as this doctor told me he did, that abnormal Pap smears are more likely to occur in sexually active young women, then this concern is embedded in his discourse. The doctor and the patient each initiate the topic of morality once (see the previous discussion of patient-initiated topics). The patient initiates more of the sequences in this category than does the doctor. However, all of the discourse about morality is provided by the doctor and in response to questions that challenge his role and authority.

Summary

Medical interviews about abnormal Pap smears are assembled into larger discourse units through the production of necessary, occasioned, and general topics of conversation about cancer, reproduction, treatment options, general information, and morality. Each such topic is structured by the asymmetry of the doctor-patient relationship and demonstrates the ways that asymmetry is enacted in the ongoing communications between them. A closer look at the initiation of these topics provides us with a clearer view of this asymmetry and of its enactment.

Who initiates topics that are not directly oriented toward a treatment decision—general information or morality topics? The doctor does. Imagine the patient on her first visit asking the doctor, who is a stranger to her, about his family life or about his wife's concern about his health. If that sounds ridiculous to you, it is because as members of this culture we share a certain view of the appropriate roles for doctor and patient. Our knowledge of these roles gives the doctor license to inquire into the private lives of patients. It does not make this privilege a reciprocal one. It could be argued that patients do not need this kind of information about the private lives of their physicians and physicians often do need this kind of information about their patients. In addition to providing background information about the patient's life, discussions about general information help the doctor assess what the patient knows and needs to know about her medical problem—her competence as a patient. But when the patient tries to assess what the doctor knows about the relationship between an abnormal Pap smear and cancer (his competence as a doctor), the inappropriateness of her actions are made visible in the shift in topic—to morality—they produce. While patients may not need to inquire about their physicians' private lives, they certainly do need to know about their medical competence.

Since it is not a routine feature of medical discourse, talk about morality provides an especially clear picture of the ways in which the doctor's authority shapes the discourse. The information the doctor provides is based on medical studies that suggest that early intercourse with multiple partners is related to an increase in abnormal Pap smears in young women. Putting aside the problems that are associated with the correlational studies upon which such findings are based (e.g., they do not consider intervening variables, such as the increased use of artificial hormones in the methods of birth control used by today's population of young women), and the problems of applying statistical aggregate data to a particular woman, the doctor did not ask about the patient's reproductive life in any detail. He did not ask when she started having intercourse or how many partners she has had. Instead he took the abnormal Pap smear as prima facie evidence of her promiscuity. I interviewed this patient after her treatment. She had been sexually active for about one year with a regular partner whom she intended to marry. On the surface, it seems that the problem for this patient is her marital status. Could it be that if she were married, her intercourse would not be seen as beginning too early and would be assumed to take place with one partner?

There is another feature of this discourse about morality that warrants comment. The patient did not call the doctor to task for it. She did not tell him that while he might be the keeper of her health, she was the keeper of her morality. Again we would not expect her to do so—why not? Because like the patient, we share a reciprocal social world with the doctor. The doctor is voicing the dominant culture's values concerning women's sexuality, which we have all learned in that shared social world.

The authority of the doctor's role also structures the discussion of the topics that are necessary to the decision making process. There appears to be an unstated expectation in medical interviews about abnormal Pap smears: that the doctor will present information about cancer and treatment options (medical information) and that the patient will provide information about her reproductive history and desires (social information). This expectation is made evident when the patient mentions cancer, talking out of turn, and produces discourse about both cancer and morality.

This asymmetry influences the topical sequences on treatment options and reproduction as well. When the patient asks questions in the sequences on treatment options, the doctor, acting on the assumption that he knows what she needs to know, controls the information she receives. When the doctor asks questions in the sequences on reproduction, the patient, acting on the assumption that full disclosure is appropriate, provides the information. The patient does not know what information about reproduction the doctor needs to know or how the information will contribute to the doctor's diagnosis and/or treatment recommendation; therefore, the patient cannot control the information she provides. The imbalance is subtle, but, subtlety notwithstanding, it has consequences for the delivery of health care.

Conclusions: Institutions, Power, and the Structure of Discourse

In this chapter, a comparison across institutional contexts shows the similarities and differences in the patterns of language use in those contexts, which further illuminate the reflexive relationship between language use and context. Teachers' authority to motivate students to learn and to behave appropriately is more direct than doctors' authority to control treatment decisions. Although doctors have the medical knowledge and technical skill to support their authority when they make a diagnosis and recommend a treatment, patients must be convinced to agree. These differences are subtly marked in the structure of discourse in both settings.

These comparisons illustrate the ways the forms and functions of institutional discourse are both situated and local productions. They are local because they are accomplished by the interactional activities of the participants. They are situated because they are produced and constrained in an institutional context. The reciprocity between the forms and the functions of institutional discourse are further evidence of a reflexive relationship between language use and context—a relationship that has consequences for the delivery of health care. Although doctors and patients negotiate medical decisions, the negotiations are heavily weighed in doctors' favor. The power imbalance, reflected and reinforced in the medical relationship, potentially places all patients at a disadvantage—a disadvantage heightened when the patient is a woman. In a society characterized by asymmetrical relationships—white/nonwhite, poor/rich, upper/lower class, professional/non-professional—the doctor-patient relationship recapitulates and reinforces this lack of symmetry and makes some patients especially vulnerable to medical persuasion.

In the next chapter, using data from the family practice clinic in the southeast, I again examine the decision-making process. Just as I argued in the last two chapters that doctors influence women to have hysterectomies that are not mandated on medical grounds, I argue in the next chapter that doctors do not influence women from a potentially high risk population to have Pap smears that are medically warranted. In each case, I ground the argument in doctors' institutionally based authority—an authority that is rooted in their technical knowledge and clinical expertise as well as in their familiarity with the medical setting. It is from this institutional base that doctors draw the power to shape discourse forms and functions and to influence treatment decisions. Every time this institutional authority is used, it does work—it reflects and reinforces the asymmetry in the medical relationship in ways that are often not in the patient's best interest.

When I talk about doctors' institutionally based authority, someone usually responds either by saying "My doctor doesn't treat me that way," or by asking "How could it be different?" In response to the first statement I point out that while exceptions are always possible, as a general rule, doctors have and use their authority, and even the decision to act differently with certain patients is under their control. How it could be different is a somewhat harder question. First, it assumes that the disparity in expertise is an essential feature of the modern practice of medicine—medicine is so complex that those without specialized training cannot grasp it—an assumption shared by many doctors and patients. Second, the question supports the view that this authority is legitimate. If patients are unable to participate in decision making about their own health care, then doctors, of necessity, must act in their behalf. But, as we have seen, doctors are little better than the rest of us at putting aside their beliefs or their financial interests to act for their patients' good.

I question both these propositions, that medical information is too complex to share and that the authority of the medical role is legitimate. While all the technical details of a medical condition may not be transmittable, the information necessary for decision making is. But if the patients acquire this information on their own, or if they ask their doctors for it, they, like Susan, run the risk of acting inappropriately—of challenging the authority of the medical role. To assume that this authority is legitimate is to ignore the social and political process by which doctors have acquired and have fought to maintain their monopoly over the delivery of health care.

4 / And Another Time, Dear, We'll Need To Do a Pap Smear

The Unfolding Phases of Medical Discourse

"Cervical cancer is a preventable disease, no woman should get it and no woman should die from it." (*Ob, Gyn News*, 1983b).

Although in the last decade the incidence of and death from cervical cancer have decreased by 20 percent, in 1982 there were 16,000 new cases of invasive cervical cancer and 7,100 deaths (Creasman and Clarke-Pearson 1983), and in 1985 15,000 cases of cancer of the cervix and 6,800 deaths are expected (American Cancer Society 1985). Since the early stages of this disease are often without symptoms, the use of a preventive health measure—the Pap smear—is critical for early detection and effective treatment. The Pap smear is a well-accepted diagnostic technique, which increases the opportunity of identifying potential disease, maximizes the likelihood of early treatment, and minimizes the potential for death from cervical cancer (Virginia Department of Health 1977). If cervical cancer is largely preventable and if Pap smears are predominantly reliable, then why do women continue to die from a preventable disease and why is incipient disease not routinely identified? These questions motivated the research I conducted in the model family practice setting in the southeast—research that is particularly timely given the ongoing controversy about the efficacy of the Pap smear.

For most of the last three decades, a Pap smear to test for cancer of the cervix has been promoted for annual use (Foltz and Kelsey 1978). In recent years, the American Cancer Society has reduced the frequency of recommended smears: "For the average risk person a Pap test is recommended once every three years after two initial negative tests one year apart" (American Cancer Society 1985:11). Despite this recommendation, the professional associations and medical practitioners in obstetrics and gynecology have retained the standard of annual Pap smears (Demarest 1985). But by any standard, the women being treated at the model family practice clinic were not at "average risk" and therefore "needed" annual Pap smears. An Appalachian population is characterized by a high risk for disease and for a low utilization of medical sources.

The analysis in the last two chapters provided vital information about the behavior that has produced the increasing hysterectomy rate in the United States. In this chapter, the focus shifts to explore the use of Pap smears in a potentially high-risk population. Once again, the data were collected in a university teaching hospital; however, the setting and the medical specialty changed—from gynecology and the subspecialty of oncology (cancer) in an urban west coast hospital to primary care in a model family medicine training program in a rural southeastern hospital. Even though the patients in both settings were women with potential cancer-related reproductive problems, both the medical task and their reasons for seeking medical care were different. In the last two chapters, we met patients who were referred to clinics with abnormal Pap smears and the medical task was a specific one—to diagnose and treat. In this chapter, we will meet women who came to the clinic for a variety of reasons, although as a group they were at a high risk for cervical cancer. Since family medicine is a primary care specialty, it seemed an ideal setting to study how, through the decision making process, the diffuse goal of providing comprehensive health care was accomplished.

This kind of analysis necessitated a reorientation in two additional ways. First, rather than examining the composite parts of the medical interview (language forms and functions), I treated the medical event as a whole to explore how the decision making process unfolded phase by phase. Second, while decisions to treat abnormal Pap smears by performing hysterectomies were consistent with the dominant medical paradigm, decisions to perform Pap smears were less so. The medical model is oriented toward high-technology treatments. To understand the context in which decisions to perform, or not to perform, Pap smears were negotiated, I describe the status of preventive medicine in the United States. Information about the commitment to and practice of preventive medicine provides a backdrop against which to display the communicational strategies through which decisions about a particular preventive procedure are negotiated—to display the linguistic accomplishment of the decision to perform or not to perform Pap smears.

The Status of Prevention

Critics of our current health care system argue that despite increasing lip service being paid to disease prevention, most funding is allocated for high-technology medicine and little is expended for prevention (Taylor 1982; Terris 1980). Although the share of the federal budget spent on health care has grown from 4.1 percent in 1940 to 8.8 percent in 1977 and most recently to 12 percent in 1979, in 1977 only two percent of the monies were spent on public health or preventive activities (Freeland and Schendler 1981; Terris 1980).

The status of preventive medicine is evidenced in another way as well. The monies allocated for prevention are extremely vulnerable to budget cuts. In the fiscal year 1980—a year when the United States was not at war—the budget for public health activities was cut by about a third, while the military budget was increased by over one half. Ostensibly these cuts were detached economic decisions, yet, as Susser (1980) points out, these decisions are laden with value judgements that reflect societal priorities.

The Sidels (1981) make a distinction between a system organized to provide medical care and one oriented toward maintaining the health of the population by preventing illness. Along with others (Taylor 1982; Terris 1980; Knowles 1977), they contend that in the United States we have a far greater investment in treatment than in prevention. We have a medical care system, which is organized to provide acute, curative, and chronic care and is becoming increasingly hospital-centered and dependent upon high technology, not a health care system, organized to maintain health and prevent illness.

Critics suggest that a medical care system controlled by the profit-making private sector and financed largely through government-supplied funds is "one of the major reasons for the overwhelmingly greater investment in treatment" (Sidel and Sidel 1981). While the public is led to believe that this is a purely economic decision (i.e., preventive care is not cost-effective), critics argue that this is not the case. Preventive medicine and a system oriented toward health would be no more costly than the one we have. On the contrary, technological methods and epidemiological findings support the widespread use of preventive measures to assure savings in terms of illness, lives, and medical costs (Terris 1980).

Although our national priorities reveal a continuing commitment to a high-technology, illness-oriented medical care system and a lack of commitment to prevention, health care and prevention are becoming the issues of the 80s. This apparent paradox is rooted in the public's growing belief that medical care is not having the desired effect on health. It is a trend accentuated by the reality of spiraling inflation. As Taylor (1982) points out, a cost-benefit analysis suggests that Americans are paying more and buying less for their money. Although official responses have varied—from the regulations suggested by the Carter administration to the competitive consumerism of the Reagan administration—dissatisfaction with the medical care system has created a consistent response: prevention is a hot issue, but not a significant practice. Several factors contribute to the illusion of prevention in a reality committed to illness-oriented medicine.

First, there is no clear-cut agreement as to what constitutes preventive medicine. Definitions of prevention vary from the cure or the arrest of disease to the identification and diagnosis of disease and the elimination of the underlying social and individual causes of disease (Taylor 1982; White 1975). Second, an ideology of individual causation prevails. Because of this ideology, disease prevention primarily entails education directed toward changing the self-destructive behaviors of individuals and treating the illnesses caused by such behaviors. Taylor (1982) suggests that the ideology of individual causation takes precedence over an ideology of social causation:

> because it is congruent with changes in other cultural ideals, because it is promoted by the organization of American medical care, and because it effectively translates, for many people, their subjective experience of the relationship between their health and aspects of their everyday lives (Taylor 1982,32).

Third, the long-range solutions of a system oriented toward health are not consistent with an individualistic ideology. Yet, in a capitalistic society, the most consistent response to any problem is to blame the individual. Industry benefits from shifting the blame from environmental and occupational hazards to individual life styles, and scientific medicine sustains these beliefs. Research illustrates a link between self-destructive habits and disease, while the biomedical model of medicine supports the belief that the etiology of a disease is a specific agent identifiable through scientific research. Medical practice is organized to identify specific disease agents and treat them—an orientation engendered by medical technology and training as well as by the reimbursement structure of the insurance industry. This short-range action orientation may satisfy the treatment expectations of doctor and patient; however, short-term relief is inconsistent with health education and disease prevention.

Finally, since health education and disease prevention demand an informed and responsible population of patients, such programs have the potential to change the balance of the doctor-patient relationship—a relationship predicated on the trust and dependence of the patient and the control and benevolence of the physician. The argument against preventive medicine made by the AMA highlights this threat. Even though the AMA agrees that preventive care has the potential to identify disease, they argue that the expense of the examination could increase, rather than reduce, the overall costs of medical care in the United States. In a time of spiraling inflation, with few, if any, controls being self-imposed by the medical profession, the argument that prevention is too costly is particularly revealing. It conceals the cost advantage associated with prevention in an ideology of cost containment, masking medical resistance. If comprehensive preventive health care is a threat, a medical system oriented toward treatment and a "vaccine model of prevention" is not (cf. Taylor 1982).

Pap Smears: A Preventative Case in Point

Pap smears are neither a treatment nor a vaccine. The Pap smear, developed by Dr. George Papanicolaou in the 1940s, is a diagnostic screening device with a good potential for detecting abnormal cells on a woman's cervix. Not long ago, cervical cancer was the number one killer of women in the United States. Today, "thanks largely to early detection from the Pap smear it ranks fourth" (Spletter 1983). When placed in the context of the practice of medicine and the status of disease prevention in the United States, it should not be surprising that the medical community divides on the issue of responsibility.

Although many physicians agree that cervical cancer is a preventable disease, medical opinion divides on who is responsible for initiating the necessary screening. Drs. Morteza Dini and Kianoosh Jafari of Cook County Hospital and Chicago Medical School place the responsibility for screening with the physician. They claim that the out-patient management of pre-invasive cervical lesions is so effective that, "physicians should offer Pap smears to all patients regardless of presenting complaint" (*Ob, Gyn News* 1983a). Here prevention as a medical responsibility is integrated into the routine delivery of care.

On the other hand, a gynecologic oncologist practicing at a university hospital places responsibility on patients. Among his remarks, quoted in a local newspaper, was a claim that women patients, by avoiding yearly physical examinations and such simple tests as Pap smears, were neglecting their own gynecological health. This "blame the victim" approach makes disease prevention an individual responsibility, isolating it from the routine delivery of medical care. Although doctors may locate the ultimate source of the problem differently, many nevertheless agree that Pap smears are essential for identifying and treating potentially cancerous cells. This doctor went on to say that in England when doctors stopped recommending physical examinations and Pap smears, the number of cancer deaths for women doubled.

Placing the primary responsibility for screening with women has not proven satisfactory. Many women experience and therefore anticipate pelvic examinations and/or Pap smears as an uncomfortable, anxiety-producing and often degrading procedure (Knopf 1976; Magee 1975; Emerson 1970). Furthermore, the preventive implications of these techniques are not always well understood by patients (Knopf 1976). Since cervical examinations are generally performed in doctors' offices and women are usually introduced to Pap smears by their physicians, doctors can and do play an important role in influencing patients to have these procedures done (McCurtis 1979; Walton *et al.* 1979; Burns *et al.* 1968; Kegeles 1967). It seems apparent that the routine performance of Pap smears and the success of cytological screening programs depend to a large extent on the interest, knowledge, and cooperation of medical providers (Kegeles 1967).

Unlike many screening devices for cancer, the Pap smear has a good potential for identifying disease. In a recent article in *Ob, Gyn News* (1983b) the effectiveness of various cancer screening devices was reviewed. Dr. Anthony Miller, the director of the National Cancer Institute of Canada, said that all screening tests for breast cancer have some disadvantages. He went on to explain that it is hard to develop effective screening when so little is known about the natural course of a disease. In a similar vein, Dr. Melvyn S. Tochman, of Johns Hopkins, spoke about the lack of success of sputum cytology for detecting lung cancer. He pointed out that mortality seemed no better for patients who were screened regularly than for those who were not screened at all. The detection of breast and lung cancer was compared with the efficacy of Pap smears for detecting cervical cancer. Dr. Neil B. Rosenstein, director of the Division of Gynecologic Oncology at the Johns Hopkins University School of Medicine, said that for cervical cancer, much is known about the course of the disease—it has a long preclinical phase, which makes early detection possible—and there is an effective screening test.

Because cervical cancer is often without symptoms in the early stages, the use of Pap smears is especially important (American Cancer Society 1985). For example, routine Pap smears identified abnormal cellular changes in each of the patients discussed in chapters 3 and 4. Numerous studies have shown that comprehensive cytological screening programs increase early detection and therefore decrease mortality from cervical cancer (Walton *et al.* 1979; Boyes *et al.* 1977; Brown 1976; Cramer 1974; Timonen *et al.* 1974; Boyes, 1972; Dickinson *et al.* 1972; Christopherson *et al.* 1970; Burnes *et al.* 1968; Sall *et al.* 1968; Handy and Wieben 1965; Lundin *et al.* 1965). Direct correlations have been demonstrated between the intensity of the screening program and reduction of this cancer (Boyes *et al.* 1977). Notwithstanding the American Cancer Society's recent suggestion that yearly Pap smears are not needed for all populations of women, no suggestion has been made to discontinue them. Instead, the populations most likely to benefit have been pinpointed. A strong case can be made for encouraging a consistent Pap smear screening program as a routine feature of medical examinations, especially in high-risk populations (Marx 1979; Shulman *et al.* 1974).

Studies suggest that a constellation of factors is prominent among women who develop cervical cancer. Richart (1980) found that this cancer is most likely in sexually active women thirty-five years of age and older. However, as patterns of sexual behavior change in the United States, a concomitant lowering of the age at which this disease is first diagnosed occurs. Richart, a pathologist at Columbia University's College of Physicians, claims that, "80 to 90 percent of young women are at risk of developing cervical cancer or its precursors" (Richart 1980). This view is echoed by the co-director of gynecological oncology at another major university. Among his remarks quoted in a newspaper was the claim that there is increasing evidence that "cervical cancer actually is a venereal disease," which today's young women are "twice as likely to get as women were 10 years ago." He goes on to explain that Pap smears for virgins almost never show an abnormality. And he concludes by saying that it is estimated that 70 percent of women who receive a positive Pap smear in the range of moderate to severe (classes three or four) will, if they do not receive appropriate treatment, "one day develop cervical cancer." (Spletter 1983). It is for this reason that doctors are calling for "early" screening—when young women seek contraception or when they enter the medical system for other reasons (Creasman and Clarke-Pearson 1983).

Although increasing attention is being paid to the likelihood that young, sexually active women will develop cervical cancer, older women continue to be at risk. In a study by Marshall (1965), the mean age at the time of discovery was 40.7 years for pre-invasive cancer and 50.3 years for invasive cancer. Furthermore, a profile developed by Walton and colleagues (1979) suggests that women with this disease are more often from the lower socio-economic classes, come from rural areas, and have had long intervals since their last pregnancy.

In a similar study, Handy and Wieben (1965) focus on a socio-economic complex of relative poverty, rapid sexual maturation, and haste—the early beginning and the early termination of the reproductive phase. In addition, the incidence of cervical cancer was significantly higher among the blacks in their study than the whites, and within the white group, higher among lower-income categories. They suggest that sexual maturation, intercourse, and pregnancy occur significantly earlier in the lives of women who develop this cancer and that age at first coitus, number of sex partners, and penile hygiene may also explain some of the variance in incidence for different populations (e.g., black/white, urban/rural, higher/lower social class).

Background Context

The model family practice clinic described in this study provided a useful setting for me to explore the performance of Pap smears in a potentially high-risk population. Appalachian women are at risk for several reasons. First, the region has the highest rate of cervical cancer in the United States (Kleinman 1979; Mason and McKay 1969). Second, the Appalachian region is a poverty area and as such has a large population of women who have a high potential for developing disease and a low utilization of medical services.[1] Third, Appalachia is a medically underserved area (Fowinkle 1975).[2] A large proportion of the primary care physicians who practice in Appalachia have been trained in medical schools and residency training programs in the area[3] and these practitioners are assumed to share a stronger orientation toward preventive care than is typically the case for those practicing in other specialties— an assumption that is particularly important, since studies have shown that women who could benefit from comprehensive screening programs are not being routinely screened.

A two-year study (Walton *et al.* 1979) of patients with advanced carcinoma of the cervix found that only 12 percent had had the disease diagnosed by a screening examination before the onset of symptoms. Furthermore, 36 percent of the women were not diagnosed even though they had been exposed to the medical care system. Another study by Fruchter *et al.* (1980) reports on the health care history of women with invasive cervical cancer. Fifty-two percent had had no previous Pap smears and 62 percent had had no Pap smears during the five-year period preceding the detection of their cancers. However, 73 percent of the unscreened women had received ambulatory medical care, including 41 percent who had had regular care for chronic conditions and 16 percent who had been hospitalized. So some women seem to be at risk even if they are receiving medical care.

Other vulnerable women are often out of the mainstream of the medical care system. The Walton *et al.* study (1979) and another by Marshall (1965) suggest that sexually active women, from the lower socio-economic classes, who are past their primary reproductive years are less likely to receive routine Pap smears (e.g., during examinations for birth control, during pre- and post-natal care, as a feature of venereal disease screening, or while being treated for vaginal infections). Many researchers agree that much of the at-risk population could be reached by routine screening in ambulatory health services and hospitals (cf. Fruchter *et al.* 1980).

Some argue that because primary care providers share a commitment to care for the whole person in the context of his/her daily life (Flannery 1982), they would be the most likely to practice preventive medicine; others disagree. For example, Dr. Lila Wallace, an internist at the University of Cornell Medical College, claims that:

> While most general practitioners listen to the patient's heart and lungs, few routinely examine female breasts—although breast cancer is the second most frequent cause of death among women. Almost none administer pelvic examinations. For these examinations women must go to a specialist—the gynecologist who is a surgeon (quoted in Schieflbein 1980, 16).

Wallace suggests educational inadequacy as the probable cause of these oversights.

Since primary care providers are often the first line of defense in patient care, especially in an underserved area, in an earlier paper Fisher and Page (1984) examined the contribution of selected variables in explaining the performance of Pap smears. Initially, the model family practice clinic in the southeast appeared to be a setting conducive to the routine performance of Pap smears. It was a teaching situation that lacked either the economic motives (residents and attending staff were salaried) or the extreme time pressures that are normally associated with private fee-for-service practices. While the medical literature stresses the importance of routine Pap smears for a high-risk population, the residents training in this setting performed relatively few.

We found that in 408 office visits, the tendency was to perform Pap smears only when they were requested, required, or convenient. Patients were more likely to receive Pap smears on their first visit to the clinic, if they were seen by second-year residents, and if they appeared to be women with low incomes or low education. Older women were the least likely to receive Pap smears. Overall, Pap smears were performed during approximately 25 percent of the 408 visits or on 39.9 percent of the patients. In a population that was by definition at high risk, this Pap smear rate appears low. And in light of the statistics reported by the U.S. Department of Health, Education, and Welfare (1975), they are low. According to this report, in 1973 almost 50 percent of women over seventeen years of age reported having had a Pap smear during the previous year. These findings lead us to join others who have questioned the adequacy of the educational background and the efficacy of family medicine as a training situation—especially as they relate to the delivery of routine preventive health care for women.

These questions are supported by research that suggests that different types of practice settings produce very different results. For example, Brown (1976), investigated the performance of Pap smears in a pre-paid medical plan—a health maintenance group—that included several gynecologists. He found a pronounced tendency on the part of all the physicians in the group routinely to do Pap smears on women being seen for a variety of reasons unrelated to cervical cancer. A pre-paid medical plan and the presence of gynecologists appeared to affect the practice of preventive medicine by all of the doctors.

Although studies highlight the risk factors associated with cervical cancer and document the performance (or lack of performance) of Pap smears in various settings, we still have very little information on how these "facts" translate into medical practices and are enacted by doctor and patient. There is evidence that this process is neither neutral nor objective. This chapter reports on how decisions to perform, or not to perform, Pap smears are negotiated as doctor and patient communicate over the course of the medical interview.

Research Context

The model family residency training program in which this research was conducted was organized as a fee-for-service group practice; however, since it was a teaching setting, medical care was provided by residents under the supervision of attending staff physicians. The patients primarily were drawn from a rural population—a small city and surrounding rural areas. Patients who could not pay (either by means of insurance, medicaid, medicare, or private funds) generally were not seen, and usually no more than 25 percent using public funds (Medicaid/ Medicare) were seen. Data were gathered over a two-year period. I spent over a year and a half establishing that I was both trustworthy and knowledgeable. During this time, I attended weekly conferences, discussed the possibility of doing the research with the attending staff, and talked informally to the residents, attending staff, and other personnel. I used this time to videotape several residents. These tapes were used for educational purposes and to diffuse some of the anxiety about the research. After each taping, we explored the tapes together, discussing how the discourse we saw influenced the delivery of care.

Finally, in the summer of 1981 I audiotaped and videotaped interactions among forty-three women patients and eighteen residents. A routine feature of the training of family medicine residents in this setting, as well as in many others in the United States, is the use of videotape. Residents and patients are videotaped during interactions and the tapes are used for teaching purposes; therefore the taping I did was not as traumatic as it might have been.

The analysis in this chapter is slightly different from the analyses in the last two chapters and, at first glance, it may seem contradictory to them. The earlier chapters suggested that whether it is intended or not, the institutional authority of physicians and the acquiescence in that authority by patients gives physicians an interactional dominance. From this position of authority, physicians have the power to impose unnecessary reproductive surgery, whether or not it is in the patient's best interest, and in the process they become the keepers of women's morality as well as their health.

In this chapter I will argue that physicians do not routinely persuade women to have medical procedures (Pap smears) that are clearly in their best interest. It may appear that at one and the same time I am criticizing medical providers for using the institutional authority of their medical role and for not using it. The argument becomes clearer if the focus is shifted to the patient. The asymmetry in the medical relationship places women at a disadvantage in the health care delivery system. Not only are they unable to evaluate their health care needs and are at risk of being negatively sanctioned if they aggressively pursue this needed information, but their primary source of information is the medical professional. As long as the medical establishment protects its institutionally based authority, it is the patient not the physician who is in a double bind; and it is medical practitioners who are subject to criticism for being too paternal and not paternal enough—a criticism that questions whether medical care is in the patient's best interest.

The Form and Function of a Medical Event

Medical interviews are organized communicational events, with an overall structure composed of four phases—an opening, a medical history, a physical examination, and a closing phase. Each phase has a characteristic form and a specific function. The task of the medical interview includes dealing with the patient's presenting complaint as well as using the specialized knowledge and technical skills at the resident's disposal to deliver medically adequate care. This task can be broken down into four phase-oriented tasks. From the doctor's point of view, the task of the opening phase (o.p.) is to get a more complete picture of the patient's presenting complaint, while the task of the medical history phase (m.h.p.) is to gather the social and medical information necessary to deal with the specific medical complaint and with more general medical problems that emerge during the discussion. Assessing the patient's health is the task of the physical examination phase (p.e.p.), while managing medical care—the patient's presenting complaint and more general emergent medical problems—is the task of the closing phase (c.p.).

In this chapter, I examine when—in what phase—Pap smears are discussed (or not discussed) and the relationship between their phase location and whether or not they are performed—the form of the medical interview. This relationship is displayed graphically in figure 4.1. There are no conflicts in the cases where women needed[4] and received, did not need and received, or did not need and did not receive Pap smears. The cases that need closer examination are those, during the medical history phase, where patients needed Pap smears, but they did not receive them. The analysis highlights communicational strategies—the functions of the medical discourse—for accomplishing and avoiding Pap smears, and discusses how the asymmetrical and reciprocal nature of the doctor-patient relationship shapes the decision making process.

There are consequences for the delivery of health care to women that

Figure 4.1. Pap Smears Across the Phases

	Needed				Did Not Need				
	o.p.	*m.h.p.*	*p.e.p.*	*c.p.*	*o.p.*	*m.h.p.*	*p.e.p.*	*c.p.*	*Total*
Received	5	3	7	0	0	1	0	0	16
Did not receive	0	5	0	0	1	5	1	1	13
Total	5	8	7	0	1	6	1	1	29

are rooted in the flow of communication: 1) an out-of-phase discussion of Pap smears precludes their performance; 2) if the need to have the patient undress has not been established before the physical examination phase of the medical interview, Pap smears are not performed;[5] and 3) once the need for a Pap smear has been established, its absence is notable and accounted for in the discourse. Of the forty-three new women patients in this study, Pap smears were discussed with twenty-four of them and performed with sixteen. Thirteen of the women with whom they were discussed did not receive them, five women did not discuss them with the doctor, yet did receive them, while an additional fourteen patients neither discussed having Pap smears nor had them performed. The data reported in this chapter add to the research findings discussed earlier by shedding light on how the decisions to do or not to do Pap smears are accomplished or avoided in the discourse that occurs as the phases of the medical interview unfold.

The Medical Interview

New women patients come to the model family practice clinic with a range of problems that require the specialized knowledge and technical expertise of a medical practitioner. When women call or walk into the clinic, they are given an appointment with one of the family practice residents, who will continue to be their physician if they so desire. This assignment of personnel is consistent with the philosophy of family medicine—continuity of care should be established and maintained

from the first visit forward. On their first visit, these patients are pro-
cessed by various staff members. They are greeted by a receptionist,
interviewed by an office worker who collects basic demographic and social information, and called into the examining room by a nurse, who
asks what their current medical needs are. Before residents walk into the
examining room, they look at the patient's chart, which includes the presenting complaint as well as demographic and social information about
the patient. Decisions to do or not to do Pap smears unfold in the communicational work the participants do together as they move through the
phases of the medical interview.

The Communicational Work of the Opening Phase

While there is some variation, the medical interview usually opens with
the resident entering the examining room, greeting the patient by name,
introducing himself or herself, and asking the patient for a more complete description of her presenting complaint. The resident establishes
the topic of this phase of the interview by asking a broad, open-ended
question, such as: "What brings you in today?" or "What can I do for
you today?" In response, the patient tells her story.

There appears to be a characteristic rhythm to the storytelling of the
opening phase. The patient tells her story in the main channel of communication, while the resident makes clucking sounds ("um-hum,"
"um," etc.) in the back channel, signaling that he or she is paying attention and encouraging the patient to continue. Occasionally the story is
interrupted by the resident asking short information-seeking questions,
such as: "Is it a sharp pain?" or "Do you wake up with the pain?" And
on other occasions, the resident directs the story with statements such
as: "Let's take one problem at a time," or "Let's go over that again."
While the patient's story dominates this phase of the interview, the resident's institutional authority has not been diminished. Residents establish the topic, control the development of the topic, and control access
to the floor.

In the cases of six of the forty-three new women patients, Pap smears
were talked about during the opening phase of the medical interview.
Three of these patients came to the clinic requesting a Pap smear, and
each received one. The Pap smear in each case was associated with a
request for a birth control prescription. The doctor entered the examin-

ing room after seeing on the patient's chart that she was there for a "Pap and pelvic." In each case, the doctor initiated the topic:

> D. OK, what brings you in today?
> P. A yearly Pap smear.

> D. OK, can you tell me the main reason you came in today?
> P. Well, I um, supposed to have another Pap smear, 'cause I ran out of the pill (birth control pills) and I didn't want to go to my doctor which was in Sayorville.

> D. Uh, let's see here (reading the file) we'll do a Pap smear and a pelvic today as well.
> P. (nods).

The other three patients came to the clinic with complaints that might have indicated the need for a Pap smear. One patient, Betty, had been told that she had a herpes infection and she wanted a second opinion. Another patient, Catherine, said that she had not had a physical examination in three years and wanted one. The last patient, Leslie, suspected that she had a vaginal infection. In each case, Pap smears were talked about during the opening phase of the medical interview. Leslie and Betty both had had recent Pap smears (within the last three months) and Catherine had not had one taken for at least three years. Betty and Catherine received Pap smears on this visit and Leslie did not. In two of the three cases, the topic of a Pap smear was initiated by the resident. Early in the discussion with Catherine, the resident said:

> D. Your last Pap smear that you know of was normal?
> P. Yeah.

Apparently this information, plus the knowledge that it had been three years since her last physical, led to a decision to do a Pap smear. During the physical exam, the resident said "what we need to do now is a pelvic" and the pelvic exam and the Pap smear were done. With Betty, the decision to do a Pap smear was more clearly reached during the opening phase. The resident initiated the topic:

> D. We need to do a, um, Pap smear. Did you have a Pap smear done yesterday? A cancer test? I guess we need to do a Pap smear then, uh, and I

guess that's about it, and the bimanual. You've had a pelvic before haven't
you? Pap smear and all that? Can I help you with any other thing today, any
other problem you are having?

    P. No just that.

After this communicational sequence, a Pap smear was taken. It appears almost as if the doctor is talking to himself, reaching the decision
and then telling the patient about it. The decision he reached implies
that in order to provide a second opinion the doctor needed to repeat all
of the diagnostic procedures that had been performed the day before. In
the next case, a Pap smear was talked about after it emerged in Leslie's
story:

    P. . . . I did have a very bad cervical problem about a year ago which
they froze, and so far has been doing all right. I was at the doctor's in April
(three months prior) and everything seemed normal then, uh//

    D. //They did a Pap smear in April?

    P. Uhm, huh, yeah.

In this case the Pap smear is part of the patient's storytelling. The doctor interrupts the story to ask for more information and the patient then
continues. Later in the medical interview (during the physical examination phase) the doctor again checks when the patient's last Pap smear
was done and that it had been normal and concludes that another Pap
smear was not necessary. He says: "Late April OK, we won't do one."

Certain contextual features seem to prompt the discussion of Pap
smears during the opening phase of the medical interview. Discussions
about Pap smears were directly related to the presenting complaint, and
less directly related to the patient's status as a sexually active young
woman. Three women came to the clinic requesting Pap smears and
three came with presenting complaints that indicated their relevance. In
one case, the request for a Pap smear went hand in hand with a desire for
birth control pills, and in another, it was related to a sexually transmitted disease—herpes. Although these data are limited, the findings support my earlier work (Fisher and Page 1984) and other data from larger-
scale quantitative studies. Pap smears are more likely to be done in the
cases of sexually active, young, unmarried women, who are routinely in
the health care delivery system; these are not necessarily the only
women at risk from cervical cancer.

Two communicational strategies seem to be operating. The first is the "patient's request." A patient who comes to the clinic requesting a Pap smear gets one. The second strategy is the "doctor's choice." The patient's having had a Pap smear recently does not automatically preclude her having another one. If the doctor decides a Pap smear is necessary, he generally does one. Sometimes he tells the patient—"I guess we need to do a Pap smear then"—and sometimes he does not—"What we need to do now is a pelvic." If the doctor decides that a Pap smear is not necessary, he does not perform one—e.g., "Late April, OK we won't do one." Requests for Pap smears and presenting complaints that entail decisions to do pelvic examinations presupposes that the patient will be undressed, thus making the occurrence of Pap smears more likely.

The Communicational Work of the Medical History
Phase

It is during the medical history phase of the interview that medical providers seek background information to provide adequate medical care. Since Pap smears are preventive health measures, we could speculate that to provide adequate care physicians would ask questions during this phase of the interview to determine whether or not patients need them. The medical history phase of the interview is opened by the doctor. At times, the topic is established explicitly, with a statement such as: "I'd like to ask you some questions about your medical background." Occasionally the transition is more subtle and marked by questions such as: "Have you ever been bothered with headaches, problems with your eyes, blurred vision?" The transition from the opening phase, whether explicit or more subtle, is usually signaled with transition markers such as: "Okay, all right, let's see, ah."

Like the opening phase, the medical history phase has a characteristic rhythm. Again, communication takes place primarily in the main channel. There are few comment or evaluation statements made. Questions are short, pointed, and generally require a yes or no answer. The answer no is usually followed with another question. A yes answer sometimes produces a probing or information-seeking question. At times, questions are chained—that is, multiple questions are asked in the same utterance—"Any problems with your heart, lungs, kidneys?" A no answer is usually understood as a no to all the questions. The questions seem to proceed as if the medical provider is moving down an internalized checklist. Pauses seem to indicate a temporary loss of place. Fast bursts of short or chained choice questions with yes/no answers give this phase of the interview a staccato quality, with interludes of probing questions providing a contrast. The resident clearly dominates the interaction. He asks the questions and the patient answers them.

During this phase of the interview, Pap smears were discussed with fourteen of the forty-three patients. Eight of the women provided information that indicated the need for a Pap smear and six of them told the resident that they had had one taken within the preceding year. Of these fourteen patients, one received a Pap smear at that time, even though she had had one within the last three months, three indicated the need for a Pap smear and then received one, and five indicated the need for a Pap smear and did not receive one (see figure 4.2).

I followed these patients' charts for six months after their initial office visits. Even when patients who needed Pap smears returned for follow-up visits, they did not usually receive one (see footnote 5). Only one of the patients whose medical history indicated the need for a Pap smear received one on a subsequent visit. While the number of patients involved is not large, these findings support earlier findings and suggest that if the mortality rate for cervical cancer is to be decreased in this population of potentially high-risk patients, Pap smears need to be conducted as a routine feature of the medical care provided.

Received Pap smears. Decisions to do Pap smears were negotiated in the discourse between resident and patient.

> D. . . . Uh, huh, How long has it been since you had a Pap smear?
> P. Uh, I had one last year.

Figure 4.2. Pap Smears in the Medical History Phase

	Needed	Not needed	
Received	3	1	4
Did not receive	5	5	10
Total	8	6	

> D. You did, about when?
> P. Ah
> D. Since, ah, since June?
> P. If I'm not mistaken it could have been June or July.
> D. Who did it?
> P. Dr. D.//
> D. //OK
> P. Anyway he and H. were the ones that did my hysterectomy.

The resident initiated the topic and in the ensuing discussion, the need for a Pap smear was established. It had been at least a year since the patient had one. Contrary to generally held beliefs, a Pap smear is indicated for a woman whether her uterus has been removed or not. The criterion of one per year established the need for a Pap smear for two of the other patients as well. The remaining patient had received a Pap smear within the prior three months; however, the discourse looks much the same.

> D. When was the last time you had a Pap smear?
> P. Three months, in a right before, right about three months ago.
> D. Have you ever had a bad report on your Pap smear?
> P. No, uh, uh.

The resident establishes the topic and in the ensuing discussion, the decision to do a Pap smear is reached. At first glance, it is hard to understand why this patient received one. The patient came to the clinic for birth control pills. This presenting complaint makes it more likely that a Pap smear will be done. Even though she has had a Pap smear three months prior to this visit, it is customary to do one whenever birth control pills are prescribed. In a slightly different way, the presenting complaint of the other three women also predisposed the decision toward a Pap smear. It had been at least a year since their previous Pap smears and their presenting complaints indicated the need for physical examinations, which, in turn, necessitate having the patients undress.

Did Not Receive Pap Smears. Decisions not to do Pap smears were also negotiated in the discussions between residents and patients.

> D. Been checked up with a good Pap smear since then?
> P. Yeah, last time it was perfect.

D. That was in May?
P. (patient nods)
D. Good, OK.

All five of the patients who did not need and did not receive Pap smears had received one in the preceding few months. Four out of the five of them had presenting complaints that did not necessitate getting undressed. One patient who presented with a complaint that indicated a need to get undressed suspected that she had a vaginal infection. It is noteworthy that a vaginal infection, while it did necessitate a pelvic examination, did not produce a decision to do a Pap smear in this case or in the case discussed earlier in relation to the opening phase. Perhaps a vaginal infection is a contraindication for a Pap smear; however, in neither case was the information about these patients' Pap smear histories entered in the patients' files for later follow-up care. The patients also shared another feature in common. Each of them had a higher-level specialist—an obstetrician gynecologist—who had provided their last Pap smear.

While talking with patients, doctors seem to make decisions that flow, one from the other. First, a decision is made about the relationship between the presenting complaint and the need to have the patient undress. Second, a discussion about the patient's past history of Pap smears involves a decision about whether the patient needs a Pap smear. Finally, a decision to do or not to do a Pap smear is reached. It appears that Pap smears are less likely to be done if the presenting complaint indicates no need for the patient to undress, if the discussion discloses no need for a Pap smear, and/or if the patient discloses that she has another physician who provided her last Pap smear. They appear to be more likely if the patient requests one, if the presenting complaint indicates the need for the patient to get undressed, and/or if the discussion indicates the need for a Pap smear (see figure 4.3). What is striking about these discussions is the paucity of information shared with patients and the absence of any attempt by patients (other than an initial request) to alter the decision making process and to affect the decision to do or not to do a Pap smear. Residents discuss neither these decisions nor the criteria upon which they are based with patients, and patients in this study did not request such information. Most often, patients are not told that they need Pap smears (or that they do not need them), nor are they asked

Figure 4.3. Decision Making Tree

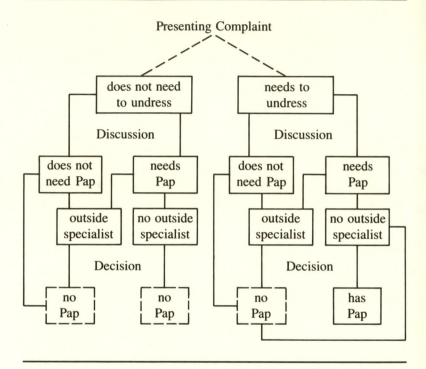

whether or not they want Pap smears. This lack of patient participation in the decision making process becomes even more obvious with the next group of patients—women who needed, but did not receive Pap smears (see footnote 4).

Needed but did not receive. Pap smears were discussed with five patients, each of whom indicated the need for a Pap smear, but who did not receive one. The first patient, Peggy, came to the clinic for a second opinion. She has been diagnosed as having hypertension, is a diabetic, did not want to be on the drugs that were prescribed, and needed to make sure that she had no other viable choices before she consented to such treatment. During the medical history the doctor asked:

D. When was your last Pap smear?
P. Uhm, about a year ago.

D. Does Dr. D. take care of all your GYN?
P. Yes.
D. Is he the one that delivered your two children?
P. He sure did.
D. Ok and you see him on a yearly basis?
P. On a yearly basis.

Toward the end of the medical history the resident concludes:

D. I'll leave the GYN part to Dr. D.
P. Ok, that's a relief.

The patient's presenting complaint suggested the need for a physical examination and hence the need for her to get undressed. The ensuing discussion disclosed that she had not had a Pap smear for approximately a year and that she had an outside physician—a higher-level specialist—who routinely takes care of her reproductive needs. The discussion about Pap smears concluded with the doctor and patient in apparent agreement that reproductive matters would remain in the hands of her specialist. Why then do I cite this patient as one who needs and does not get a Pap smear, implying that there is a problem? I do so for several reasons. First, as I have already discussed, the doctor's choice is made in a series of stages that flow one from the other. The decision to do or not to do a Pap smear is the culmination of these choices. In this case, the doctor does not use the authority of his role to persuade the patient. Instead he bows to the authority of a higher-level specialist. If we conceptualize the decision making process in terms of the decision making tree discussed earlier, the juncture between one branch and another becomes more obvious (see figure 4.4).

An interesting question is raised here about the relationship between the internal structure of the profession of medicine and the routine delivery of adequate medical care. In the medical hierarchy, family medicine is designated as a lower-level specialty than obstetrics/gynecology. Perhaps a part of what we are seeing in this interaction is a manifestation of this stratification. It is as if there is an unwritten rule, "If there is a higher-level practitioner on the case, do not step on his/her turf."

The sidestepping involved in bowing to a higher-level specialist is compounded by the discomfort doctor and patient display in their talk. The patient quite clearly expresses her relief that a Pap smear will not be done. The doctor's discomfort is more subtle. As we have seen, when

Figure 4.4. Decision Making Juncture

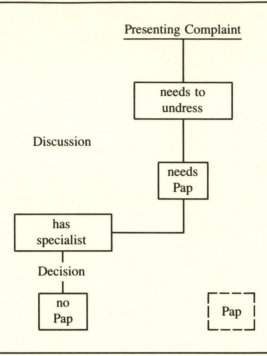

doctors want to do a Pap smear, they use the authority of their role to do one. Since Pap smears are neither dangerous nor expensive procedures, the absence of a Pap smear is notable and may, at least in part, reflect the doctor's discomfort. Not only is the authority of the doctor's role not used to persuade the patient to have a Pap smear, but he does not take responsibility for her health care by informing her that she needs one. As the holder of medical knowledge and technical skill, it is his responsibility to inform her of the risks for women her age and either to offer to do a Pap smear or to suggest that she make an appointment with a specialist for one.

With the second, third, and fourth patients, the results were much the same. The strategies used to accomplish them were, however, different. One patient, Wendy, had a presenting complaint of a body rash (a complaint that indicated the need for her to undress); the other two patients, Denise and Lucia, presented with complaints that at first did not indicate a need for them to undress (an ear ache and a leg injury). The discussion with both of these patients clearly established that they needed a Pap smear, yet Pap smears were not done on these visits, nor were they performed on subsequent visits.

Wendy

D. Uh, when was your last Pap and pelvic?
P. Uh, it's been about a year and three months.
D. Ok, do you intend to keep going in for your Pap and pelvic or do you want to have that done here?
P. Well . . .
D. So it really doesn't matter.

Denise

D. Uh, we're somewhat limited in terms of time; initially with new patients I like to do a complete history and complete examination; sometimes we have to break the exam up into pieces.
P. Right.
D. If you haven't had a Pap smear in a year then sometime in the near future we need to do that.
P. Yeah, it's been a year.

Lucia

D. When was the last time you were at Planned Parenthood?
P. Sixteen months ago.
D. Well you need another Pap smear.
P. Yeah, definitely.
D. As many times as you've been pregnant.

In each of these cases it was established that the patient needed a physical examination, which entailed getting undressed. One of the patients did get undressed and the other two did not. The discussion about Pap smears also established that none of the patients had an outside doctor and that each of them needed a Pap smear, yet none of the patients received one. If we examine these decisions in terms of the decision making tree discussed earlier, we find a disjuncture. It is as if the doctor were progressing down the decision making branch that should have produced a decision to do a Pap smear, then he suddenly crossed over, having decided not to do one (see figure 4.5).

In each of these cases, doctors initiated a discussion about Pap smears and established that the patients needed them. They then used their authority to take away what they had just established the need for, and the patients colluded in this process. With Wendy, the doctor asked whether she wanted to continue going elsewhere for her reproductive needs or if she wanted her Pap smear performed at this clinic. The patient started to respond. She says "well," and as her voice trailed off, the doctor drew the conclusion for her. He said, "it really doesn't matter," and the patient let this conclusion stand. Although she was already undressed for the examination, a Pap smear was not performed; nor was one performed when she returned on subsequent visits. The "unsell" seems to have a permanent quality to it.[6]

Figure 4.5. Decision Making Disjuncture

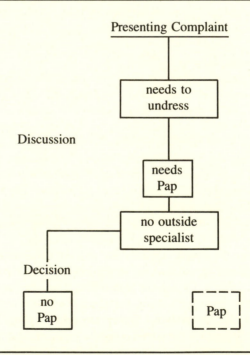

With Denise, the decision making process is less clear on the face of it, from the transcript. Just before the section of dialogue discussed, the doctor asked the patient to "hop up" on the examining table. This little hop had big consequences. By asking the patient to sit dressed on the examining table, instead of asking her to undress for an examination, the doctor made a decision that influenced the rest of the interaction. This section of data opened with the doctor accounting for his decision. He explains that sometimes exams are broken into little pieces. The patient agrees. She is agreeing to remain dressed and to have a superficial examination.

Once this has been agreed, the ensuing discussion about Pap smears is begun. The discussion is characterized by its conditional character. The doctor does not establish whether or not the patient needs a Pap smear. She volunteers this information. He says: "If you haven't had a Pap smear in a year, then sometime in the future we need to do that." The doctor provides the information that women need Pap smears once a year, but he provides it in a way that makes it highly unlikely one will be performed at this time. The patient did not receive a Pap smear on that visit; nor did she receive one on subsequent visits. In both of these cases, the disjuncture in the decision making process influences the adequacy of the health care provided.[7]

In the next case, a similar, but even more subtle, avoidance strategy is used to negotiate the decision not to do a Pap smear. The patient, Lucia, came to the clinic because she injured her leg in a motorcycle accident. An injured leg does not indicate that the patient needs a physical examination; however, the patient quickly lets the doctor know that she fears she is pregnant, may need an abortion, and is interested in obtaining some form of birth control. Had the doctor taken these complaints seriously, the patient would have been asked to undress. She was not, and once again, decisions made early influenced the outcome of this and subsequent visits. Although the patient returned for subsequent visits, she never received a Pap smear.

In this case, the doctor informs the patient that she needs a Pap smear. The patient agrees and the stage appears set for her to receive one, but she does not. In part this may reflect the earlier decision not to have her undress; however, this cannot be the whole story. A decision making tree, again, is clarifying. During the opening phase of the medical interview, the patient presented several complaints that indicated the need to have her undress, yet she remained dressed. During the medical history phase, the resident established that she needed a Pap smear, yet he did not provide one. At each decision making juncture, there occurred a disjuncture. The resident's silence speaks and functions to avoid a procedure that appears to be agreed upon—a Pap smear. Despite the evidence, he moved toward the narrow definition of her problem—an injured leg. She has injured her leg and has come to the clinic to have it treated. The resident provides no medication for her pain and does not treat any of the other medical problems that have emerged during the medical interview. Why not? The answer to this question is the subject of another paper (Fisher and Groce 1983). In brief, the patient triggers a negative response from the resident.

The woman has had a motorcycle accident. She was the driver, not the passenger, of a large motorcycle. During the taking of her medical history, she told the doctor that she is not married, has moved to this area with a boyfriend and lives with him, has had several abortions, is not currently using birth control, feels she may be pregnant again, and wants to know about abortions. The doctor she is talking with is a fundamentalist Christian, whose attitudes about morality and abortion are well known in the clinic. It seems clear that his attitudes about "this kind of woman" colored his decision making and influenced the quality of care she received.

Needed but did not receive. The next patient, Connie, is the only one who did not receive a Pap smear on her initial visit, but did receive one on a subsequent visit. The patient is an epileptic. She was looking for a new doctor and had come to the clinic for a physical examination.

> D. . . . so, uh, are you going to be seeing somebody else for like pelvics and things like that? I, uh, think it's important for women to have a yearly Pap smear. Uh, I'd be glad to do it. If you feel uncomfortable, you know, be glad to let you go to somebody else, because, I think it is important that you have it done.
> P. Ok.
> D. So, if its, uh, you know we don't need to do that today, but, ah, I think that your next visit we ought to do that. Ok? Otherwise I'll just, you know, no need to undress, I'll just listen to your heart and lungs and tap on you.
> P. All right.

At first glance, the exchange in this case looks much like the exchanges in the cases just discussed. The resident established the topic, gathered the information that the patient needed a Pap smear and then decided not to do one. However, there are several significant differences. First, the resident provided the information for the patient to make an independent decision. He told her that women needed a Pap smear once a year and that he would be glad to do one for her. Second, he informed her that if she is uncomfortable, she can choose to go to another doctor.[8] Third, he told the patient he will not do a complete physical on this visit, so there is no need for her to undress, and gave her until the next visit to decide who she wants to provide reproductive care. Finally, he entered the need for a Pap smear on the patient's chart, and on the next visit, he did a complete physical with a pelvic and Pap smear.

During the history-taking phase of the medical interview, certain contextual features, such as the presenting complaint and its consequences (being able to examine patients while dressed or needing them to be undressed), requests for birth control prescriptions, the time elapsed since the last Pap smear, and patients having a higher-level specialist who usually cares for reproductive problems all contribute to decisions to do or not to do Pap smears. The strategies employed to accomplish the decision are most obvious in the cases in which patients need, but do not receive, Pap smears. In these cases, the doctor's choice is strategically expressed in the discourse through practices such as bowing to a higher-level specialist, selling and unselling a Pap smear, and letting silence speak to accomplish a decision not to perform a Pap smear. Each of these practices functions as an avoidance mechanism. That is, they produce a decision not to do a Pap smear, when the discussion has already determined that one is necessary. These decisions are not challenged by patients.

*The Communicational Work of the Physical
Examination Phase*

It is during the physical examination phase of the medical interview that residents gather the information to reach a physical assessment of the patient and her medical problem. More superficial examinations (looking in patients' ears, eyes, and throat, listening to their hearts and lungs, palpating their abdomens, etc.) can be done while the patient remains dressed. More complete examinations require that the patient gets undressed. As I have already shown, whether or not the patient gets undressed is usually the doctor's decision, and as such, is partially shaped by the presenting complaint, as well as by information that emerges during the medical history discussion.

Again, this phase of the interview is opened by the doctor. At times the topic is established by asking a dressed patient to move to the examining table. If the patient is already on the examining table, the topic is often initiated with a statement such as: "I'm going to have a look at you now." If the patient is to get undressed, residents can hand them the paper gown, tell them how to change into it, and leave while they do so. Or residents can make such statements as: "I'll step out now and get my nurse to help you get undressed." The nurse will then reach into the drawer and get the paper gown, etc. The doctor's attitude toward his/her own authority is expressed in this interaction.

As in the other phases of the medical interview, there is a characteristic rhythm to the physical examination. It is characterized by directive statements such as: "Lie down, sit up, take a breath" and behavioristic responses (patients lie down and take breaths, etc.). It is also marked by evaluations. The patient complains of an ear ache. The doctor tells her to turn her head; as she does so, the doctor says: "good." While the doctor is looking in the ear, he or she says "uhm" (with medical intonation this ranges from neutral to anxiety producing). The dual nature of the physical examination—talking and doing—is reflected in the discourse as well. There are frequent pauses, casual talk to fill in some of the "doing time," and a blurring of the medical history and physical examination phases. It is not uncommon as doctors are doing a breast examination for them to be taking further medical history about breast cancer in the family. Nor is it uncommon for doctors, while doing a pelvic examination, to fill the auditory channel with talk about the weather or the new movies in town.

Eight patients had Pap smears talked about, not talked about, and/or done during the physical examination phases of their interviews. All of these patients had presenting complaints that indicated a need to have the patient undress for a physical examination. Pap smears done during this phase came about in different ways. In the first case, it is as if the doctor realized during the examination that he has forgotten to take a history about Pap smears and compensates by taking one then.

D. When was the last time you had a pelvic, a Pap smear done?

P. It's been a year ago. I was supposed to have one in May, but we had a death in the family and I had to cancel it so . . . ,

D. (points arm and index finger at the nurse and snaps his fingers)

N. Pap smear?

D. Yes ma'am, (to nurse)

D. We'll do that too since we got you here.

Not all of the doctors who discover that patients need Pap smears during the physical examination point and snap their fingers for the nurse to set up for one. Nor do all of them tell the patients what they are going to do. The next patient was a pregnant woman. During the pelvic examination, the resident did a Pap smear and a gonorrhea culture (GC) without telling the patient that she was doing either procedure. The patient heard about the Pap smear as the doctor and nurse talked, but while she paid for the GC culture, she was not told about it, nor did she consent to it.

D. Now put your feet in the stirrups hon. You're going to have to scoot down before you do that I'm afraid.

P. Well I can't scoot either (laughs).

D. Ooh it's hot (referring to the just warmed speculum), come on down just a little bit more. You're getting there. Slow but sure. That's good. These things are so uncomfortable (this is a woman doctor and she is sharing the discomfort of pelvic examinations with the patient).

P. They sure are!

D. Ok, now I'll tell you before I do anything.

P. Ok.

D. I'm going to touch your legs. Have you been having itching or burning?

P. No.

D. You have a slight inflammation of your vagina. This looks like a little yeast infection or something. I'm going to insert a finger into your vagina and push down on that muscle. You try to relax that muscle, Ok?

P. Ok.

D. I'm putting the speculum in.

N. You want to do the wet prep or which?

D. Now the wet prep I guess (pause). Now the Pap.

In spite of the fact that the doctor told the patient that she would tell her before she did anything, she did not tell her about the Pap smear, the GC culture, or the wet prep (a test to check for vaginal infections). If the patient knew what a Pap smear and wet prep were, she would have known from overhearing the doctor and nurse talk that one was done. The next case was similar in that the doctor performed a Pap smear and a wet prep without asking or telling the patient before doing so. After the patient is sitting up, the resident said:

> D. . . . the other specimen I took for a Pap smear, Ok? Even though you've had your uterus taken out, you need to have a Pap smear taken about every year. Ok?
> P. Ok.

This patient came in complaining of vaginal bleeding seven years after having had a hysterectomy. A pelvic examination and a Pap smear were clearly called for and were done. What is astonishing about this transaction is that with a presenting complaint of this kind, the doctor did not ask about the patient's Pap smear history or discuss the need to do one with her during the medical history phase of the examination. Nor did he tell the patient what he was doing during the physical examination. He just did it and told her about it after the fact.

Certain contextual features mark the performance of Pap smears during the physical examination phase of the medical interview. The decision to have a patient undress allows for the later decision to do a Pap smear. The reverse does not seem as easily accomplished. We have seen several examples of crossovers in the decision making process from the branch more likely to produce a decision to do a Pap smear to the branch less likely to do so. I saw no crossovers in the other direction (see figure 4.1). A decision not to have the patient undress seems to preclude a later decision to do a Pap smear. Although it is possible for this to be renegotiated, it is time-consuming and could be construed as mismanagement of the situation—the doctor did not elicit the necessary information at the appropriate time and needed to remedy the situation after the fact by interrupting the physical examination to have the patient undress for a Pap smear.

The Communicational Work of the Closing Phase

The last phase of the medical interview is the closing phase. It is during this phase that the problem the patient brought to the clinic is dealt with. If the patient has been undressed, the doctor often leaves the examining room to allow her to dress. When the doctor returns, he or she characteristically sums up his/her findings, prescribes or distributes medicine, and discusses future appointments. Again the switch to this phase is initiated by the doctor.

The rhythm of this phase is much like that of the opening phase, except that there is a reversal of roles. It is the doctor, not the patient, who provides information in a storytelling fashion. The story is told by the doctor in the main channel of communication and the patient signals her understanding in the back channel with clucking sounds (um hum, uh, yeah, etc.). Just before the medical interview ends, the patient is given a chance to introduce a topic or clarify her understanding. During this pre-closing phase, doctors ask questions such as: "Is there anything else bothering you?" "Anything else I can do for you today?" or "Do you have any questions?" If a topic is initiated, the doctor ends the interview after having dealt with it.

With one patient, a Pap smear was discussed during the closing phase. The topic was initiated by the resident prior to his pre-closing question. He said:

D. Do you have a gynecologist that you go to?
P. Yeah.
D. Ok, do you have Pap smears, wet smears?
P. Yeah.
D. You're all up on those?
P. Um hum.

This patient came to the clinic with a presenting complaint of headaches. After a short medical history in which no reproduction-related questions were asked (she was not asked if she was taking birth control pills—a relevant question—or about Pap smears), she received a superficial physical examination while sitting dressed on the examining table. When the physical examination was completed, the doctor summed up, prescribed medication, and before asking his pre-closing questions, asked this last set of questions. He established that the patient has a higher-level physician who performs her Pap smears and that she thinks she is up to date with them. What could his purpose be for asking these questions? Surely it is not to gather the information to decide whether or not the patient needs a Pap smear on this visit. It is highly unlikely at this point in the medical interview that he would have her get undressed and that he would do a Pap smear if she needs one. Perhaps, because it is her first visit, he wants to gather a complete medical history and has realized that he has not discussed reproduction or related questions with her. But the form of the questioning belies this supposition. He does not ask her when her last Pap smear was performed, whether the results were normal, who did it, or if she wants to continue to have them done by the same person. Nor does he enter any information from this discussion onto her chart. I suspect that these questions were asked because I am audiotaping the interview and the resident knows from my participation in the clinic of my interest in the topic. But regardless of why they were asked, these out-of-phase questions still function to avoid the decision to do a Pap smear.

No Communicational Work

There are fourteen patients with whom Pap smears were neither discussed nor performed; thirteen came to the clinic with presenting complaints that did not indicate a need for the patients to get undressed. These patients did not get undressed nor did they discuss a need for having Pap smears taken. The fourteenth patient came to the clinic with a presenting complaint of abdominal pains with vaginal bleeding and was suspected of being in the process of having a spontaneous abortion. The seriousness of her presenting complaint may have prohibited a discussion about her Pap smear history. However, on her second and third return visits, even though pelvic examinations were performed, a Pap smear was not. The tendency toward not talking about Pap smears on first visits and not doing them on subsequent visits was evident with the other thirteen patients as well (see also Fisher and Page 1984). Four of them returned for second and/or third visits and did not receive Pap smears on these visits either. When Pap smears were not discussed with patients during their initial visits, generally no notation was entered onto the patients' charts to remind the physician to bring up the topic on subsequent visits. The absence of this discussion during a first visit contributes to their avoidance on subsequent visits as well. Doctors' silence on the topic of Pap smears speaks quite loudly to the issue of the inadequacy of medical care routinely provided to women patients.

The Politics of Preventive Medicine[9]

Pap smears are a case in point in relation to the politics of preventive medicine in the United States. Although they have the potential to impact on the health of the population in a way that neither prophylactic nor elective hysterectomies do, they are not performed routinely with women in the health care delivery system. Why not? The number in this data sample is small and no definitive answers are possible; however, the data are nevertheless revealing. They suggest that medical practice continues to be rooted in a commitment to high technology, to illness-oriented medical care and tertiary prevention (cure) rather than to health-oriented primary or secondary prevention (diagnosis and/or identification of social or individual causation). And this commitment, reinforced by medical education and training as well as by the reimbursement structure of the insurance industry, holds strongly even with a population of potentially high-risk patients.

When an ideology of individual responsibility is added to this commitment, Pap smears come to be provided primarily when patients request them or doctors choose to do them. There appears to be no consistent policy that guides their performance. The only exception is in relation to young, sexually active women. Younger women were more likely to receive Pap smears, even though the older age groups—especially women between 40–60—continue to be at high risk. Although the incidence of reproduction disease is increasing in the younger population and this increase might account for some of the increase in Pap smears, other factors also play a part. Many doctors take it as their responsibility to protect the reproductive capacities of young women. Perhaps this responsibility accounts, in part, for the increase. Or perhaps it is just that these women are more likely to come to the clinic with presenting complaints that place doctors in the pelvic area—a position from which Pap smears seem more likely to be done.

Even in a residency training program designed to model the actual practice of family medicine in an underserved area with a potentially high-risk population of patients, relatively few Pap smears were done. Residents examined, diagnosed, and prescribed treatments, primarily practicing on their own initiative, while the attending staff functioned mainly as consultants. These attendings seldom had direct contact with patients. They monitored residents' performances by reviewing patients' charts. Yet, comments about patients' Pap smear histories were not routinely entered into the files. The only notations about Pap smears regularly entered into the files were the lab results, which were appended to the records. When patients' charts were reviewed by staff physicians, the absence of information about a patient's Pap smear history was not interpreted as noteworthy. The limited performance of Pap smears in this training setting leads me to question whether these residents wouldn't be more likely to perform even fewer Pap smears when they enter private practice.

While preventive care may be the ideal in family medicine, private practice is constrained by a more concrete economic reality. As more physicians enter the profession, competition for patients and income obviously increases. These concerns necessarily affect medical treatment. From the physician's point of view, Pap smears take time, they are not profitable, and they usually do not contribute to patient satisfaction—women generally do not understand or like them. By comparison, acute and chronic care is more lucrative and contributes to patient satisfaction—patients tend to see them as "real" medical care.

Beyond competitive concerns, there are other, less apparent, economic factors that also may influence the performance of preventive procedures (see also Fisher and Page 1984). For example, health insurance companies do not routinely pay for such procedures and new federal cost control programs also discourage them. Pharmaceutical and medical supply companies, which have a vested interest in supplying information to doctors about profit-related matters, do not have a comparable interest in providing information about Pap smears. There is little immediate profit from this procedure for these companies or for hospitals. All of these economic interests (i.e., pharmaceutical and medical supply companies, the insurance industry, and hospitals) serve an important function: they provide information to and, in some sense, create pressure on doctors to use particular drugs and to perform specific procedures. At the very least, they affect the awareness of the physicians.

But, for whatever reasons, the data suggest that family medicine may provide a context that is unfavorable for the routine performance of preventive health measures. This kind of a context would exist and would be sustained because it was, as Taylor (1982) pointed out, congruent with other cultural and structural factors, promoted by the institutional structures of the medical profession, and enacted in social relationships that are consistent with the beliefs of both doctors and patients. Although doctors are charged with the responsibility to provide adequate medical care, the illness-orientation and treatment focus of modern medicine puts them in blinders. Patients too have their vision obscured. It is obscured by trust and by the dependency of the patient's role and it is maintained in the asymmetrical structure of the medical relationship. This pattern is reflected in the stages of the medical decision making process. The first stage of the decision making process occurs during the opening phase of the medical interview and involves a decision about the presenting complaint and the need for a more complete physical examination. If the decision is made not to have the patient undress, this often structures the rest of the medical interview. For many patients, this means that discussions about prior Pap smear histories will not take place nor will Pap smears be done. With some patients, the decision not to have them undress does not block the discussion of prior Pap smear histories, but it does block the performance of these procedures.

The second stage of the decision making process occurs during the medical history phase of the medical interview and involves discussion about the patient's prior Pap smear history. During this discussion, some patients provide the information that they have had a recent Pap smear and do not need another one, while others provide information that suggests the need for a Pap smear. Often there is a time dimension involved in determining the need for a Pap smear—has it been a year or more since a previous smear. A request for birth control pills can also signal the need to do a Pap smear, regardless of the time elapsed since the prior smear. If the patient has a presenting complaint that does not require getting undressed, and if her prior Pap smear history is discussed and the patient does not indicate a need for a Pap smear, no conflict arises— a Pap smear is not needed and it is not done. There is a similar lack of conflict in regard to patients whose presenting complaints indicates the need for them to be undressed during the physical examination. If the discussion with these patients reveals a need for a Pap smear and they receive one, or if discussion with them indicates no need for a Pap smear and they do not receive one, there is no conflict.

However, as we have seen, the issues are not always so clear cut. When there is conflict, it is notable. Avoidance strategies emerge in the discourse—strategies that function to accomplish the decision to do, or not to do, a Pap smear. I have identified three such strategies—bowing to higher-level specialists, influencing patients to have or not to have Pap smears, and letting silence speak to accomplish the decision not to do Pap smears. In each case, the presenting complaint or the information that emerged during the medical history disclosed a need to have the patient undress as well as the need for a Pap smear, yet Pap smears were not performed. Using a decision making tree, I pointed out that these conflicts can be represented in terms of a crossover in the expected decision making process. Factors have emerged in the first two phases of the medical interview that seem to direct the decision toward doing a Pap smear, yet one is not performed.

The third stage occurs during the physical examination phase of the medical interview and involves a discussion about Pap smears and a decision to do or not to do one. Decisions made during this phase are shaped by those made earlier. In each case, an earlier decision that patients needed to be undressed for their physical examinations allowed the later discussion about prior Pap smear histories or the performance of Pap smears with or without this discussion.

The final stage occurs during the closing phase of the medical interview. Pap smears discussed here are out-of-phase and as such, they are unlikely to produce a decision to do one. By using a decision making tree, I pointed out that there are no instances in the data of a crossover in the expected decision making process. If the patient is dressed for the physical examination or if the physical examination has been completed, decisions to do Pap smears seem to be precluded.

Both the doctor's control and the patient's trust are expressed in the data. Every phase of the medical interview was initiated by doctors. They generated each topic, controlled their development, and controlled the decision making process. Except when patients requested a Pap smear, it was the doctors who decided whether or not patients should undress, whether or not prior Pap smear histories would be discussed, and whether or not Pap smears would be done (sometimes without discussing the decision with patients). When the doctors made these choices, the patients usually agreed. Patients neither questioned the lack of information shared with them nor used interactional strategies to move the decision making process toward getting a Pap smear.

I have discussed the ways the form and function of the medical inter-view reflects and reveals the asymmetry in the doctor-patient relation-ship, shapes the decision making process, and has significant conse-quences for the delivery of health care to women. In the next chapter, I move away from the data to discuss further how decisions to perform Pap smears and elective or prophylactic hysterectomies, or not to per-form these procedures, are influenced by the institutional setting, the structural context and the cultural arena in which the decision making process occurs.

5 / Spinning the Contextual Web

Bridging the Gap Between Social Structure and Social Interaction

Last week, as I was preparing to write this final chapter, two women friends talked to me about their recent medical experiences. For me these tales exemplify the story this book is telling.

One woman, Adrian, called to say that on a routine appointment for an annual Pap smear and pelvic examination, a nurse-practitioner found an ovarian mass and referred her to a local Ob-Gyn for diagnosis and treatment. The doctor confirmed the mass and proposed that she enter the hospital as soon as possible for tests, to be followed by a "pelvic clean out." He claimed that whatever was found, the mass would need to be removed anyway, and since she did not want children, she might as well get cleaned out at the same time. Although an ovarian mass is always cause for concern, Adrian is 37 and her age, her presenting complaint, and her physical examination were not suggestive of cancer. In fact, when she consulted another doctor, she was assured that the likelihood of cancer was certainly less than 5 percent and probably less than 1 percent. Although the earlier recommendation relied on the emotional impact of cancer, there was no actual discussion of whether or not the mass was likely to be cancerous. Instead, the recommendation of a pelvic clean out sent a message that suggested that Adrian's reproductive organs were at least dirty if not dangerous (what could be dirtier or more dangerous than cancer) and needed to be removed.

Jannett, a friend in her late 50s, told me a very different story. For the past two years, she had been watched closely by her Ob-Gyn for irregular bleeding. Spotting in a woman past menopause is always cause for concern about cancer. Yet, her doctor never discussed the possibility of cancer with her and neither suggested nor performed any diagnostic tests. After two years of recurrent bleeding, a hysterectomy was suggested and performed to get rid of the offending uterus. During surgery, extensive, possibly life-threatening cancer was found.

It would not be hard to dismiss these tales—to see them as isolated events or to claim that there are bad apples everywhere. Instead, I am asking you to consider how, as the medical profession developed, doctors have increasingly gained and patients have progressively lost control. They lost the information to participate fully in the medical process. It is doctors, not patients, who define and legitimize health and illness. Doctors can, as in Adrian's case, intensify symptoms, medicalize problems, and encourage patients to have procedures not warranted on medical grounds alone. Or, as in Jannett's case, doctors can ignore symptoms, psychologize problems, and fail to perform diagnostic procedures and/or to provide treatments that could be life-saving. Many doctors and most patients seem to agree that since doctors have medical knowledge and technical skill, they also have control. Patients are both encouraged and expected to trust that their doctor knows what is best for them and will act in their best interests. There are at least two assumptions built into this expectation: 1) that medical decisions are governed by medical expertise, and 2) that medical relationships are not characterized by conflicts of interest. Yet, the data in this book provide repeated examples that suggest that: 1) both scientific information and the medical decisions that flow from them are value-laden social accomplishments. And 2) for as long as medicine is practiced for profit by primarily white middle-class men, there will be conflicts of interest rooted in economics as well as in race, class, and gender.

Much has been written in the last few years by feminists and others who are critical of the way health care is delivered in the United States today; however, very little research has documented how the assumptions just addressed influence the delivery of health care. My first task has been to provide an empirical analysis that highlighted *how* the delivery of health care was enacted as the doctor-patient relationship unfolded over the course of medical interviews. The analytic focus has been on the ways the language used was social as well as micropolitical—it not only accomplished interactional work, but it simultaneously functioned to sustain and helped to support the status quo. Language use, or communication, provided a window on both the internal dynamics of the medical process and the larger landscape of our society. However, if the earlier promise to elevate context to a researchable topic is to be kept, it is now time to change the direction of the analysis from one that focused on an empirical discussion of the local production and situated accomplishment of medical events to one that will focus on the ways context sets the stage for medical interactions—to spin a contextual web. Taken together, these relationships facilitate the development of sociological knowledge and of political action by suggesting how social interaction and social structure are related to each other.

In this chapter, I will trace the fibers of this web from interacting individuals—doctors and patients—to the organization of the clinical setting and the profession of medicine and from there to the structural and cultural arrangements of society. Once the contextual web is spun, I will draw out both the theoretical implications and the policy ramifications of these patterns.

Extending the Web: The Organizational Nexus

Freidson (1970), arguing from a sociology of knowledge perspective, claims that the organization of the medical profession (its professional autonomy) and the structure of medical services (fee-for-service) or prepaid health maintenance) impacts on the definition of illness and influences the delivery of health care. Decisions to perform (or not to perform) prophylactic or elective hysterectomies and diagnostic Pap smears take place in an organizational nexus. While it would be hard to document that either the clinical settings or the structure of the profession *caused* the medical decisions discussed in earlier chapters, it seems eminently reasonable to suggest that both the organization of the specific clinical setting and the more general structure of the medical profession provided a context that influenced the decision making process and was in turn reinforced by it. Because this organizational context developed over time and in response to particular moments in history, it is amenable to change—time has passed and we are now facing a new historical moment. To gain a better understanding of the factors that produced and constrained the medical interactions discussed earlier, I discuss how the autonomy of the profession was shaped to achieve its current form, as well as how the current configuration of the profession provides new opportunities for reshaping it.

Today the practice of medicine is monopolistic, with doctors, as a group, controlling who gains access to the profession—obtains a medical education and a license—as well as how non-physician providers practice. Physicians set the limits and evaluate the performances of most medical workers, themselves included. Their domination over the definition of illness and the practice of medicine contributes to the ever growing trend toward medicalization, and when this trend is combined with a mentality of individualism, it produces a medical care system that resists social responsibility. Health care is seen as an individual responsibility and illness is understood to result from specific agents (germs or viruses) or from an unhealthy life style. Neither the social causes of disease (poverty, pollution, etc.) nor a social or public responsibility for health care are consistent with a mentality of individualism, especially when the private fee-for-service practice of medicine reimburses physicians for caring for individuals regardless of the cause of their illness.

It might be argued that doctors' control and autonomy rightfully developed along with their scientific and medical knowledge, technical skill, and the clinical achievements that flowed from them. History does not support this conclusion. The medical profession in the United States consolidated its monopoly over the delivery of health care during the 19th century, when medical techniques were both limited and dangerous and improvements in health were more related to social changes (improvements in the standard of living and public health measures such as improved sanitation) than to the practice of medicine (McKeown 1976). It has been argued that the process of consolidation had more to do with social and political factors than it did with medical achievements (Starr 1982; Stevens 1966). Medical practitioners as we know them today emerged as "regular doctors" in competition with an array of other healers. Although the regular doctors of the nineteenth century had neither superior knowledge nor greater numbers than the other healers, as urban, university-educated, male members of the upper classes, they had social standing as well as ties (cemented in class and gender interests) with the newly formed foundations—e.g., Rockefeller and Carnegie (Brown 1979) and with governmental bodies.

Until the later part of the 19th century, regular doctors and various healers existed side by side, competing for legitimacy and financial resources. Early efforts by the regulars to pass laws limiting the practice of medicine failed because the temper of the time was hostile to elitism, whether it was based on class or education. In their drive for professional and economic control, regular doctors banded together first in guilds and later in a national organization—The American Medical Association. As the century unfolded and the climate of opinion turned toward social reform, the AMA pushed again for licensing laws and educational reforms to create and enforce standards in medical education and practice (Starr 1982; Stevens 1966).

The process of reform began with licensing laws. As Starr (1982) points out, the regular doctors, often in conjunction with their competitors, convinced state legislatures to pass laws limiting who could practice medicine. While at first these laws protected both regular doctors and sectarian practitioners, as the laws grew more rigorous they began to discriminate against those without university training— those who were not regular doctors. Licensing in conjunction with the growing strength of the AMA finally allowed the medical profession to gain control of medical education and in so doing to control the supply of physicians and to achieve financial security for their members.

These changes came about slowly and were the result of a constellation of factors. First, the rise of hospitals moved the locus of care out of the home. Second, the increasing development of university training produced a greater specialization and an increased interdependence among physicians. Third, with the growth of medical practice came the growth of malpractice suits. Once the courts had established the standard of care in the local community as the measure of quality, doctors became increasingly dependent on each other and on their local medical societies. These societies not only adjudicated the standard of practice in the community, but they effectively controlled their members' behavior, so that it became almost impossible for patients to find doctors willing to testify in a malpractice suit. Through collective efforts, regular doctors could protect their hospital privileges, their incomes, and their licenses (Starr 1982).

By late in the nineteenth century, licensing and collective support were established and the AMA returned to educational reform. Based on its own surveys, there was a considerable disparity in the medical education available from the various medical schools in the country at that time. Armed with this information, the AMA approached the Carnegie Foundation and asked them officially to gather information on which to base reform measures. Abraham Flexner, a man with a university education and the protégé of the president of the Rockefeller Institute for Medical Research, was selected to conduct the investigation. There is little doubt that working for the Carnegie Foundation facilitated his entry into many schools. The foundation controlled financial resources that would allow schools to compete in an increasingly competitive market (Starr 1982).

Taken together, the licensing laws, the consolidation of the AMA, and the Flexner report had far-reaching consequences: 1) Many medical schools closed, reducing the number of doctors and improving the market position of those who remained; 2) With financial support from foundations, the remaining medical schools improved their facilities and the remaining practitioners improved their status and skill; 3) The direction of medical education changed, becoming increasingly scientific and oriented toward research and specialty care, rather than toward primary care or disease prevention; 4) Under the guise of eliminating the "quacks," variety was quelled. For example, instead of teaching homeopathic, osteopathic, and allopathic medicine, allopathic medicine alone became the standard taught in all university medical schools, and instead of training generalists and specialists, specialty training became the norm; 5) Access to medical education decreased, increasing the homogeneity and coalescence of physicians by encouraging the development of common values; 6) Lower- and working-class individuals, as well as Jews, women, and blacks were largely excluded from medical education, either by deliberate discrimination or through policies that functioned to discriminate against them (higher costs, increased entrance requirements, increased duration of education, etc.); 7) The hospital-based university training, which produced scientists and researchers, the social homogeneity of medical practitioners, and the declining output of medical schools contributed to a geographic maldistribution of physicians, which aggravated the shortage of physicians in poor and rural areas (Starr 1982); and 8) The elimination of alternatives led to a monopoly over the definition and practice of medicine. Many of these factors continue to shape the delivery of medical care even today.

As the medical profession consolidated its power, women were largely excluded from being licensed to practice medicine. Women physicians, or would-be physicians, were not the only women to feel the growing power of the profession. Women's roles as providers and consumers of health care were also shaped in this process. At the heart of the struggle between women and the male-dominated profession was economics. As a group, the regular physicians of the 19th century, while originating in the upper classes, were not affluent. In fact they were often unable to earn a living practicing their profession. Birthing women held the key.

One of the first tasks of the burgeoning medical profession was to convince the public that they had a valuable service to offer—to gain what Starr (1982) calls cultural authority. Although physicians did not know a lot about the birth process, it was in their interest to convince women—particularly upper-class women—that the drugs and technology at their disposal were indispensable for a safe birth. Physicians and upper-class women, joined together by the concept of a medically managed birth as a safe birth, converted public perceptions, and in the process they discredited midwives and elevated physicians to the role of medical experts. In little more than a century, birth was redefined from a natural process in which women helped each other give birth to a dangerous, high-risk activity in which birthing women needed the medical ministrations and the interventionist practices of the male physicians who would "deliver" their babies (Riessman 1983; Rothman 1982; Wertz and Wertz 1977).

It is important to remember that at its beginnings, the domination of the medical profession by male physicians was not achieved through medical expertise. In fact, Wertz and Wertz (1979) argued that the transition from midwives to physicians as birth attendants did not result in greater safety. Both maternal and infant mortality rose as midwives' participation in the birth process declined (Riessman 1983). Even as physicians were consolidating their power and establishing their credibility, they were struggling financially. The management of birth, while not always lucrative in itself, was both a guaranteed income and, more importantly, a gateway to family practice and what Riessman (1983) calls "the healing market."

In the process of creating birth as a medical event, class and race joined gender and economics and contributed to the consolidation of male medical power. Existing midwives, who were predominantly women of the lower classes, many of whom were immigrant and black women, were described as ignorant and dirty and all women were discredited as unsafe. They were considered weak, unfit to act, and unable to think. To seal their fate, women were told that if they knew their place, they would not want to compete with physicians, who were mainly men of the upper classes, for to do so would unsex them. These same factors (class, race, and the potential for economic gain) contributed to defining the appropriate patient population. Women of the upper classes were seen as weak and in need of a medically managed birth, while immigrant women, minority women, and women of the lower classes were viewed as stronger—more animal-like—and better able to manage on their own. Patients responded in kind. Women of the upper classes flocked to physicians because they wanted the best available care and physicians had sold themselves as the best, both in terms of safety and fashionableness, while women of the lower classes as well as immigrant and black women were in a no-win position. They could continue to use discredited midwives or they could become the teaching material in the new hospital-based university programs (c.f. Riessman 1983; Wertz and Wertz 1977).

This historic process shaped the health care delivery system and had consequences that are evident today. Physicians historically provided care for those best able to pay for it, leaving poor women with little choice. The poverty-stricken today are still caught in a double bind with few options. One of the most striking things about the patterning of disease and the access to medical care in the United States today is its relationship to poverty. By-and-large, the poorer one is, the more likely one is to be sick, and the less likely one is to receive adequate medical care (Conrad and Kern 1981). We have today what has been described as a dual health care system; one for the indigent (primarily non-white, poor, and elderly) and one for the affluent (Scully 1980). And in this system, physicians continue to provide medical care for those best able to pay for it. As a consequence, poorer, rural areas like Appalachia have experienced extreme shortages of health care providers, and poorer patients often have to use emergency rooms and outpatient clinics in public hospitals, because private practitioners either refuse to take non-paying patients or refuse to accept Medicaid or Medicare (Waitzken 1983).

The consolidation of the medical profession reflected in the dual health care system is reiterated in the continuing domination of health care workers by higher-class male physicians. Although the medical labor force has expanded considerably in the last two decades, gender and class remain all too evident in the distribution of power and privilege. In the 1970s, "98 percent of U.S. physicians were white, 91 percent were male and predominantly from middle and upper-middle class families" (Sidel and Sidel 1981, 214). In addition Conrad and Kern (1981, 199), drawing from DHEW statistics, point out that while physicians make up less than 6 percent of the medical work force, they are among the highest paid workers. Navarro (1981) claims that as a group, physicians' earnings place them in the top 5 percent of earners in the United States.

As income drops, the composition of the medical work force changes, increasingly coming to include women and non-white workers. Seventy-five percent of all medical workers are women, many of whom are drawn from minority groups and working- and lower-middle-class backgrounds. These women workers not only earn less than the higher status male professionals, but they also have little or no decision making power in the health care delivery system. In addition, there is very little movement from one job category to another in the medical work force. Each group of workers receives specialized training to qualify for their licenses and the licensing process is authorized by the AMA's Committee on Education. This stratification of health care workers has been described as a pyramid:

> with the usually white male on top, his orders carried out by middle-level professionals who are generally women and with the patient and the "dirty work" left to low paid, frequently alienated, largely black paraprofessionals with still lower status (Sidel and Sidel 1981, 215).

There has been some change in recent years. For example, while application and admission rates of women to medical schools have increased from 8.9 percent in 1972–1973 to 16.2 percent in 1975–1976 (an increase of 82 percent) the absolute and proportionate numbers of women and non-whites remains low compared to their numbers in the population as a whole and this holds true for all major health professions (Weaver and Garrett 1983). Although women and non-whites continue to earn lower salaries and have more limited occupational mobility than white males, whether in male-dominated or female-dominated segments of the medical profession, when men enter the lower status, traditionally female occupational slots, they seem to garner the best-paying jobs and a disproportionate share of administrative positions. In addition, discrimination in the medical work force by class continues almost unabated. People from working-class and low-income families continue to be overrepresented as a teaching population for the medical profession, underrepresented in medical schools and in certain medical specialties—those from higher class backgrounds are more likely to choose higher-level medical specialties and those from lower class backgrounds are more likely to become primary care physicians (Strelnick 1980).

As history has unfolded, the medical profession has consolidated its power by: 1) sustaining its economic position and supporting a dual health care system; 2) maintaining the hierarchical stratification of the medical force by class, gender, and race; 3) generating new markets (e.g. birth); and 4) discrediting competing practitioners. Today all of these factors remain in evidence. As the medical professionals face the 80s, they are threatened with the loss of patient confidence, the specter of government regulations, as well as the threat of increased competition and declining economic prospects.

Signs of trouble are strewn throughout the media. The journal, *Medical Economics,* carries articles advising doctors of effective ways to collect fees and affect their income (Kirchner 1983a) and warning them that patients' support for fee-for-service medicine is being eroded by rising costs (Kirchner 1983b). Doctors are told that since 1976 " . . . more people have come to favor government regulation of doctors' fees, more prefer prepaid care and many now hold physicians responsible for the escalation of medical costs" (Ibid.). These words strike fear into the collective heart of the profession. Articles in other medical journals explain that although doctors are taking the heat, they are not to be blamed. Doctors' costs, it is argued, reflect " . . . the influence of government policies, third-party reimbursements and consumer demand" (Murphy 1983). And while the arguments continue, doctors worry about declining economic prospects and the lack, in real terms, of any increase in disposable income since 1977 (*Ob, Gyn News* 1983c).

Today the delivery of health care is increasingly becoming a big business, with large corporations at the helm managing hospitals, retirement homes, nursing homes, home health care, and even health spas (Dentzer 1983). Coupled with the growing glut of doctors and the mounting public concern about costs, the new medical-industrial complex has set the stage for a fiercely competitive battle. In the past, as the profession has fought to maintain control, it has consistently resisted the intrusion of others into its domain. And so it is today. The medical profession continues to resist the intrusion of nontraditional applicants to medical schools, non-physician providers in the health care delivery system, and government regulation of its turf. The profession stands strongly on its individual freedoms, often without even paying lip service to the rights of others—most notably patients' rights to health care.

Once again as physicians move to consolidate their power, women's bodies make good targets. History seems to be repeating itself. As a variety of medical services competes for patients' dollars, a new business has developed—a business that diseases women's bodies and medicalizes their reproductive systems (Todd 1983b; Riessman 1983). For example, the medical profession has entered the beauty business, taking responsibility for keeping women thin, has turned its attention and considerable resources to treating a new disease—premenstrual syndrome—and has made birth a high technology event (Riessman 1983; Rothman 1982).

Medicalizing women's bodies and eliminating women as competition again seem to be going hand in hand. Nurse-practitioners, who are predominantly women, are being sued for inserting IUD's (intra-uterian devices), dispensing birth control, and for administering vaginal medication—for the unauthorized practice of medicine. And the physicians who write the standing orders and protocols under which these nurses perform their duties are being charged with aiding and abetting this illegal practice of medicine. In the more affluent times of the late 60s and 70s, the nurse-practitioner movement was seen as a solution to the shortage of doctors in many underserved areas and as a response to the increasing specialization of medicine, which has resulted in fewer physicians willing to provide primary care. Today as the economic market shrinks, the medical profession is telling us that the nurse-practitioner is inadequately trained. Their lack of training, it is argued, subjects the patients under their care to inferior medical practices. But unlike the midwives of the past, nurses are fighting back and disclosing the economic motivations that underlie the accusations and suits (Donovan 1983).

How does extending the contextual web to examine the historical development of the organizational nexus in which health care is provided help to clarify the paradoxes discussed in the three data chapters? How does it make us more able to address the ways women are influenced to have elective and prophylactic hysterectomies when these procedures are not mandated on medical grounds, and how women are not influenced to have routine Pap smears when, in a high-risk population, they are warranted on medical grounds? Several factors that emerged during the development of the medical profession make these paradoxes more understandable.

As the medical profession has consolidated its power, its hold has become stronger, until doctors have become the sole arbitrators of medical knowledge and technical skill. In this process, patients have lost—they have lost the information to make independent decisions and the skill to care for themselves. Patients must rely, at least to some degree, on their physicians—physicians who control the information they receive as well as the decisions they reach. Patients' access to independent health care providers who could offer alternative sources of medical information is also limited. And in many cases, they have lost the ability to choose the setting in which they will receive care—a loss that is significant. Repeatedly, setting has been identified as an important factor in the delivery of health care (Freidson and Lorber 1972; Freidson 1970). For example, Rothman (1982) claims that a home delivery is a very different birthing experience from a hospital delivery. And, while the sample is not large, the last three data chapters also illustrate the importance of setting: In the clinic staffed by residents, hysterectomies were more likely to be recommended and performed than they were in the clinic staffed by professors of medicine (attending staff); and residents in a family practice clinic did not routinely perform Pap smears, even in a potentially high-risk population.

In addition, once their training is complete, gynecological specialists are more likely to practice in urban areas and family practitioners trained in rural areas are more likely to stay in these areas—a fact of life over which patients have little control, but one which potentially influences the care they receive. Middle-class women living in urban areas who are statistically less at risk from cervical cancer have access to specialists, including gynecologists—an access that is often denied to poorer, rural women who are statistically at the greatest risk of cervical cancer. Middle-class women also have the resources to pay for care—resources poorer, rural women often lack. It seems reasonable to argue that this differential access has potential consequences for patients. Middle-class women can choose to go to gynecologists, who, because of their training and experience, which exposes them almost daily to the life-threatening consequences of reproductive cancer, may be more likely to perform routine Pap smears than family practitioners whose training and experience were different. But if gynecologists are more sensitive to women's potential reproductive problems and if patients reap the benefits in terms of Pap smears, there are also potential penalties. Gynecologists are surgeons—a fact that is reflected in the increased incidence of Caesarean sections as well as in the rising hysterectomy rates. If for middle-class women there are at least potential benefits to offset the costs of their choices, poorer, rural women have few choices and fewer benefits.

Patients lose in another way as well. Although differences in training, experience, and setting undoubtedly influence the delivery of care, the consolidation of the profession and the legitimation provided by science create an overall commitment to certain beliefs and practices: that the uterus is a dangerous organ and needs to be removed; Birth is a dangerous event and needs to occur in the hospital with the aid of a well-trained physician; Women can be maintained as well on exogenous estrogens as they can on the estrogens their bodies produce naturally; High-technology cures take precedence over routine preventive procedures; and medical responsibility extends to individuals, not to the social roots of their problems. Perhaps if the Flexner report had not recommended the development of scientific medicine and research to the exclusion of alternative practitioners, we might have had a medical system today in which social responsibility and preventive care were integrated into a multi-level system. Instead, our priorities continue to be high-technology treatments—a priority reflected in the ways doctors in this study influenced women to have hysterectomies and did not influence them to have routine Pap smears.

The development and growth of corporate medicine and the additional stress it places on the profession of medicine is creating a new historical moment and new opportunities for change. Before addressing these, I want to expand the contextual web to discuss the way structural contradictions influence the doctor-patient relationship and then to show how the cultural milieu shapes the delivery of care.

Extending the Web Further: Structural Contradictions

As the web is spun, it becomes increasingly evident that there is a relationship between the structure of society, the organization of the profession of medicine, the ways in which medical care is delivered, and the types and distribution of disease. Yet, most sociological analyses emphasize one aspect of the problem or another without spotlighting the connective tissue that joins them. It seems self-evident that decisions to perform (or not to perform) elective or prophylactic hysterectomies and diagnostic Pap smears take place within the current economic and political system. Even though it would be hard to document that the economic context of capitalism *caused* the medical decisions discussed in earlier chapters (and that is not my intent), it seems reasonable to suggest that the organization of medicine and the delivery of health care both reflect and foster the capitalist economic structure. If, as I argue, health problems are at least partially rooted in the larger society, then strategies for change should, of necessity, address the contradictions inherent in such a system.

Today emerging developments jeopardize the sovereignty of the medical profession. While to date the profession has been able to garner both state protection and political accommodation of its interests, its ability to continue to do so is now being threatened. The consolidation of the profession came about through the development of a strong collective organization with a cohesive membership. Today the rapidly increasing supply of physicians and the increasing competition for patients and economic rewards promises to create severe strains. In addition, the mantle of power so long held by the profession is now at risk. Physicians are no longer the sole dominant voices of the medical industry. Increasingly, corporate powers are getting involved in the medical market place and using their considerable power to influence the state to accommodate their interests—interests that do not always coincide with those of the medical profession. And this is occurring at a time when both government and employers are concerned about the seemingly unlimited growth of medical expenditures (Starr 1982). The cost-benefit analysis of the corporate model is especially seductive in a climate of opinion that looks at costs without considering the structural configurations that underlie spiraling medical inflation.

Waitzken (1983) argues that the private accumulation of capital sets the stage both for problems in the health care delivery system and in society. At one and the same time, the state assumes contradictory roles and ideologies to justify, legitimize, and sustain the status quo. On the one hand, the state protects the ability of private enterprise to accumulate wealth, espousing an ideology of individual achievement as the basis of equality, while masking continued inequalities. On the other hand, the state provides public services—especially health and welfare services—while again espousing the same ideology of individualism that masks continued systematic oppression. Both the protection of private enterprise and the provision of public services function in support of the status quo. A healthy economy sustains the social system and welfare benefits can be manipulated so that, in economically hard times, services can be cut, and when social unrest threatens, services can be extended.

The same balancing act influences health care, reflecting national priorities. In a society that pays lip service to equality, health care is a commodity to be bought and sold like any other. And while we claim to be a peace-loving nation, the relatively small portion of the national budget devoted to health reveals political and economic priorities that more whole-heartedly support the military and related industries. Within the health care delivery system, the state continues to protect an economic system based on private property by means of social policies that support the private medical sector by scrimping in the public sector: Federal grants have subsidized private hospital construction; Public programs (e.g., Medicaid and Medicare) use public funds (tax revenues) to support the private practice of medicine; Funds for indigent patients that could support public facilities (public health programs and municipal hospitals) get syphoned off by the private sector while the public sector faces severe financial problems often leading to the closing of medical facilities. And the state assures payment, while costs continue to rise (Waitzken 1983). All this occurs in a system where doctors in fee-for-service practices maintain the right to refuse to treat anyone and for-profit hospitals claim the privilege of refusing to accept patients (Starr 1982).

These inequalities and others are supported by the structure of third-party reimbursements. Bodenheimer and colleagues (1981) argue that the insurance industry plays a critical role in the health care delivery system. Almost all third-party payments are made by public (Medicare and Medicaid) and private insurers, with nearly half of each medical dollar coming from public funds. And these insurance dollars are primarily spent in the private sector for the fee-for-service practice of medicine. In theory, private insurance for those who can afford the premiums (often provided for workers as part of their benefit package) and public insurance for the needy paid for by tax revenues should go a long way toward resolving inequities in the delivery of care. Instead, the combination of private and public insurance enriches the insurance industry at the cost of continued inequities. Why?

Starr (1982) points out that the insurance industry in this country grew up as a response to middle-class interests rather than to relieve the economic plight of the working class. During the 20s and again during the 30s, when physicians and hospitals were hard-hit economically, insurance companies developed to help middle-class patients pay their medical costs—so from its inception the intent was not egalitarian. Traditionally, those locked out of the mainstream of society—the poor, the unemployed, the chronically ill, and the old—were also locked out of the health care delivery system. During the affluent years of the early Johnson administration, Medicaid and Medicare were developed as liberal responses to this problem of distributive justice. Medicare was an insurance program directed toward providing medical care for people over sixty-five (and other qualified recipients of social security) and Medicaid was developed to help the indigent obtain health care. Although these programs looked good in theory, they were flawed in predictable ways: programs to help the poor simultaneously functioned to funnel public funds into private pockets, because the contradictions of a capitalist system—self-interest versus social responsibility—were built into them from their inception (Waitzken 1983).

Early on the government allowed insurance companies—most notably Blue Cross and Blue Shield—to act as fiscal intermediaries, and, in so doing, the administration of a public program was lodged in the hands of a private industry—an industry with a long history of serving the private interests of doctors and hospitals. But concessions did not end there. Not only was control of the program and its costs surrendered to the insurance industry, but the government also entered into a financial agreement with hospitals that was extremely favorable to the hospital industry. The government agreed to pay costs as they were established by hospitals (including depreciation on hospital assets, even if they were acquired through public funds) (Starr 1982). And in the process, the door was left open for costs to increase, taxes to rise, and benefits to shrink.

Today the regressive nature of third-party payments is becoming evident in a variety of ways: deductibles (uncovered or partially covered care), co-insurance and limited coverage (sharing the costs), and experience ratings by which companies competitively seek the best risks. In addition, most insurance policies leave many services uncovered, i.e., dental care, outpatient psychiatric care, and preventive care are the most frequently uncovered services (Bodenheimer *et al.* 1981). These limitations increase the out-of-pocket costs—costs that often exceed those covered by insurance benefits. Bodenheimer and colleagues (1981) claim that only 42 percent of the health costs of the average person are covered by insurance. And again, those in greatest need are hardest hit. Medicare fails to pay for eye and hearing examinations, glasses or hearing aids, routine checkups, or out-patient drugs. And these are not the only inequities. Just as licensing laws were used during earlier historical periods to eliminate competition, today third-party payments serve the same function (Starr 1982).

Waitzkin (1983) claims that contradictions such as these are not only inherent in a capitalist system, but also reverberate through the scientific practice of medicine. As the role of the state has increased within the health care system, the state has chosen again and again to reinforce the dominant framework of scientific medicine—a framework that is consistent with the current economic system—and to surpress alternative frameworks that might threaten the system. Since cancer is the "plague of the 20th century" (Epstein 1979, 11), a closer look at the politics of cancer displays how the framework of scientific medicine is used to justify sacrificing safety for profit.

At least since 1970, it has been generally accepted that the majority—70–90 percent—of cancer is caused by environmental factors (Epstein 1979). Yet policy makers—some top economists, the current administration, some people in government and industry—have resisted funding research or enforcing policies directed at cleaning up the environment. The reasons given: "economic considerations." How much are the millions of lives lost to cancer each year worth? Why is it more cost-efficient for individual cancer victims, their families, and society to bear the enormous economic burdens of cancer? Could it be because these costs do not effect the profits of the companies polluting air, water, and food?

The exploitation of illness for profit is legitimized in social policies and in the ideology that underlies the practice of scientific medicine. Generous funding is available for research on chemotherapeutic agents or medical procedures to treat cancer, but very little research is funded on the social or environmental causes of cancer. Funding for research is more likely in studies that focus on the problems associated with individual life styles—smoking, diets, etc. Funding is less likely for studies that focus on the relationship between cancer and industrial pesticidal or hormonal residues in food and water or in air- or water-borne pollutants. Research is responsive to narrowly defined special interest groups, who exaggerate both claims for safety and the costs associated with increased safety controls—and do so in the interest of profit (Waitzkin 1983; Epstein 1979).

The exploitation of illness and the scientific practice of medicine also go hand in hand with an increasing abuse of technological approaches to medical problems. Medical science encourages the development and use of technologically complex treatments, often without a rigorous scientific appraisal of their effectiveness. Waitzkin (1983) discusses intensive care units for patients suffering heart attacks as an example. The proliferation of extremely expensive technologies, such as intensive care units, while consistent with an economic system oriented toward profit, reinforces the economic and ideological contradictions of the practice of medicine. Sustained corporate profits demand expansion, diversification, and the creation of new markets. A new technology is profitable. With time, the market becomes saturated, the rate of profit falls, and newer technological developments are called for. Each technology, once developed and distributed, creates a demand for its use.

Meanwhile cheaper, more mundane practices, such as home care, often receive little attention, even though they may be more effective. Waitzkin talks about studies that show that "the cumulative one-year mortality was not different in home and hospital groups and there was no evidence that MI patients did better in the hospital" (Waitzkin 1983: 94).

In earlier chapters, I discussed a paradox in medical treatment: Patients were encouraged to have elective and prophylactic hysterectomies—hysterectomies not required on medical grounds alone—and patients, who were potentially at high risk, were not encouraged to have preventive procedures—Pap smears—even though such procedures might prove to be life-saving. Perhaps a closer look at the uses of technology and the tendency toward medicalization will help to shed light on this paradox.

Expensive medical technology, as Waitzkin (1983) points out, conveys a symbolic expression of technical efficiency. Could it be that a hysterectomy to prevent the future possibility of disease (cancer), because it involves the mystique of surgery and a hospital stay, has the symbolic trappings of effectiveness? Could it be that a Pap smear, as a more mundane office procedure, does not convey this symbolic aura? Could this be so even in the face of medical evidence that suggests that routine Pap smears are effective screening procedures, which are recommended for most women, even after a hysterectomy, because abnormal cell changes can recur without the presence of a uterus? And if it is so, do such decisions simultaneously convey messages of social control— ideological messages—as a feature of the medical decision making process?

I have argued that to influence women to have prophylactic and elective hysterectomies is to disease their reproductive systems and medicalize their lives. It seems clear that a reasonable argument can be made against this increasing scope of medicine. However "demedicalization" (Waitzkin 1983), which may influence the decision not to perform Pap smears, has even more potentially severe repercussions. Pap smears left undone invite cancer and place women's lives at risk. Furthermore, in an economy such as ours, demedicalization may have differential effects. Affluent women from middle- and upper-class, largely urban backgrounds may be less affected than are lower- and lower-middle-class women from primarily rural backgrounds. Not only are lower-class women from rural backgrounds at a higher statistical risk from cervical cancer, but poorer women, in underserved areas, have been shown to underutilize medical services. Perhaps one reason they do involves insurance coverage. For example, even though preventive procedures such as Pap smears are not covered by most insurance policies, public (Medicaid or Medicare) or private, middle-class women often have additional resources at their disposal. When poor, rural women do go to the doctor, they are more likely to be seen by primary care physicians in fee-for-service practices and there is some indication that these physicians, delivering care in this kind of practice, are not the doctors or the situations most likely to produce Pap smears (Brown 1976). Geographic maldistribution, underutilization of medical services, insurance coverage, underserved areas, the lack of balance of general and specialty services, and greater likelihood of disease all serve to place lower-class women at greater risk, and each of these factors individually and collectively are part and parcel of a capitalist economic system.

We are at a turning point. As various segments of our society—government, employers, doctors, and the public—increasingly come to realize that spiraling medical inflation hurts everyone, the call for change grows stronger. Before discussing strategies for change, I want to develop the last spiral of the contextual web—the cultural milieu.

The Web's Outer Spiral: The Cultural Milieu

As the web is spun, the spirals get larger and the weave gets looser. I have moved from a discussion of the development of the medical profession and its relationship to class, gender, and economic interests to a discussion of how the practice of medicine is shaped by the contradictions inherent in a capitalist economic system. And now I want to pull the threads of these discussions into the outer spiral to address the ways the doctor-patient relationship and the practice of medicine are, as Ruzek (1978) points out, "embedded in and an embodiment of" a patriarchal culture. I will discuss the ways male dominance is interwoven with professional dominance and how in the process, the practice of medicine acquires a basic distortion. In so doing, I am combining my interest in sociology with my commitment as a feminist to create an alternative paradigm—one which takes relations between men and women as a critical feature of social life, sociological understanding, and political action.

As I have pointed out, it is well within the tradition of western thought to consider the role of ideas on behavior. From the idealism of Plato to Weber's analysis of the influence of religion on social structure and continuing with the more recent analyses of patriarchy (Daly 1978) an emphasis on the relationship between ideas and our everyday lives has been developed. It is consistent with this tradition to suggest that decisions to perform (or not to perform) elective or prophylactic hysterectomies and diagnostic Pap smears take place in a cultural context. Although it would be hard to map specific aspects of the culture onto the behavior of doctors and/or patients and harder yet to claim that culture, or some aspect of it, caused the medical decisions discussed in earlier chapters, this is not my intent. It seems reasonable, however, to suggest that the culture provides a context, which influences and is reinforced in the medical decision making process. If, as I will argue, the medical relationship is at least partly rooted in a cultural context, then strategies for change should, of necessity, be addressed toward relevant aspects of our common culture.

Fee (1983) suggests that medical domination is a kind of "extended patriarchy," which reinforces male dominance. Therefore, we ought to be able to identify systematic patterns of sexist behavior in the practice of medicine and these sexist practices ought to serve social control functions. History is replete with such examples. It was medicine in the 19th century that declared middle- and upper-class women too weak to think and reproduce. Since the uterus was at war with the brain for a limited supply of energy, education, it was claimed, would interfere with the development of a woman's reproductive system and, hence, her ability to bear children. From puberty on, elite women were described as emotionally high strung and sickly. The cure, rest and isolation, led to a life of invalidism. And always there was the ever-present physician to "help" women over the rough spots. Menstruation required a rest cure. Pregnancy and child birth were diseases to be treated by the physician and menopause called for death rites, as it signaled the symbolic end of a woman's meaningful life. Masturbation was an evil to be rooted out surgically by removing the clitoris and/or the clitoral hood. But by far the most popular of the medical procedures—touted as a cure-all—was the removal of the ovaries. While it was prescribed for many supposed ailments, including: "practically anything untoward in female behavior" (Barker-Benfield 1976), its most pervasive use was to make women more woman-like. The underlying assumption was that by removing the ovaries, women would become more tractable (Ehrenreich and English 1979; Ruzek 1978; Barker-Benfield 1976).

It has been argued that while the male medical establishment legitimized and enriched itself as it diseased women's bodies, there were additional motivations. Barker-Benfield (1976) points out that the interests of doctors and those of the dominant society were in accord. Both wanted to control women and their reproductive capacities (cf. Ruzek 1978). And Daly (1978) suggests why. Men, who were unable to create life, responded to the first wave of feminism with a violent, medical "enforcement of the sexual caste system" (Daly 1978, 227). She goes on to draw parallels between gynecologists, who specialize in diseases of women's bodies (body gynecologists) and mental health professionals, who specialize in reshaping women's minds (mind gynecologists). And while she says that some specialists are at times helpful to women, this occurs in spite of "loyalties to their patriarchally identified fields" (Daly 1978, 224).

Others (Ehrenreich and English 1979; Ruzek 1978) have pointed out that by the 20th century, the social control functions had shifted to include psychiatry. And again there is evidence (of systematic patterns of sexist behavior) that professional dominance functioned to reinforce male dominance. The upper- and middle-class "sickly" women of the 19th century and their doctors set the stage for this transition. Women in increasing numbers went from the gentle invalidism encouraged by their physicians to hysteria. And hysteria created a crisis for the medical profession. If it was a disease and if they were the masters of disease, why could they not cure it. Ehrenreich and English (1978) point out that the deadlock over hysteria ushered in a new era—an era that removed women's emotional lives from the arena of gynecology.

Although Freudian theory replaced the gynecological view of women, it was not much of an improvement (see Chodorow 1978; Dinnerstein 1978; Mitchell 1978 for a more complete feminist analysis of the psychoanalytic tradition). Women were still flawed and the flaw was still associated with their reproductive organs. Whereas for the gynecologists, women's reproductive systems were at fault, for Freudian theorists, it was the absence of a penis that caused women's problems (see also Ruzek 1978). When in the 19th century women did not meet standards of societal behavior, their reproductive systems were brought into line surgically. When women in the 20th century were nonconforming, the diagnosis was "madness" and the cure, psychotherapy. And in each case, the inappropriate behavior was similar: the women in question were not sufficiently passive and acquiescent. They did not do the job of daughter, wife, and/or mother with enough vigor, self-sacrifice, and dependence (cf. Ruzek 1978).

How tempting it is to think that women were browbeaten then (at an earlier period in history), but that today we know better. But do we? In the early 1970s when Cheslter wrote *Women and Madness,* she argued that husbands, fathers, and therapists institutionalized women for breaking sex role expectations—for being too independent, for failing to do housework well enough, and/or for participating in lesbian relationships (Chesler 1972). Psychosurgery was one solution for women who failed to adjust. Today's most prevalent solution is psychoactive (or mood altering) drugs. The lobotomized woman of yesterday and the tranquilized woman of today share something in common: they are tractable and better able to be good housewives (Ruzek 1978). Daly, working in the late 1970s, suggests that today's escalation of gynecological surgery and psychotherapy are related to the re-emergence of feminism. Drawing on Christian theological paradigms, she argues that there are only two possibilities for women:

> First there is the fallen state, formerly named sinful and symbolized by Eve, presently known as sick and typified in the powerless but sometimes difficult and problematic patient. Second, there is the restored/redeemed state of perfect femininity, formerly named saintly and symbolized by Mary, presently typified in the weak "normal" woman whose normality is so elusive that it must constantly be reinforced (Daly 1978, 231).

The strength of this Christian paradigm was graphically brought home to me as I did the research for this book. The 1970 edition of *Novak's Textbook of Gynecology* has etched into its cover a picture of a naked woman walking forward, one hand covering her pubic area, the other across her breasts, and pain screaming from her face (see illustration 1). The picture stuck with me. I was bothered by the naked helplessness of the woman; the way her body seemed to hunch forward as if to hide her bare skin; the futility of the hands not quite covering breasts and pubic region; the cry escaping from her lips and the look of absolute agony on her face. What was a woman like this doing on the cover of a gynecology textbook, even in the relatively unenlightened time of the

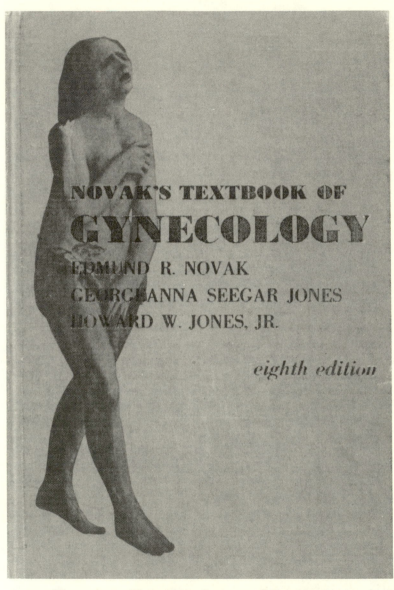

Illustration 1. Picture from the cover of *Novak's Textbook of Gynecology*

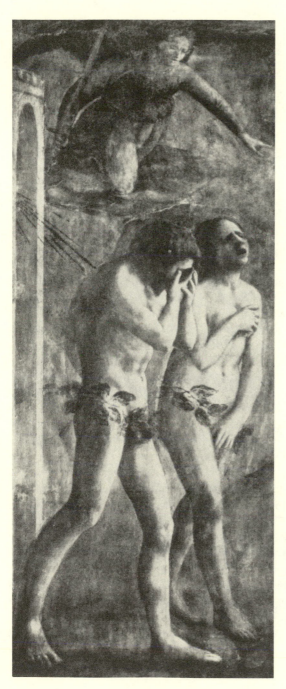

Illustration 2.
Masaccio. *Expulsion
of Adam and Eve*.
Florence, Church of
the Carmine, Bran-
cacci Chapel

early 1970s? I was disheartened by the message about women the picture conveyed—the message of Eve, the fallen woman in need of medical management.

Still the picture nagged at the corner of my mind asking to be remembered. I finally found her—the woman entombed on the cover of a textbook. She had originally been painted by a Florentine, Masaccio, about 1427 and had adorned the left-hand entrance pilaster of the Brancacci Chapel. The painting is called the "Expulsion of Adam and Eve." In it an angel, bearing a threatening sword, hovers above Adam and Eve as they make their way "from the portals of paradise" (see illustration 2). This painting has been acclaimed for its emotional and psychological reality: "Adam's gesture in covering his face is eloquent of the soul shattering reality of the finality of the punishment, and Eve conceals her shame with an instinctive motion as old in art as "Aphrodites of pagan antiquity" (Robb 1951, 221).

So at least into the 1970s, the age-old dichotomy between Eve and Mary—bad woman and good woman—was still being conveyed to the body gynecologist. And these sexist messages about women learned in society were amplified in medical education (cf. Ruzek 1978). Mary Howell, former associate dean of Harvard Medical School, writing under the pseudonym Margaret Campbell, M.D., documents sexist behavior and discriminatory practices directed against women medical students. She argues that the treatment of these students brings to light attitudes about women that are incubated in future physicians during their educations—attitudes that still portray women as dominated by their reproductive functions and that continue to assume that women are neurotic and likely to have predominantly psychosomatic illnesses (Campbell 1973). Scully and Bart (1973) have found evidence to support Dr. Howell's position. In reviewing gynecological texts, they found that physicians are still being encouraged to maintain traditional attitudes about women's sexuality and their sex role behavior. Once doctors-in-training are out of school, drug company advertisements take over. Drug ads perpetuate society's prejudices about women by portraying women in ways that maintain traditional sex roles (Prather and Fidell 1975).

Not only are sexist messages sent, but they appear to be received as well. In 1970, the Broverman *et al.,* study probed the sexist stereotypes held by mental health clinicians of both sexes. Clinicians were presented with a checklist of bipolar characteristics—not at all aggressive, very aggressive, etc.—and asked to pick the ones that best described a normal, healthy, mature, competent man, adult, and woman. Their findings documented that mental health clinicians shared a societal concensus about sex role stereotypes and their social desirability. The characteristics picked for a normal, healthy, mature, competent man and adult were substantially the same (e.g., dominant). The characteristics picked for a normal, healthy, mature, competent woman were substantially different (e.g., passive). Women were not depicted as competent adults (Browerman *et al.* 1970). As Richardson (1981) points out, women continue to be associated with characteristics that, in our culture, are considered negative. She describes more recent work on clinicians and suggests that these studies show that while stereotyping has declined in the last ten years, women continue to be typecast as more emotional, more passive, more excitable, and less aggressive. My recent look at drug advertisements in medical journals finds sex role stereotypes writ large.

During 1982, a drug company ran a series of ads for an oral contraceptive in several major medical journals—ads addressed to physicians. These ads oriented health care providers to "today's women." As I describe the ads, I'm sure many of us, doctors or laypersons, men or women, of reproductive age or beyond, will recognize issues that are of concern to us. At first glance, it is tempting to argue that progress has been made—that the values of the women's movement have infiltrated the consciousness of doctors and pharmaceutical companies and that it is these values that are reflected in the ads. Unfortunately, I do not think this is the case. A closer look shows how the values of the women's movement have been co-opted. At a deeper level, the language of these ads reflects and sustains stereotypic images. While playing off the image of today's women, they reinforce commonly held cultural assumptions about women. In addition, the ads, at one and the same time, influence doctors to prescribe brand x contraceptive, legitimize the prescription of birth control pills for both married and unmarried women, and maximize the doctor's role as an agent of social control—the preserver of the status quo.

The first ad in the series depicts a young woman in jeans and a close-fitting low-cut t-shirt. She is sitting in a large armchair with one leg thrown over the arm of her chair, looking up through her eyelashes while fingering her single blond braid. At one and the same time, this young woman looks innocent and enticing, sweet and seductive. But if the physicians reading the ad have any doubts about the woman or their responsibility to her, the copy dispels it. The heading in bold type reads, "She's 16 years old" (*Journal of Reproductive Medicine* 1982:102–103). The text continues by sending the message that doctors have a responsibility perhaps even a moral responsibility to "protect" young, sexually active women from pregnancy. Since, according to the ad, young women today choose to be "sexually active," but not "sexually informed or responsible" doctors must "help" them by prescribing birth control (brand x, of course).

The next ad shows the same woman sitting in the same chair, but she has grown up. Her hair is no longer hanging over her shoulder in one long braid. Instead, it falls loosely to her shoulders. She is more conservatively dressed in a tailored skirt and blouse and she looks straight out of the picture at the reader. There are files in the chair with her, a pad of writing paper on her lap and a pen in her hand. Why does this woman need a doctor? Again the text clears up any confusion. The bold type reads, "She's 24 years old," and in smaller type continues by again sending the message that doctors have a responsibility to "help" unmarried women—whether they be sixteen or twenty-four. The woman in this ad is "thinking about" a variety of options—careers ranging from science to the arts or other social and community activities. She is also "thinking about motherhood." But since she decides "not yet" for motherhood, the doctor's task is to "help" her carry out her choice by prescribing brand x (Ibid., 104–105).

In the next ad, the same woman, now depicted against a dark, somber background, sits in the same chair. She is obviously older, more mature. Her hair is shorter and well coifed. She is dressed in a long robe, has a child's storybook open in her lap, and her arm around a smiling little girl that looks just like her. Why does this well settled woman need a doctor? The bold type of the ad says, "She's 30 years old," and once again the smaller print continues by sending the message that the doctor needs to "help" this woman too. She is described in the ad as a woman who may want more children someday, "but not this year." For now she is choosing to be a loving wife and mother and an "active woman" (Ibid., 106–107). To "help" her preserve her choice, while retaining the option of having more children later, she needs a prescription of brand x—a prescription only the doctor can provide.

Each of these ads typifies the choices of today's women. Women have fought for the right to choose to be sexually active without being married. They have fought to control their reproduction by choosing whether to have children, when to have children, and how many children to have. The sixteen-year-old woman depicted in the ad is free today to choose to be sexually active. In earlier times, her sexuality would have been more closely controlled. As the woman in the ad matures, she appears to be making her own choices in other ways as well. At twenty-four, while remaining sexually active, she is choosing between motherhood and a career. At thirty, married and with a child, she is choosing when and if she wants to have another child. With these choices represented in the ads, why do I claim that the values of the women's movement have been co-opted—that these ads, and others like them, parade stereotypic images of women behind the facade of the more liberated woman. Let's look more closely.

First, at each stage of the woman's life she is shown as dependent. No matter what her age, she is unable to accomplish the choices she sets for herself without the "help" of her physician. At sixteen, she needed her/his protection as well—protection from her own irresponsibility. She is "sexually active," but not "sexually informed or responsible" (Ibid., 102–103). At twenty-four and thirty, her ability to control her reproductive choices is influenced by the doctor's willingness to prescribe. So while at first glance the woman in these ads appears to be making choices about her life, at a closer look, she is dependent upon the prevailing cultural attitudes about women and the good will of her physician. This is an old woman in new garb. There is no such duplicity in the depiction of the appropriate role for doctors. They are today, as they were yesterday, agents of social control, gatekeepers of the moral order.

Second, she is an old woman in new garb in another way as well. While her sexuality is played up, her maturity is downplayed. At sixteen, she is depicted as neither informed nor responsible, and at twenty-four, while she is ostensibly choosing between a career and motherhood, her career choice is at best unfocused. She has no sense of what kind of a career she wants and is not sure she wants a career at all. Perhaps being active in social and community life will do. This lack of focus is carried forth to the last ad. At thirty, her role as wife and mother is sharply drawn in both the picture and the text of the ad. But while we are told that she is "an active woman," (Ibid. 106–107) we are not told in what ways. The ad seems intentionally vague on this point.

Finally, Mary Daly (1978), faced with these ads might argue that at

sixteen she is a fallen woman, and at twenty-four she is somewhat re-
stored. Although she is thinking about a career, she is also thinking
about motherhood. By thirty, she is redeemed: "A loving wife and
mother." While today's woman may think about a career, and even have
one, her societal worth is to be found by fulfilling traditional sex role
expectations: she is a good woman because she has found a man, gotten
married, and had a beautiful child. And clearly the physician played a
pivotal role in her redemption. It was the doctor who "helped" her use
contraception at sixteen and thus "helped" her avoid an unwanted pregnancy that might have hindered her own rebirth. And it was the doctor
who continued to "help" her find contraception and to allow her the illusion of making choices about her life. The ads, when looked at in this
light, display very consistent messages about women: there is Eve the
fallen woman; there is Mary in the "restored/redeemed state of perfect
femininity" (Daly 1978); and there is medical domination functioning
to reinforce male domination.

   If we apply these messages to the data discussed in earlier chapters,
the same process is evident: By controlling women and their reproductive capacities, medical domination functioned to sustain male domination. In chapter two, hysterectomies were recommended to women who
had finished their child-bearing—to Mary-like women, who no longer
need their potentially disease-producing reproductive organs. Hysterectomies were also recommended to women who were more like the fallen
Eve: women who did not want to have children, who had had abortions,
who had given children up for adoption, who had left children with their
divorced husbands—was their "sin" failing to meet societal expectations about motherhood? And women who had fallen from grace, even
though they were married and had children, also had hysterectomies
recommended—their "sin": poverty or government assistance. Societal
expectations about women were all too evident in chapter three, when
the doctor implied that the patient had caused her abnormal Pap smear
with her inappropriate sexual behavior—was her "sin" sex without marriage? And the same expectations, in slightly different form, were also
apparent in chapter four. Young, sexually active women were more
likely to receive Pap smears in conjunction with prescriptions for birth
control than were older women. And while these women were at risk,
cervical cancer is still much more prevalent in women past their reproductive prime of life. Yet, such women were not as likely to receive

Pap smears—was their "sin" approaching old age? But in each case, the decision to perform or not to perform a Pap smear functioned, with the "help" of doctors, to sustain traditional sex role expectations. Doctors protected the reproductive capacity of young sexually active women until they could be redeemed by marriage and motherhood (or motherhood if they were already married). But for older women, however they had lived their lives, reproduction was almost over and so were their opportunities for redemption.

So the Eve and Mary of the Christian theological paradigm appear to be alive and well in the 19th and in the 20th centuries. The medical profession grew to dominance on these images. If, as Fee (1983) suggests, medical domination is a kind of "extended patriarchy," then these images have not only maintained the profession, but also they have functioned to sustain a male-dominated society. This understanding is supported by Mary Daly, who argues that the dominant, who she refers to as "Mind Managers," oppress women to maintain the patriarchical patterning of society. She claims that:

> Mind Managers are able to penetrate their victims' minds/imaginations only by seeing to it that their deceptive myths are acted out over and over again in performances that draw participants into emotional complicity. Such re-enactments train both victims and victimizers to perform uncritically their preordained roles (Daly 1978, 109).

Daly goes on to point out that gynecological practices of the 19th and 20th centuries are only one example of the enactment of "deceptive myths." She outlines several others: Indian suttee (or the burning of Indian widows with their dead husbands), Chinese footbinding, African genital mutilation, and European witchburning. And in each of these cases, women are drawn into complicity with their oppressors, believing that to do otherwise would show them to be unnatural women. From this perspective, the perpetuation of patriarchal notions about women and their proper place in society can be understood as strategies for explaining, justifying, legitimating, glamorizing, and enforcing prevailing conditions. Such strategies are almost unnecessary when one concept of reality permeates throughout society, its institutions, and its individual members. But when popular support for the dominant view slips, when some people begin to see that prevailing conditions do not serve their interests, manipulation is carried out in earnest for the minds and hearts of the defectors, to win them back to an acceptance of the status quo.

In the 19th century with the birth of feminism, the "mind-binding" (Daly 1978) of women began to slip and the medical profession joined with their fellow patriarchs in helping to reinstate it. And again with the rebirth of feminism in the 20th century, the patriarchs are explaining, justifying, legitimating, glamorizing, and enforcing prevailing myths about women and the traditional family. "Pro-family" spokespersons of the New Right take changes in the line of authority between man, woman, and child as evidence of an anti-family trend. Each change is proclaimed a threat to the family and each threat is seized upon as an opportunity to forecast doom and in so doing to legitimize and glamorize the status quo. Why? Is it because the hierarchical family is critical for the preservation of the status quo? Could it be because dominance depends on hierarchy, and as a hierarchical institution, the family provides an essential model for other authoritarian patriarchal structures (Porgrebin 1983)? Are the dependence of women and children on men the only acceptable pro-family forms? Do women who want to control their reproductive lives, who want more decision making power or who want careers threaten the delicate balance of power (Luker 1984) the same way children do who break with tradition or strive for autonomy? Is normalcy as Daly (1978) suggests, so elusive it needs constant reinforcement? If these questions are answered affirmatively, does that speak of a conspiracy? I am not suggesting a conspiracy. Physicians, spokespersons for the New Right, and other patriarchs do not sit down together and plan how they are going to punish or recapture today's defectors. Rather, most of us act out socialized complicity, performing uncritically our "preordained roles" (see also Chodorow 1978; Daly 1978; Dinnerstein 1978; Mitchell 1978).

Theoretical Implications: Building Sociological Understanding

I have argued that in order to understand the medical decision making process discussed in earlier chapters, it is necessary to extend the concept of context—to build a contextual web. Neither language nor the immediate environment as a focus of analysis allow discussion of how history and competing interests infiltrate examining rooms and the practice of medicine that occurs within them. Again, at the risk of being redundant, I am not claiming that organizational, structural and/or cultural factors caused the medical interactions discussed earlier. Rather my aim is to balance the sociological equation. Instead of the more traditional view of an external and constraining social world, which shapes the actions of individuals within it, or the newer conception of reality as an interactional accomplishment, I want to suggest that social structure and social interaction are intimately connected. Language does interactional work. It transmits messages that blend features of the social structure with interactional cues and, in the process, informs the social accomplishments of events like medical decisions. Simultaneously, the interactional work of participants during medical encounters reinforces and sustains the social structure, while also embodying a collaborative potential for social change. Theoretical implications with the potential to influence sociological understanding are possible when the relationship between language and context, social structure and social interaction, are reinterpreted as reflexively related—each informing the other.

Research on the sexual politics of talk examines the relationship between certain features of social structure and language. Using a variety of methods—informants, anecdotes, observation, and content analysis—researchers have questioned who has power, how it is expressed, and why the expression is patterned in relatively constant ways. They claim that a fallacy is built into the study of language if communication is assumed to be a social production that occurs between equals. Rather, they suggest that power and status are reflected in talk. By examining the effects of gender on the allocation of speaking turns, patterns of interpretations, the choice and development of topic and words, chosen patterns of verbal and nonverbal behavior have been identified. For example, Henley (1975) points out that when nonverbal behavior is examined, touching, smiling, eye contact, intonation, and interruptions "establish, express and maintain power relations." In a similar vein, researchers have found that as subordinates, women smile and use their eyes to appease or to seek approval. They smile and submissively avert their gaze to send messages of appeasement, and they use their eyes and their faces to express emotions seeking approval from those who have the power to provide it (cf. Eakins and Eakins 1978; Thorn and Henley 1975 for a review of this literature).

In addition, when conversation is examined, men and women are found to talk differently. Men interrupt women more often (Zimmerman and West 1975) and are more talkative in general. This talkativeness is attributed, at least in part, to their answering questions that are not addressed to them (Eakins and Eakins 1978). By contrast Thorne and Henley (1975) report on research that finds that women use "mmhmm" more often than men do. "Mmhmm" does not interrupt a turn of talk. It is a supportive utterance, consistent with the ways women are socialized. Subordination, and therefore gender, affects the ways English is spoken in other ways as well (Lakoff 1973). Who says "God dammit" and who says "Oh dear"? What image is projected when the following kind of statements are made: "It's such a lovely day."; "It's a nice day, isn't it?" or "This may sound crazy, but . . ."? Intensifiers ("such a lovely day"), tag questions ("isn't it") and qualifiers ("This may sound crazy but") are less forceful modes of expression, which display patterns of weakness and uncertainty. It is these modes of expression that characterize women's speech in the United States, reflecting their place in society.

In a society in which men and women are seen to have different spheres of activities, these differences are also reflected in language. In the United States, men are assumed to work, and women, notwithstanding the fact that almost half of them are employed full-time outside the home, are presumed to be at home taking care of house and family. If women do work, their jobs are assumed to be lower status than those of men—an assumption that is basically correct. These assumptions are reflected in language. Regardless of the setting, women are defined primarily by their relationship to men. They are titled Miss if they are not married, and Mrs. if they are. While men also have families, they are not primarily identified by these roles. Men remain Mr. whether married or not. Similarly, the majority of titles for occupations and professions carry a masculine presumption. Gender is generally not specified in reference to physicians, lawyers, or professors, if the person occupying that position is male. However, gender is marked if the person occupying the position does not conform to the unstated gender-appropriate assumption. Male nurse and woman lawyer, doctor, or professor display these assumptions and speak eloquently about the sexual division of labor as well as the status associated with gender-specific occupations and professions (cf. Eakins and Eakins 1978; Thorne and Henley 1975).

These findings point to the social production of gender differences in language and suggest that they are intimately connected to a structural reality. Thorne and Henley (1975) depict speech as a kind of action, which reveals the fabric of social life. They argue that this life, characterized by the "social elaboration of gender," reveals a society shaped by male dominance—a dominance "built into the economic, family, political and legal structures of society."

The analysis of language in the data chapters in this work is similar to and also different from the work of Thorne and Henley. I examine the way institutional authority (institutionally produced status and power) is reflected in the way language is used, how the way language is used reflects and sustains features of social structure, and how consequences are socially accomplished in and through language use. The similarities in our work lie in our conception of language as reflecting and sustaining features of the social system. What is different? I look at naturally occurring talk, analyze the interactional work that the talk does and the consequences produced in the process. Although research on the sexual politics of talk and my analysis move in the same direction, their primary focus is on language use. Context, albeit an important aspect of the analysis, is not fully developed. The conceptual web just discussed illustrates the organization of the profession and the practice of medicine, the structural contradictions of capitalism, and the cultural milieu of patriarchy and provides a context that helps make sense out of the medical decision making process. What is needed now is a theory that is capable of integrating social structure and social interaction.

Recently, efforts have been made to generate a theory that can reintegrate what Knorr-Cetina and Cicourel (1981) call "macro- and microsociologies."[1] In this effort, language is used as a critical link in the bridge between social interaction and social structure. In the introduction to her book, Knorr-Cetina states:

> Macro-social theories and methodologies have generally focused their interest on the interrelationship of social action. They have promoted conceptions of (macro) social order which start from an interrelation hypothesis and em-

ployed notions such as social system and social structure to deal with this interrelation. In contrast, micro-social theories and methodologies favour conceptions which start from the ontological and methodological primacy of micro-social situations. While this has resulted in a long-standing challenge of macro-approaches to social reality, attempts to *reconstruct* macro-sociology from a microsociological perspective are new. (1981, 40)

She identifies three hypotheses for reconstructing the macro- from micro-sociological insights. First, in relation to the aggregation hypothesis stemming from the work of Collins (1981), Knorr-Cetina asserts that the macro-realm of social order and structure are composed of aggregations of micro-moments in everyday life. This is the most extreme of the micro-theories, as it posits that all understandings of macro-phenomena are aggregated from *in situ* micro-data. In other words, the whole is the sum of the parts.

Second, in relation to the hypothesis of unintended consequences suggested by the work of Harre (1981) and Giddens (1981), Knorr-Cetina claims that there are unintended as well as intended consequences of micro-experiences. Micro-events must be studied in order to know the macro-world. But in contrast to the position of the aggregation hypothesis, she argues that the entire global (macro) picture cannot be gleaned from the intended (micro). She acknowledges that there are influences on social life that transcend empirical evidence. We can try to understand the unintended by studying micro-actions and one can study unintended consequences to see the emergent macro-world, but there is no assurance that this will provide us with the whole picture. In this case, the whole is more than the sum of its parts, but only the parts are researchable.

Third, in relation to the representation hypothesis drawn from the work of Cicourel (1981), Knorr-Cetina suggests relationships and connections between situations and the construction of accounts, or between the represented and the representation.

The macro emerges from such work not as the sum of unintended consequences of micro-episodes nor as their aggregate or network of interrelations, but rather as a summary representation actively constructed and pursued within micro-situations. In other words, the macro appears no longer as a *particular layer* of social reality *on top* of micro-episodes composed of their interrelation (macro-sociologies), their aggregation (aggregation hy-

pothesis), or their unforeseen effects (hypothesis of unintended consequences). Rather, it is seen to reside *within* these micro-episodes where it
results from the *structuring practices* of agents. (1981, 34)

The macro-order becomes a part of micro-action. An integral meshing
of the two occurs, rather than the emergence of macro from micro, as
espoused in the two earlier hypotheses.

In the introduction to *Discourse and Institutional Authority,* (1986)
Alexandra Todd and I join in the call for a reintegration between micro-
and macro-sociologies; however, there are distinctions between our conception and Knorr-Cetina's in terms of the status of social structure and
social interaction (what she refers to as their ontological primacy), and
therefore, of necessity, with our suggestions for how the gap should be
bridged. Since proponents from both macro- and micro-sociologies have
tried to make these connections, perhaps a comparison between their
proposals will illuminate this distinction.

Habermas (1981), a traditional macro-theorist, calls for integration;
however, for him, macro-structures (institutional arrangements) have
priority. Social integration is rooted in a historical location in the political order: macro-institutional arrangements are interrelated with micro-
social actions. However, since he is interested in social change, he
posits a micro-process for creating new forms of social integration. He
suggests that alternative interpretive systems develop in marginal
groups and spread to other societal members. Once spread, they create a
shared cognitive potential for reorganizing society. Institutions change
by embodying this shared interpretation. Language and interaction are,
of course, features of this interactive transformation. Although it
appears that Habermas is calling for an integration between macro-
structures and micro-processes, the weaving of these micro-processes
into the larger picture is weak. Habermas' forté is social systems—his
theory of language and interaction remains underdeveloped.

By comparison, the position Knorr-Cetina claims is the most viable of
the micro-positions, the representational hypothesis, turns Habermas'
vision on its head. Whereas, for Habermas, the macro—institutional
arrangements—takes priority, for the representational hypothesis, the
micro has primacy. Macro-structures reside within "micro-episodes"
and are accomplished through the social activities of the participants in
these episodes. The strength of this work is the detailed analysis of the

ways individuals accomplish events or create social realities. Power, structures, and social order are all alluded to, but when the hypothesis has been fully unveiled, its strength lies in the development of the micro-world—the larger concerns of social structure remain vague.

Taking power as an example, as does Knorr-Cetina, two opposing arguments can be made: Power is depicted as a macro-phenomenon arising out of concrete social relationships. Here, power is truncated from interpersonal relationships and individuals' actions. Or, power is seen as accomplished through the actions of individuals. Here, power is isolated from concrete institutional arrangements. We suggest, by contrast, that power is both a micro- and macro-phenomenon. If one were to break the law, get arrested, be tried and sentenced, the power of police, law enforcement agencies, and the courts would be both interactional and institutional. Although aspects of this power would reside in micro-episodes of social action, the reality of power could not be captured totally in these micro-scenes. Power is more than a summary representation. It is a concrete, political reality realized and reflected in social actions, which in turn often help to support the status quo.

To say that the macro resides within micro-episodes, established by people's actions, leads to a possible conclusion that individuals control their activities, abstracted from concrete social reality. A "blame the victim" ideology, useful to maintaining status relationships, is the logical conclusion of this view. Once again we do not mean to imply that human beings are societally preprogrammed robots, but neither are they free agents. To borrow from Marx, individuals make their own society and history, but not just as they please.

Duster (1981) outlines an alternative proposal for reintegrating micro- and macro-sociologies. Taking micro-episodes of interaction as the starting point, he suggests that a composite of micro-episodes can extend our understanding of social life. He proposes a picture made up of multi-levels of data as a way to bridge micro and macro. Using the metaphor of the ladder, he specifies the rungs necessary to complete a broader view of society than is usually envisioned in any one research project. His research suggestions include studying law, lobbying, and government; administration and organization; and interaction and community, all grounded in historical context. This is a rather large order. Collective work or the combination of studies across settings, perspectives, and methodologies are required to create a broader vision than single efforts can provide.

The contextual web outlined earlier attempts to move in the direction Duster suggests. This web is a heuristic device—a device for reintegrating language with context, social structure with social interaction. As a heuristic device, it poses social interaction and social structure in a reflexive relationship in which each influences the other, and it gives priority to neither level of analysis. It is influenced by recommendations from both micro- and macro-sociologies. With Knorr-Cetina's representation hypothesis, the reflexive model envisions macro-influences reflected in micro-episodes of interaction, rather than conceptualizing the macro as a layer of reality on top of these interactional events. With Habermas' more macro perspective, the reflexive model sees social reality as rooted in a historical location in the political order.

If the relationship between social structure and social interaction is reflexive, how is social change to be conceptualized? Again, some of the insights of macro- and micro-sociologies are informative. The reflexive model draws from macro-theorists who see the hierarchical arrangements of society mirrored in the organizational structure of institutions (see for example Navarro 1976) and recapitulated in language (see for example Henley 1977) and concurs with the micro-theorists who display how individuals acting in concert accomplish events, producing social reality in the process. Drawing from the strengths of both perspectives, it suggests a contextual, hermeneutic mode of analysis in which causality resides in a dynamic, reflexive process.

Policy Ramifications: Directions for Social Action

In a seminal paper, Waitzkin and Stoeckle (1976) state that policy changes at the macro-level of social structure are implemented at the micro-level of social interaction. The implication is that if we want social change, it is not sufficient just to change social policies. It is also insufficient just to change the ways people interact. We can teach patients to take more responsibility for their health and to be more assertive during medical encounters. It also may be possible to teach doctors to communicate more effectively. However, without policy changes, the delivery of health care will still function to support the status quo.

Up to this point the argument has been that: 1) The way health care is delivered in the U.S. may not be in the patient's best interest, especially if the patient is a woman; 2) The organizational nexus, structural contradictions, and cultural milieu contribute to the problem and 3) Language use both reflects and sustains structures of dominance. The conceptual web allows us to visualize interrelationships between organizational, structural and cultural factors, and micro-episodes of interaction, and in so doing suggests policy ramifications and directions for social change. The problems under discussion are obviously complex and there can be no easy solutions. However, there may be hope.

Earlier when I discussed the organization of the profession of medicine, I stated that change may be on the horizon. Starr (1982) argues that a historical process is underway. Just as the medical profession consolidated its autonomy by wrestling power away from competing practitioners, so today this autonomy is being threatened. The signs are there for all to read: the increasing growth of the corporate medical establishment, projections forecasting an oversupply of physicians and increasing competition among them, and burgeoning patient dissatisfaction with rising medical costs, a dissatisfaction that has physicians at its epicenter.

It is not hard to imagine that physicians could become today's scapegoats, as midwives were yesterday's. Individuals have direct contact with physicians, not with amorphous bureaucratic structures, and they have learned to blame other individuals, not the social structure, for the problems they experience. If patients feel ripped off by spiraling medical inflation, and there is every indication that they do, physicians are ideally situated to be blamed. Today the problem is couched in terms of medical fees. Doctors' fees are too high. The voluntary freeze on medical fees for 1984 is little more than a symbolic gesture—a gesture aimed at reassuring patients without challenging the economic status quo. If cutting costs were a real issue, doctors' fees would not be the only area targeted. For every health dollar spent, and in 1982 286,610 billion dollars were spent, nineteen cents, or 54,780 billion dollars, went for the services of physicians, while more than twice that amount, forty-one cents, or 117,995 billion dollars, were spent on hospital care (Murphy 1983, based on figures supplied by the Department of Health and Human Services, Health Care Financing Administration).

There is a double irony in today's threat to the status and power of the medical profession. First, the profession has been locked in battle with the government, fighting for the state to protect its interests without regulating its performances. Second, physicians have resisted attempts to change the nature of the doctor-patient relationship. Patients' rights, patients' advocates, and even package inserts in prescription drugs have each been seen as a threat and fought against. Although the profession has been on guard against government invasion of and consumer demands upon its privileged position, the threat is coming from another direction—from the increasing power of the corporate medical establishment.

If, as Starr (1982) points out, this threat comes to be realized, there are potentially serious consequences for the medical profession as well as for the rest of society. Doctors working for corporations are likely to have less autonomy than they did. In the interests of controlling costs and maximizing profits, corporations are more than likely to interfere in the ways health care is practiced. In this process, it may beome increasingly difficult to separate "business" and "medical" considerations. In addition, as corporations gain control over the delivery of care, they will become an even more powerful force within the state. If their lobbying efforts are successful, the influence of the medical profession will be reduced even further.

Corporate encroachment will not only effect medical autonomy, it will also aggravate inequalities in the health care delivery system. Corporations are likely to oppose any national health program that might threaten their profits. In addition, differential access to health care and the maldistribution of medical services are likely to be exacerbated, because corporations will not be interested in providing care for those who cannot pay for it or in locating facilities in unprofitable areas. Thus the corporate cost-benefit analysis is likely to sharpen the contrast between those who have resources and those who do not—to strengthen the duality of the health care system. Finally, there is no evidence that cost savings for either tax payers or consumers will result from this, because there is no evidence that there will be significant savings with corporate medicine.

The picture Starr (1982) paints is gloomy. He says:

> This turn of events is the fruit of a history of accommodating professional and institutional interests, failing to exercise public control over public programs, then adopting piecemeal regulation to control the inflationary consequences, and, as a final resort, cutting back programs and turning them to

the private sector. The failure to rationalize medical services under public control meant that sooner or later they would be rationalized under private control. Instead of public regulation, there will be private regulation, and instead of public planning, there will be corporate planning. Instead of public financing for prepaid plans that might be managed by the subscribers' chosen representatives, there will be corporate financing for private plans controlled by conglomerates whose interests will be determined by the rate of return on investments. That is the future toward which American medicine now seems to be heading (Starr 1982, 449).

But the picture is not without hope: If we take medicine back into the public domain, we can salvage it. Starr (1982) calls us to action, but specifies neither the courses available to us nor the consequences of our choices. Waitzkin (1983) is much clearer on these points. He advocates a national health service plan, saying that other choices (community clinics, health maintenance organizations or national health insurance) that might be in the public domain are piecemeal solutions that preserve the inequalities in our current system.

Prepaid plans managed by whomever subscribers choose leave most of the problems in our current system unmet. Waitzkin (1983) claims that while a national health insurance plan or a system of health maintenance organizations (HMOs) promise fundamental change, they primarily modify payment mechanisms, and while community clinics improve medical accessibility for some patients, without a unified health system, they are at best stop-gap measures. Since the structure of the health care system is not changed in basic ways with any of these approaches, problems such as the maldistribution of medical facilities and personnel remain relatively untouched. Each plan, however, holds out a different hope.

HMOs are said to facilitate peer review and to offer other administrative advantages. Yet, there is little evidence of either increased efficiency or better quality care in them (Waitzkin 1983). While some doctors would be drawn away from the private fee-for-service practice of medicine and hired by HMOs, the fee-for-service system, with all its inequalities, would not be modified greatly. Furthermore, since the professionals in these settings have historically played major roles in the development of policy, professional dominance would not be diminished in meaningful ways.

National health insurance plans, while reducing financial difficulties for some patients, would do little to control costs, minimize profits, or change the broad structure of the health care system. Like Medicaid and Medicare, a national health insurance plan promises to reduce inequalities, but would leave the nature of private practice and the structure of the corporate medical establishment intact. Since insurance companies would still be the most likely fiscal intermediaries and fees would still be set by professional organizations, there would be little incentive for cutting costs. Inequalities would be maintained in other ways as well. The plan would primarily be financed by payroll taxes—a largely regressive method of taxation—and since all costs would not be covered by the plan, those with more resources would still have the advantage. Accessibility would not be improved and profit would not be controlled (also see Bodenheimer *et al.* 1981).

While community clinics improve medical accessibility, they are an even more piecemeal solution. Historically, community-based clinics have developed in rural and urban areas that lacked services or in order to meet the needs of those systematically oppressed in the medical system—women, minorities, and the poor. Clinics have been funded as a response to political unrest or political pressure, but when that pressure has been reduced, their funds have been cut. Without a unified health care system, the clinic's ability to continue to provide care is fragile and the patient population vulnerable.

Using the Dellums bill as a model, Waitzkin (1983) argues that only a national health service plan suggests major changes in the system. By limiting profit and rechanneling control, health care could be elevated from a commodity to a right of citizenship. The plan calls for comprehensive health care, free at the point of delivery, financed by taxation on individual and corporate incomes as well as by gift and estate taxes—a more progressive form of taxation. With profit no longer a major consideration, the maldistribution of facilities and personnel would be more amenable to solution. Free medical education and training would be provided in return for periods of service in underserved areas and hospitals. Rather than duplicating services and competing with each other, hospitals could coordinate services on a regional basis. To mitigate against continued professional dominance, users (⅔) and health workers (⅓) would cooperate in more democratic policy making. To

minimize the effects of bureaucracy, planning would be done nation-
wide, but control and implementation would be at the local level. Cost
containment could be facilitated by strict budgeting and by nationaliza-
tion. With the opportunity for profits reduced, profiteering (by professionals and corporations) could be contained as well.

After outlining the advantages, Waitzkin (1983) suggests some other
problems. While a national health service plan could support major
changes in the pattern of power and could reduce financial and geographic inequalities, in a capitalist society, it still leaves many problems
unaddressed. Opportunities for private gain and professional dominance, while weakened, still remain. The Dellums bill neither abolishes
the private fee-for-service practice of medicine, nor provides a stable
solution for the maldistribution of physicians. But perhaps the biggest
problem lies in an inherent weakness. Private practitioners and corporations would predictably see a national health service plan as not in their
interest and fight against it. This is an inevitable problem associated with
"a single sector reform within the broad context of class structure and
the capitalist economy." To combat this problem, Waitzkin (1983) suggests education, organization, activism, advocacy, and politicization.

I read him to be suggesting that we become active, we organize, educate and politicize each other as we become advocates for both a national health service plan and for other more far-reaching changes. He
seems to be suggesting that we band together and pit ourselves against
the medical profession and corporate establishment. But perhaps we
will not be alone. Increasingly, as corporate power threatens to overtake
medical autonomy, it is becoming in doctors' interests to join in the
battle against corporate encroachment. It may indeed be in all of our
interests to have public control over public medical programs rather than
private corporate control over private medical programs, to have public
rather than private regulation, and to have public planning and financing
rather than corporate planning and financing.

While the battle for a national health service plan would be a long and
arduous one, even if won it would not eliminate women's problems in the
health care delivery system. Taking profit out of health care will not
produce a withering away of patriarchy. Because, as I argued, decisions
to perform (or not to perform) elective or prophylactic hysterectomies
and diagnostic Pap smears were expressed at the intersection of the organization of the medical profession, capitalism, and patriarchy, it is to

this intersection that we must address ourselves. As women we need to mount a double campaign. While advocating a national health service and other changes in the capitalist economic system, we need to become active and remain active, to organize, to educate, to politicize and to become and remain advocates, breaking down the myths and structures that bind women.

Appendix

In chapter one, I outlined the relationship between language and context both in linguistics and in sociology. I argued that for the most part even when context is incorporated into an analysis of language, the status of context is ambiguous. The question I want to ask here is how does context function in an analysis of language? Is it a resource against which language behavior can be discussed? Or is it a topic of analysis in its own right? For example, when research presents a description of the ways people talk differently in different settings, is the focus on the linguistic behavior or does it address the ways the situation produces and constrains conversations? It is my contention that in the former case, language is the topic of the analysis and context is a largely unexamined background resource. Only when the relationship between language and context is addressed specifically does context become a research topic, having equal status with language.

In each of the three data chapters in this book, I show how language is a kind of "spoken interaction" (Labov and Fanshel 1977) oriented toward a particular goal—making a diagnosis and reaching a treatment decision. In these interactions, institutional arrangements and communicational strategies merge as doctors orchestrate the diagnostic treatment process. Highlighted in this kind of analysis are three important points: 1) How the institutional authority of medicine influences the decision making process; 2) How this institutional authority is reflected in the structure and function of medical discourse as well as in medical outcomes; and 3) How the information gained in these analyses is connected to cultural, structural, and institutional factors.

The purpose of this appendix is to provide background information about the development of an analysis that elevates context to an analytic status equal to language. I do this in several ways: 1) I provide more detail on the transition from linguistics to sociolinguistics, focusing on the increasing importance of context in the analysis. Using the work of Shuy (1983) and Labov and Fanshel (1977) as cases in point, I discuss how the relationship between language and context is managed by them in a specific setting—a medical and a therapeutic setting; and 3) I shift the focus to recent sociological work. While for most sociologists, language has been an unexamined background resource, these conversational and discourse analysts have explicitly taken it as a topic of inquiry. To see how context is managed by these researchers, I discuss research that treats language use as an essentially local production and as a situated process.

The Transition: Linguistics to Sociolinguistics

Linguists like Chomsky (1965) and philosophers of ordinary language such as Searle (1969), Austin (1962), and Wittgenstein (1953) contributed to the development of a perspective that in method and findings moved away from the perspective held by the early theoretical linguists. The focus for these linguists was on context-free linguistic rules, which could account for homogeneous linguistic behavior. The data brought to bear in this analysis were surface utterances drawn from experimental situations, texts, introspection, and informants.

Chomsky (1965) proposed an alternative course of linguistic study. While lending support to theoretical linguists who studied the linguistic structures (rules) available to every biologically intact individual—what Chomsky called the study of "competence" or "deep structure"—he recommended another level of analysis, which he called "performance" or "surface structure." At the less abstract surface level, researchers could study the way individuals selected and executed the rules of the deep structure—how they performed. The dichotomy between competence and performance—deep and surface structure—simultaneously supported the acontextual position of the theoretical linguists and legitimized the more contextual argument that language use was patterned by external environments. On the one hand, Chomsky accepted the assumption of a homogenous speech community in which individuals have an equal opportunity to learn to speak in a like manner—an implicitly conservative, blame-the-victim approach that supports the status quo while claiming political neutrality. On the other hand, by addressing the relationship between linguistic form (surface structure/performance) and the internal processes that produce them (deep structures/competence), he also provided a theoretical foundation from which to explore the relationship between language use and context.

In a parallel way, philosophers of ordinary language (Searle 1969; Austin 1962; and Wittgenstein 1953) supported an exploration of language use in its more contextual environment. Although Wittgenstein did not discuss context directly, his interest in language use and meaning as shared practices both implied context as necessary for understanding and refuted an earlier philosophical tradition with a passive view of language in which words stood for objects in the world. Wittgenstein suggested a more active conception of language. His focus was on the way words are used and what they mean. However, it was not until the work of Austin and Searle that a theory of language use was incorporated into a general theory of action.

Austin (1962) and Searle (1969) view speech acts as activities through which individuals construct social actions. To speak an utterance is to carry out an act. To use an often cited example, the utterance "I promise" is a speech act that accomplishes the action of promising. This act only has meaning within a social context; however, neither Austin or Searle made this contextual world explicit. Their contribution was rather to provide a way to analyze language as normatively ordered patterns of interaction. It is the work of sociolinguists that most explicitly examines language as a form of social behavior.

A Case in Point: Sociolinguistics and Medicine

Shuy applies linguistic knowledge to other fields, among them education, medicine, and law (Shuy 1983, 1976, 1970). In a recent article addressing effective communication in medical interviews, he discusses three types of interference: the use of vocabularies or jargon, the effect of cultural differences, and differences between the structure of discourse in medical settings and "normal conversation" (Shuy 1983). The first two are more obvious than the third.

Doctors and patients often use different vocabularies or codes. Communicating with different codes, or code-switching, interferes with effective communication. This is a relatively straightforward issue. An associated problem is the expectation that patients should accept and learn the language of doctors without there being an equal expectation for doctors. There is little demand for doctors to learn to speak or understand the language of patients.

The second point Shuy makes is that even though culturally different patients use their best standard English when they go to the doctor, the dialects they speak and the vocabularies they use have an effect. Not only do they produce an expected gap in understanding, but they also underline a less expected assumption of ignorance, which is reflected in the ways patients are communicated with and treated.

Finally, Shuy suggests that a different picture emerges when normal conversations and medical discourse are compared. Although both are structured, predictable, and organized around topics, medical dialogue is not characterized, as is normal conversation, by an expectation of balanced participation. Doctors, not patients, usually begin and end medical interviews. They also introduce and recycle most topics and hold on to the floor while switching topics. Doctors' styles do vary—some exercise more control and some less—however, there is a constant factor in medical interviews: they are characterized by the patients' lack of control. While there is a range of responses available to conversational partners—they can expand, amend, or argue with the topics—patients' responses are more limited. Their options are to request clarification, interrupt, express uncertainty, agree, or respond directly. The usual pattern in conversation is for the more dominant partner to interrupt the less dominant one. Shuy (1983) finds this pattern reversed in the medical situation. He finds frequent interruptions of the doctor by the patient. However, when the patient interrupts, the doctor retains the floor and by winning out in this way displays his/her dominance.

Shuy's findings illuminate the importance of context for the study of language use. His analysis highlights the asymmetry in the doctor-patient relationship—an asymmetry reflected in the discourse. The medical vocabulary is the dominant mode of communication and patients are expected to learn to use it. Medical practice is influenced by physicians' assumptions about patients' social worth—assumptions rooted in class, race, and ethnic differences. The structure of medical discourse displays these power relationships. Not only do people speak differently in different situations, but these differences are shaped by the institutions in which they occur.

Although the work of Labov and Fanshel (1977) is different from Shuy's, they share several central points of agreement: the therapeutic event, like the medical interview, is asymmetrical. The asymmetry is structured by who initiates and who is helped by the encounter. Discourse in medical and therapeutic settings is patterned in predictable ways. Relying on Hymes' definition of an event, Labov and Fanshel (1977) depict a therapeutic interview as a speech event with a routinized form of behavior, well-defined boundaries, and clearly delineated sets of behavioral expectations. In both studies, the importance of context for understanding medical and therapeutic relationships is illustrated.

Labov and Fanshel claim that particular features of the therapeutic interview—its conflicts and pressures—shape the discourse and inform the analyst's expansion of it. Expansions bring together information that facilitates understanding the production, interpretation, and sequencing of utterances in the event. Although they analyze five episodes occurring during the first fifteen minutes of the interview and address a limited number of actions, e.g., requests, challenges, etc., they provide a close analysis of both the actions performed by speakers through their utterances—"what is said" and "what is done"—and the linguistic structures that govern language use. In so doing, they highlight some of the devices speakers use to cope with one another, some of the rules of interpretation and production, and they address as well the ways both are influenced by the character of the psychiatric event.

Although the researchers just discussed take their analyses in different directions, they both take linguistic performance in therapeutic settings as the topic of their inquiry. Shuy describes medical discourse, highlights the linguistic variation between the language used in everyday situations and in medical settings, and discusses how these differences interfere with successful communication. The global picture he provides contrasts with the more detailed description provided by Labov and Fanshel. Their discussion simultaneously moves to ground the analysis in two directions. First, they specify how speakers use language and then they go underneath this use to expand on the cognitive assumptions used to make sense out of the interactions. In each case, language provides the data, and context, while important, is an analytic resource.

Recent Sociological Work: Conversational and Discourse Analyses

Conversational and discourse analysts, like the philosophers of ordinary language, focus on the interactional/communicational "work" done by participants to accomplish reality. However, rather than concentrating on the abstract, context-free theoretical approach of the philosophers of ordinary language, they, like sociolinguists, extend the unit of analysis beyond the sentence used by Chomsky and the theoretical linguists, to study naturally occurring talk. Just as sociolinguists grapple with the analytic status of context and divide on the issue of structure and function, so too do these analysts.

The Local Production: An Analysis Focused on Language

For the more structural sociolinguists, the central concern is with linguistic rules, and context is an analytic resource. Conversational analysts (Sacks, Schegloff, and Jefferson 1974; Sacks 1968, 1966; Schegloff 1968) also examine the structure of talk. They explore the ways speakers select utterances and locate the sequential structure of ordinary conversation in "adjacency pairs"—conversational forms that are related to one another and usually occur side by side. These forms are structured by a reciprocal relationship, which converts separate speech acts into unfolding social acts requiring cooperative participation. Given the first pair-part of an adjacency sequence, the second part is linked to it. The first statement sets the stage for the second, and the second reaffirms the meaning of the first. For example, if a question is the first pair-part, the expected second is an answer. If an answer is not forthcoming, its absence is noticeable. The first pair-part then sets the stage for the second, and the second retrospectively establishes the appropriateness of the first.

The recognition of this relationship as a reflexive one changes the definition of communication. Rather than being seen as the transmission and reception of distinct acts (the speech acts of the philosophers of ordinary language), communication becomes a social act, accomplished as speaker and hearer cooperatively interact. Yet, as with the more structural sociolinguists, the central concern of conversational analysts is the local production of structures—greeting pairs, summons and response pairs, question and answer pairs, as well as other conversational structures like interruptions and overlapping speech.

Perhaps another example drawn from work done in medicine would be clarifying. Conversational analyses of discourse during medical interviews demonstrate that while it is not necessary or usual in casual conversation for one party to do most of the questioning and the other most of the answering, this is indeed the characteristic form of most medical interviews. Frankel (forthcoming), in analyzing 3,517 utterances collected during medical interviews, claims that there is a general "dispreference" for patient-initiated questions. Not only do doctors ask most of the questions, but as West (1983) points out, they also frequently interrupt while patients are speaking. This practice, she reports, is especially common with male physicians, but less common when the "doctor is a lady" (West, 1984). The close scrutiny given to the dynamics of actual exchanges between participants during medical interviews begins to document the ways context is enacted in the doctor-patient relationship. Yet, since the focus is on the local production of discourse structures—questions and answers—the relationship between context and discourse is not well specified. Discourse is the research topic and context is an analytic resource.

The Situated Production: A Reflexive Analysis
Focused on Language and Context

Discourse analysts, like the more functional sociolinguists, examine "the organization of verbal means and the ends they serve" (Hymes 1974, 8). They take as their central concern the situated production of both the forms and functions of discourse. While for conversational analysts the focus is on the local production of discourse, for discourse analyses, the focus shifts to how this local production is influenced by its placement in an institutional order. They extend the unit of analysis beyond the adjacency pairs located by conversational analysts to explore the social organization of events such as classroom lessons and medical interviews (see for example, Cosaro 1985; Todd 1983a; Mehan 1979; Fisher 1979; Griffin and Humphrey 1978). By so doing, language and context are accorded equal status in a reflexive analysis.

Again, examples are clarifying. Discourse analysts have identified two levels of organization—one sequential and the other hierarchical. Mehan (1979) reports that the basic sequential unit of discourse during classroom lessons is a three-part sequence.

While conversational analysts do not draw out the relationship between linguistic structures and the institutional function they serve, Frankel (1984) confirms the occurrence of a third pair-part. In analyzing the first three to five minutes of medical ambulatory care encounters, he finds this pair-part to be marked by the virtual nonexistence of assessment or value statements. The third pair-part, he claims, functions to invite the speaker to continue, to legitimize the information the patient presents, as well as to downgrade and reformulate the patient's concern. He posits a rule to account for this lack of evaluations: "When necessary accept and extend patients' responses, but do not evaluate them."

Frankel's findings are consistent with Mehan's in two ways. The presence of the third pair-part indicates that the reflexive relationship among utterances is not limited to two utterances that are next to each other. Second, while this is not specifically addressed by Frankel, the lack of assessment or value statements during the first three to five minutes of a medical interview is consistent with Mehan's findings. Mehan describes classroom lessons as organized hierarchically. They have a layered phase structure organized into opening, instructional, and closing phases, each with characteristic sequences that perform distinctive functions. For instance, directive and informative sequences contribute to opening and closing phases, while elicitation sequences compose the instructional phase. Given this organization, we would not expect value statements to occur most often during the opening phase. Consistent with this expectation, Frankel did not find evaluations in medical discourse during what could be characterized as the opening phase.

We would not expect to find evaluations in medical interviews for another reason as well. Medical interviews occur in a different context than classroom lessons. In classrooms, teachers are concerned with controlling students' behavior and motivating them to learn (Mehan 1979; Eder 1981). In examining rooms, doctors are concerned with making a diagnosis and reaching a treatment decision. These concerns are evidenced in the forms of the discourse and in the ways they function to accomplish educational and medical tasks. This point is highlighted in the preceding chapters, where I found many similarities and differences—similarities and differences arising out of setting and task, which were reflected in the structure of the discourse and the interactional work of the participants.

Work in medical and educational fields suggests that language use is both a local and a situated production. Participants in concert produce discourse structures (forms) and interact in meaningful ways to accomplish tasks (functions). However, this work also highlights how language use is situated in an institutional setting, which structures the discourse, influences the flow of information, and has consequences for educational and medical outcomes. The relationship between discourse and context emerges most clearly in comparisons: casual conversations with institutional discourse, and across institutional contexts. Such comparisons reveal that while casual conversation is relatively symmetrical, institutional discourse is more asymmetrical. This discourse, at least in part, reflects and reveals the authority the institution lends its dominant actors.

Notes

1. Whisper, Whisper, Whisper

1. The American Cancer Society establishes criteria for those who need to have Pap smears and how often they are needed. In a potentially high-risk population of women, Pap smears are recommended at least once a year.

2. Pap smears take a sampling of cells from the cervix to provide information about abnormal cell changes. (See chapter 2 for a more complete description.)

3. I am not the only one to make this observation. For example, in an article on paternalism in the delivery of health care, Graber (1978) observed that while there are social and legal strictures preserving patients' rights, some health care providers view them as "excessive and arbitrary barriers to their legitimate rights, legitimate exercise of paternalism" (238–239). He goes on to point out that sometimes the restrictions are ignored, sometimes they are honored begrudgingly, and sometimes they are followed minimally, usually out of the fear of legal reprisal. The arguments that flow from these observations do not question whether doctors act paternalistically—do something for or to patients without their fully informed and voluntary consent (Graber's definition). Rather they question whether paternalism is ever justified (Beauchamp and Childress 1980; Graber 1978). Whether paternalism is central to the doctor's ability to deliver health care—the ability to act beneficently in the interests of the patient (Thomasma 1983) and/or whether patient autonomy (patients acting in their own interests based on full medical disclosure and voluntary participation) is consistent with the cognitive, social, and psychological constraints imposed by illness (Ackerman 1982; Pellegrino 1979; Cassell 1976).

While these issues have been raised by philosophers during discussions of medical ethics, similar issues have been addressed by sociologists. Those critical of the institutional authority of the doctor's role (their paternalism) argue that the superior knowledge of physicians combined with the institutional arrangements of the profession of medicine, the influence of the corporate medical establishment, and state support provide power for physicians while placing patients at a disadvantage (Navarro 1976; Waitzkin and Waterman 1974; Ehrenreich and Ehrenreich 1970). There are other sociologists who support the status quo both in society and in the practice of medicine. Parsons (1951) typifies this uncritical approach. For him the interests of doctor, patient, and society are adequately served in current health care arrangements. The sick role entails an obligation on the part of the patient to seek technically competent medical help, to cooperate in trying to get well, and to trust the beneficence of the physician—he/she will act in your best interest. Doctors serve the interests of both patients and society by legitimizing and controlling illness. These observations of philosophers and sociologists are once removed from the beliefs of doctors and patients and the medical practices that flow from them. Doctors argue, and clinical observations support, that many patients rely on the medical use of paternalism. Patients defer to the physician's superior education and social status—the authority of his/her medical role—and act as if they expect the physician to take responsibility for them. This should not be surprising. The perception that the doctor knows best and will act in the patient's best interest is a socially acquired, taken-for-granted feature of our common stock of knowledge.

4. The technological explosion is quickly taking the pain out of this kind of analysis. While I had to identify patterns by reading and rereading thousands of pages of manuscripts and analyze by choosing prototypical instances to discuss, microcomputers are making it possible to type the transcripts, code the patterns, and quickly recall all instances of a particular pattern. The programs to do this are not yet sufficiently sophisticated to handle the kind of analysis done in this book, but that day is not far away. I anticipate having such a program for my next research project.

5. Just as the technology was not advanced enough to computerize the analysis of the data I did, the technology was not available to do a systematic analysis of the non-verbal aspects of communication. Although it is possible to outfit an examining room with two cameras and to position them so that they capture the non-verbal behavior of both doctors and patients, I was lucky to have video equipment in the examining room at all. It was focused on the examining table and could not be manipulated from outside of the examining room. When doctor and

patient were seated to discuss the medical problem and take a history they were sometimes on camera and sometimes not; when the patient was on the examining table, she faced the camera; the doctor's back was to the camera. So that while non-verbal aspects of the interaction contributed to the stock of knowledge with which I analyzed the data, technological limitations made a systematic analysis of these factors impossible.

2. No More Uterus, No More Babies

1. This is the inductive process characterized by Glaser and Strauss (1967) as "grounded theory." I entered the setting with some preconceptions, but without a firm hypothesis. I used these preconceptions as "sensitizing concepts" as I began to gather the data. Grounded theory is sufficiently open-ended so that along with the discovery process I could reformulate initial preconceptions and develop substantive theory to account for my findings.

2. The sample population in this study only includes women to age forty-four. Yet, the population most at risk from cervical cancer are women in the fourth and fifth decades of life.

3. While this is one of the textbooks used most prevalently in medical education and resident training, there are many who would disagree with the conclusion that there are no drastic results following the removal of the uterus. Is death not a risk worth mentioning? Citing an article in the New York *Times,* Scully (1980) reports that out of the 787,000 hysterectomies performed in 1975, there were 1,700 deaths. In addition, the morbidity rate is not inconsequential. Complications may occur with a vaginal hysterectomy in up to 25 percent of patients and with an abdominal hysterectomy in up to 50 percent of patients (Thompson and Birch 1981). In addition, Sloan (1978) reviews studies that find increased psychic stress with hysterectomy. While there is fear, ambivalence, and anxiety associated with any surgical procedure, the number of postoperative psychiatric hospital admissions for hysterectomy patients is double that of any other surgery. He cites another study that finds an increase in menopausal symptoms—hot flashes, depression— in patients whose ovaries were preserved; then moves on to discuss other problems. A loss in sexual desire and function is found to be associated with the loss of an intact self. He argues that menstruation is a

visible means of identifying one's self as female. It signals the potential to bear children, even to women who want no (or no more) children. Finally, a hysterectomy is an irreversible procedure. He concludes that "drastic" is not a benign description of the potential consequences of hysterectomy.

4. In this discussion, competence is not intended to index the patient's overall ability, but rather to indicate the more specific ability of the patient to show herself as appropriate (able to understand the medical information and to use the technology, e.g., birth control pills, at her disposal) within the doctor's medical framework.

5. At the time I did my research, the faculty clinic was staffed by two oncologists, Doctors M. and Q. Although I observed both doctors interacting with patients, I only discuss Doctor M's interactions. There are several reasons for this. I was interested in following patients from their initial visits through the diagnostic/treatment process and I was not interested in patients who had invasive disease. As the senior physician, Doctor Q. accepted fewer, more advanced cases and saw many more continuing cases with invasive, life-threatening cancer. Dr. M., who by contrast was just establishing his reputation and building his practice, accepted many new patients, most of whom did not have life-threatening disease. The fact that I only talk about Dr. M's interactions is a reflection of their different patient loads rather than differences in the communicational patterns I observed. As Cicourel (1983) points out, in analyzing one of my tapes in which Dr. Q. is interacting with a patient, a common consequence of asymmetrical communicative power is that it shapes the discourse and influences medical outcomes.

3. What Brings You in Today?

1. Doctors also need medical information about the location and extent of the lesion, which they acquire on physical examination.

2. I use the male pronoun throughout this chapter intentionally. Doctors in the United States are predominantly male and this is even more true in the specialty of Obstetrics and Gynecology. The doctors and residents in this study were not an exception to this rule.

3. Dysplasia is a change in the cellular structure in the transformation zone of the cervix. These changes are believed to be precursors to the development of cervical cancer.

4. Reproductive capacities are differentially protected. They are protected for those women who are of childbearing age and who want or are seen to deserve more children.

5. Another kind of occasioned talk that did not occur in this transcript but does occur in others is a discussion of the patient's ability to pay for the medical care under consideration. In most cases the information about the patient's ability to pay is coded onto an information sheet on the patient's chart. The receptionist gets this information from all new women patients and records it on the chart. However, if the chart indicates that patients have no insurance or that they are not eligible for public funds, then doctors and patients engage in "ability to pay talk," which establishes how medical care will be paid for and in some cases which treatment, if any, will be provided.

6. Cancer and option talk are established in initiations that provide information. By contrast, reproduction and morality talk are established in initiations that request information, and general information talk can be established in either.

7. I am indebted to Candace West and her in-depth understanding of the Sacks, Schegloff and Jefferson mode of conversational analysis for her observation that the patient's "uhm" could be a turn-holder, allowing the user a brief interval in which to figure out what could be used to fill the turn space.

8. The doctor marked the noticeable absence of the patient's response by beginning a new initiation. This was the only initiation act not followed by a response act in this transcript.

9. In the hall before examining the patient the doctor described her as a cry-baby. He intimated that if she is old enough to get herself into such predicaments, she should be responsible enough to accept the consequences.

10. I am indebted to Peg Griffin for the view of "keeper of the moral order talk" as occasioned by the inappropriate cancer talk of the patient. She suggested that "keeper of the moral order talk" repaired the breach.

4. And Another Time, Dear, We'll Need to Do A Pap Smear

1. Because the region is characterized by a low utilization of medical services, each patient visit is important. If women do not receive

Pap smears on such visits, studies (Burns *et al.* 1968; Kegeles 1967) have shown that they are not likely to return for tests or for other preventive procedures.

2. The federal government's definition of a "medically underserved area" is based on several criteria, including the number of non-federal physicians per 100,000 population, the number of primary physicians per 100,000 population, the number of specialists per 100,000 population, and the number of hospital beds per 100,000 population.

3. By August 31, 1982, the family practice program described in this study had produced forty-six graduates. Forty of the doctors are currently practicing in the state where the program is located. Three are elsewhere in the Appalachian region and three are in rural areas outside the region.

4. While this criterion was not applied evenly by the residents in the study, "need" is, or should be, a medical criterion. The American Cancer Society establishes criteria for who needs to have Pap smears and how often they are needed. In a potentially high-risk population of women, like the Appalachian population, Pap smears are recommended at least once a year. In addition, Pap smears in this setting are "needed" medically as a routine feature of prenatal care and to accompany the prescription of birth control pills (see also Virginia Health Bulletin 1977).

5. As the data are unfolded, this point becomes clearer. A decision to have a patient undress can be made in the opening phase of the medical interview on the basis of the presenting complaint. For example, if a patient comes to the clinic with the presenting complaint of a vaginal infection, getting undressed is essential for diagnosis and treatment. If the presenting complaint is an ear ache, undressing is not essential to manage the presenting complaint. Decisions to have patients undress can also be reached during the medical history phases of the interview. Suppose that during this phase the patient who came to the clinic with the presenting complaint of an ear ache discloses that she also has irregular vaginal bleeding. While it is unnecessary to have the patient undress to manage her original presenting complaint, to deal effectively with the complaint that has emerged during the medical history the doctor needs to have her undress. Decisions to have patients undress during the opening or medical history phases of their interviews allow a later decision during the physical examination to conduct a Pap smear. Once a physical examination has begun on a dressed patient, undressing no

longer appears to be an option, and the opportunity to do a Pap smear is lost. While it is logically possible for patients to undress during any phase of the medical interview, the data suggest that decisions to have patients undress or remain dressed are made early in the medical interview and, at least to some extent, structure the medical care that follows.

6. This finding is significant. The number of patients discussed in this paper is small—forty-three doctor-patient interactions captured on audio and video tape and transcribed for analysis. However, for over a year the files of a much larger sample of patients were followed (see Fisher and Page 1984). For a year from their first visit to the clinic, or until three consecutive office visits had been completed or a Pap smear conducted, the files of all new women patients were monitored. Findings from this larger sample support the argument presented in this paper—Pap smears should be conducted as a routine feature of medical examinations. On the first office visit, out of 253 patients, 77 (30.4 percent) received a Pap smear and 176 (69.6 percent) did not. Of the 176 women who did not receive Pap smears, 72 (40.9 percent) were lost to follow-up—they did not return to the clinic for the duration of the study. On the second office visit, out of 104 patients, 20 (19.2 percent) received a Pap smear and 84 (80.8 percent) did not. Of the 84 women who did not receive Pap smears, 33 (39.3 percent) were lost to follow-up. On the third office visit, out of 51 patients, 4 (7.8 percent) received a Pap smear and 47 (92.2 percent) did not. While the argument can be made that not all of the women who came to the clinic were in need of Pap smears, the findings are still dramatic. Studies have shown that routine Pap smears increase early case findings and decrease mortality (Boyes *et al.* 1977). The patients who come to this clinic are from a geographic region of the country that has the highest mortality rate from cervical cancer, yet in a population of new women patients followed for three office visits in family practice settings, only 101 (39.9 percent) of the patients received Pap smears, while 152 (60.1 percent) did not.

7. Studies have disclosed that one of the most important factors influencing patients to have Pap smears is the physician (McCurtis 1979). Given the importance of the physician's role in conducting Pap smears, it seems reasonable to conclude that at least part of the reason Pap smears are not performed routinely in the population of patients studied is the

doctor's attitude toward them. As we have seen, when doctors decide a Pap smear is necessary, a Pap smear is usually performed. One manifestation of doctors' lack of commitment to routine Pap smears is evidenced in the record-keeping activities of the residents in this study. Pap smears when performed were entered on the patient's chart. However, when Pap smears had been discussed and found to be needed, no notation was made in the chart. Similarly, when Pap smears were discussed and found not to be needed (the patient had recently had one or had an outside specialist who routinely performed them) no notation was made in the chart. So taken for granted was this practice that when supervising medical staff conducted chart reviews, the absence of information on Pap smear histories was not noted.

8. The authority of his role is quite evident while telling her this. If she is uncomfortable, he will *let* her go to someone else for her Pap smear. While only those with power can *let* others make their own decisions, there are interesting differences. When parents let children make their own decisions, the assumption is that children are developing the competencies to assume responsibility for themselves. These patients were not children, yet they were treated as if they were children who had not developed the competency to assume responsibility for themselves. For a doctor to tell a patient that he will let her make a decision about her own health care is to assume that the patient, even if provided with the necessary information, could not make a responsible decision for herself.

9. I am indebted to Rosemary Taylor for the title of this section as well as for the seminal insights in her article, "The Politics of Prevention," *Social Policy* 1982 (Summer): 32–41.

5. *Spinning the Contextual Web*

1. The original discussion of macro- and micro-sociologies was written by Alexandra Dundas Todd and myself for the introduction to *Discourse and Institutional Authority,* Sue Fisher and Alexandra Dundas Todd, eds. (New Jersey: Ablex, 1986). It is included here with the permission of both Alexandra and Ablex. I am indebted to them both.

Bibliography

Ackerman, T. F. 1982. "Why Doctors Should Intervene." *The Hastings Center Report* 12, 4 (August): 14–17.

American Cancer Society. 1985. *Cancer Facts and Figures*. New York: American Cancer Society.

Austin, J. L. 1961. *Philosophical Papers*. London: Oxford Press.

Austin, J. L. 1962. *How to Do Things With Words*. Cambridge: Harvard University Press.

Barker-Benfield, G. J. 1976. *The Horrors of the Half-Known Life*. New York: Harper Colophon Books.

Beauchamp, T. and J. F. Childress. 1980. *Principles of Biomedical Ethics*. New York: Oxford University Press.

Bodenheimer, T., *et al.* 1981. "Capitalizing on Illness: The Health Insurance Industry." In *The Sociology of Health and Illness*, edited by P. Conrad and R. Kern, 273–279. New York: St. Martin's Press.

Boyes, D. A. 1972. "Guest Editorial." *Mayo Clinic Proceedings* 47 (August): 533.

Boyes, D. A., T. M. Nichols, A. M. Miller and A. J. Worth. 1977. "Recent Results from the British Columbia Screening Program for Cervical Cancer." *American Journal of Obstetrics and Gynecology* 128:692–693.

Braun, P., and E. Druckman. 1976. "Public Health Rounds at the Harvard School of Public Health." *New England Journal of Medicine* 295, no. 5: 264–268.

Broverman, I. K., *et al.* 1970. "Sex Role Stereotypes and Clinical Judgements of Mental Health." *Journal of Consulting and Clinical Psychology* 34:1–7.

Brown, A. J. 1976. "Awareness and Use of Cervical Cancer Tests in a Southern Appalachian Community." *Public Health Reports* 91, no. 3: 236–242.

Brown, E. R. 1979. *Rockefeller Medicine Men: Medicine and Capi-*

talism in the Progressive Era. Berkeley and Los Angeles: University of California Press.

Bunker, J. 1970. "Surgical Manpower: A Comparison of Operations and Surgeons in the United States and in England and Wales." *New England Journal of Medicine* 282, no. 3: 135–144.

———. 1976. "Elective Hysterectomy: Pro and Con," in "Public Health Rounds at the Harvard School of Public Health," edited by P. Braun and E. Druckman, *New England Journal of Medicine* 295, no. 5: 264–268.

Burns, E. L., *et al.* 1968. "Detections of Uterine Cancer: Results of a Community Program of 17 Years." *Cancer* 22: 1108–1119.

Campbell, M. 1973. *"Why Would a Girl Go Into Medicine?" Medical Education in the United States: A Guide For Women.* Old Westbury, N.Y.: The Feminist Press.

Caress, B. 1977. "Womb-boom." *Health/Pac Bulletin,* reprint, July/August.

Cassell, E. 1976. *The Healer's Art.* New York: Lippincott. Center for Disease Control. 1981. "Hysterectomy in Women Aged 15–44, United States, 1970–1978." *Morbidity and Mortality Weekly Report* 30, no. 15: 173–176.

Chesler, P. 1972. *Women and Madness.* Garden City, N.Y.: Doubleday.

Chodorow, N. 1978. *The Reproduction of Mothering: Psychoanalysis and the Sociology of Gender.* Berkeley and Los Angeles: University of California Press.

Chomsky, N. 1965. *Aspects of the Theory of Syntax.* Cambridge: MIT Press.

Christopherson, W. M., *et al.* 1970. "Cervix Cancer Control in Louisville, Kentucky." *Cancer* 26:29–38.

Cicourel, A. V. 1964. *Method and Measurement in Sociology.* New York: The Free Press.

———. 1970. "The Acquisition of Social Structure: Toward a Developmental Sociology of Language and Meaning." In *Understanding Everyday Life,* edited by J. D. Douglas, 136–168. Chicago: Aldine Publishing Co.

———. 1973. *Cognitive Sociology: Language and Meaning in Social Interaction.* London: Macmillan.

———. 1975. "Discourse and Text: Cognitive and Linguistic Processes in Studies of Social Structure." *Versus Quaderni di Studi Semiotica* (Sept.–Dec.): 33–84.

————. 1981. "Notes on the Integration of Micro- and Macro-Levels of Analysis." In *Advances in Social Theory and Methodology: Toward an Integration of Micro- and Macro-Sociologies*, edited by K. Knorr-Cetina and A. V. Cicourel, 51–80. Boston: Routledge and Kegan Paul.

————. 1983. "Language and the Structure of Belief in Medical Communication." In *The Social Organization of Doctor-Patient Communication*, edited by S. Fisher and A. D. Todd, 221–240. Washington, D.C.: The Center for Applied Linguistics and Harcourt Brace Jovanovich.

Collins, R. 1981. "Micro-Translation as a Theory-Building Strategy." In *Advances in Social Theory and Methodology: Toward an Integration of Micro- and Macro-Sociologies*, edited by K. Knorr-Cetina and A. V. Cicourel, 81–108. Boston: Routledge and Kegan Paul.

Conrad, P., and R. Kern, eds. 1981. *The Sociology of Health and Illness: Critical Perspectives*. New York: St. Martin's Press.

Cosaro, W. 1985. *Friendship and Peer Culture*. Norwood, N.J.: Ablex.

Cramer, D. W. 1974. "The Role of Cervical Cytology in the Declining Morbidity and Mortality of Cervical Cancer." *Cancer* 34: 2018–2027.

Creasman, W. T., M.D., and D. L. Clarke-Pearson, M.D. 1983. "Abnormal Cervical Cytology: Spotting It, Treating It." *Contemporary OB/GYN* 27 (June): 53–76.

Daly, M. 1978. *Gyn/Ecology*. Boston: Beacon Press.

Demarest, C. B. 1985. "Getting the Most From the Pap Smear." In *Patient Care* (February).

Dentzer, S., *et al.* 1983. "The Big Business of Medicine." *Newsweek* 102: 62–66.

Dicker, R. D., M.D., *et al.* 1982. "Hysterectomy Among Women of Reproductive Age. Trends in the United States, 1970–1978." *Journal of The American Medical Association* 248, no. 3: 323–327.

Dickinson, L., *et al.* 1972. "Evaluation of the Effectiveness of Cytologic Screening for Cervical Cancer." *Mayo Clinic Proceedings* 47 (Aug.): 534–544.

Dinnerstein, D. 1976. *The Mermaid and the Minotaur: Sexual Arrangements and the Human Malaise*. New York: Harper & Row.

Donovan, P. 1983. "Medical Societies vs. Nurse Practitioners." *Family Planning Perspectives* 15, no. 4: 166–171.

Duncan, S., Jr. 1972. "Some Signals and Rules for Taking Speaking Turns in Conversation." *Journal of Personality and Social Psychology* 23: 283–292.

Duster, T. 1981. "Intermediate Steps Between Micro- and Macro-Integration: the Case of Screening for Inherited Disorders." In *Advances In Social Theory and Methodology: Toward An Integration of Micro- and Macro-Sociologies* edited by K. Knorr-Cetina and A. V. Cicourel, 109–135. Boston: Routledge and Kegan Paul.

Eakins, B. W., and R. G. Eakins. 1978. *Sex Differences in Human Communication*. Boston: Houghton Mifflin Co.

Eder, D. 1981. "Ability Grouping as a Self-Fulfilling Prophesy: A Micro-Analysis of Teacher-Student Interaction, 3." *Sociology of Education* 54:151–162.

Ehrenreich, B., and J. Ehrenreich. 1970. *The American Health Empire*. A Health-Pac Book. New York: Vintage Books.

Ehrenreich, B., and D. English. 1979. *For Her Own Good*. Garden City, N.Y.: Anchor Press/Doubleday.

Emerson, J. 1970. "Behavior in Private Places: Sustaining Definitions of Reality in Gynecological Examinations." In *Recent Sociology No. 2* edited by H. P. Dreitzel, 73–113. London: Macmillan and Co.

Epstein, S. 1979. *The Politics of Cancer*. Garden City, N.Y.: Anchor Books.

Fee, E. 1983. *Women and Health: The Politics of Sex in Medicine*. Farmingdale: Baywood Publishing Company.

Fisher S. 1979. "The Negotiation of Treatment Decisions in Doctor/Patient Communications and Their Impact on Identity on Women Patients." Ph.D. diss., University of California, San Diego.

———. 1984. "Institutional Authority and the Structure of Discourse." *Discourse Processes* 7:201–224.

Fisher, S., and S. B. Groce. 1983. "Doctor-Patient Negotiation of Cultural Assumptions." Paper presented at Southern Sociological Society, Atlanta, Georgia.

Fisher, S., and A. Page. 1984. "Women and Preventative Health Care: An Exploratory Study of the Use of Pap Smears in a Potentially High-Risk Applachian Population." Paper presented at Southern Sociological Association, Knoxville, Tennessee.

Fisher, S., and A. Todd, eds. 1983. "Friendly Persuasion: The Negotiation of Decisions to Use Oral Contraceptions." Paper presented at the American Sociological Association, Detroit, Michigan.

Fisher, S., and A. D. Todd. 1986. "Communication in Institutional Contexts: Social Interaction and Social Structure." In *Discourse and Institutional Authority: Medicine, Education and Law,* edited by S. Fisher and A. D. Todd, Norwood, N.J.: Ablex.

Flannery, M. A. 1982. "Primary Care in Rural Appalachia: Simple Living and Hard Choices." *The Hastings Center Report* (August): 9–12.

Foltz, A., and J. Kelsey. 1978. "The Annual Pap Test: A Dubious Policy Success." *Milbank Memorial Fund Quarterly/Health and Society* 56, no. 4: 426–462.

Forester, J. 1981. "Critical Theory and Organizational Analysis." *Working Papers in Planning. Department of City and Regional Planning in Conjunction with the Program in Urban and Regional Studies.* Ithaca, N.Y.: Cornell University.

Fowinkle, E. 1975. *Health in Tennessee—A Statistical Overview,* 2nd ed. Nashville: Office of Comprehensive Health Planning (July): 93–96.

Frankel, R. M. 1984. "From Sentence to Sequence: Understanding the Medical Encounter Through Micro-Interactional Analysis." *Discourse Processes* 7, no. 2: 135–170.

Frankel, R. Forthcoming. "Talking in Interviews: A Dispreference for Patient Initiated Questions in Physician-Patient Encounters." In *Interactional Competence,* edited by G. Psathas, G. Coulter, and R. Frankel. Norwood, N.J.: Ablex.

Freeland, M. S., and C. E. Schendler. 1981. "National Health Expenditures: Short-term Outlook and Long-term Projections." *Health Care Financing Review* 2 (Winter): 97–126.

Freidson, E. 1970. *Profession of Medicine.* New York: Dodd, Mead.

Freidson, E., and J. Lorber, eds. 1972. *Medical Men and Their Work.* Chicago: Aldine Publishing Co.

Fruchter, G., *et al.* 1980. "Missed Opportunities for Early Diagnosis of Cancer of the Cervix." *American Journal of Public Health* 70: 418–420.

Garfinkel, H. 1967. *Studies in Ethnomethodology.* New Jersey: Prentice-Hall.

Giddens, A. 1981. "Agency, Institution and Time-Space Analysis." In *Advances In Social Theory and Methodology: Toward an Integration of Micro- and Macro-Sociologies,* edited by K. Knorr-Cetina and A. V. Cicourel, 161–174. Boston: Routledge and Kegan Paul.

Giglioli, P. P. 1972. *Language and Social Contexts.* Middlesex, England: Penguin Books.

Glaser, B. G., and A. L. Strauss. 1967. *The Discovery of Grounded Theory: Strategies for Qualitative Research.* Chicago: Aldine Publishing Co.

Graber, G. C. 1978. "On Paternalism and Health Care." *Contemporary Issues in Biomedical Ethics,* edited by J. W. Davis, B. Hoffmaster, and S. Shorten, 233–244. Clifton, N.J.: The Humana Press.

Griffin, P., and F. Humphrey. 1978. "Task and Talk." In *Children's Functional Language and Education in the Early Years,* edited by R. Shuy and P. Griffin. Final Report to the Carnegie Corporation of New York. Arlington, Va.: Center for Applied Linguistics.

Habermas, J. 1981. "Toward a Reconstruction of Historical Materialism." In *Advances in Social Theory and Methodology: Toward an Integration of Micro- and Macro-Sociologies,* edited by K. Knorr-Cetina and A. V. Cicourel, 259–276. Boston: Routledge and Kegan Paul.

Handy, V. H., and E. Wieben. 1965. "Detection of Cancer of the Cervix: A Public Health Approach." *Obstetrics and Gynecology* 25: 348–355.

Harre, R. 1981. "Philosophical Aspects of the Micro-Macro Problem." In *Advances in Social Theory and Methodology: Toward an Integration of Micro- and Macro-Sociologies,* edited by K. Knorr-Cetina and A. V. Cicourel, 139–160. Boston: Routledge and Kegan Paul.

Harrison, M., M.D. 1982. *A Woman in Residence.* New York: Random House.

Henley, N. M. 1975. "Power, Sex, and Nonverbal Communication." In

Language and Sex: Difference and Domination, edited by B. Thorne and N. M. Henley, 184–202. Rowley, Mass.: Newbury House Publishers.

———. 1977. *Body Politics: Power, Sex and Nonverbal Communication.* Englewood Cliffs, N.J.: Prentice-Hall.

Hymes, D. 1962. "The Ethnography of Speaking." *Anthropology and Human Behavior.* Washington, D.C.: Anthropological Society of Washington.

———. 1974. *Foundations of Sociolinguistics.* Philadelphia: University of Pennsylvania Press.

Johnson, J. M. 1975. *Doing Field Research.* New York: The Free Press.

Jones, H., and G. Jones. 1981. *Novak's Textbook of Gynecology* (10th ed.) 153–156. Baltimore: Williams and Wilkins.

Journal of Reproductive Medicine. 1982. 27 (June): 102–107.

Kegeles, S. S. 1967. "Attitudes and Behavior of the Public Regarding Cervical Cytology: Current Findings and New Directions for Research." *Journal of Chronic Disease* 20: 911–922.

Keller, E. F. 1985. *Reflections on Science and Gender.* New Haven: Yale University Press.

Kirchner, M. 1983a. "Nice Guys Collect First." *Medical Economics* (May): 24–36.

———. 1983b. "Special Report: How the Health-Cost Backlash is Hurting You." *Medical Economics* (May): 47–52.

Kleinman, J. C. 1979. "Death Rates From Cervical Cancer by Health Service Area, 1968–79." *Statistical Notes for Health Planners.* U.S. Department of Health, Education and Welfare, (August).

Knopf, A. 1976. "Changes in Women's Opinions About Cancer." *Social Science and Medicine* 10: 191–195.

Knorr-Cetina, K. and A. V. Cicourel, eds. 1981. *Advances in Social Theory and Methodology: Toward an Integration of Micro- and Macro-Sociologies.* Boston: Routledge and Kegan Paul.

Knowles, J. H., M.D. 1977a. "Introduction: Doing Better and Feeling Worse: Health Care in the United States." *Daedalus* 106: 1–8.

———. 1977b. "The Responsibility of the Individual." *Daedalus* 106: 57–80.

Krause, E. A. 1977. *Power and Illness.* New York: Elsevier.

Labov, W. 1972. *Sociolinguistic Patterns.* Philadelphia: University of Pennsylvania Press.

Labov, W., and D. Fanshel. 1977. *Therapeutic Discourse: Psychotherapy as Conversation.* New York: Academic Press.

Lakoff, R. 1973. *Language and Woman's Place.* New York: Harper Colophon Books.

Larned, D. 1977. "The Epidemic in Unnecessary Hysterectomy." In *Seizing Our Bodies: The Politics of Women's Health.* Edited by C. Dreifus 195–208. New York: Vintage Books.

Luker, K. 1984. *Abortion and the Politics of Motherhood.* Berkeley and Los Angeles: University of California Press.

Lundin, F. E., Jr., *et al.* 1965. "Morbidity from Cervical Cancer: Effects of Cervical Cytology and Socioeconomic Status." *Journal of the National Cancer Institute* 35: 1015–1025.

Magee, J. 1975. "The Pelvic Examination: A View from the Other End of the Table." *Annals of Internal Medicine* 83: 563–564.

Marshall, C. E. 1965. "Effect of Cytologic Screening on the Incidence of Invasive Carcinoma of the Cervix in a Semi-Closed Community." *Cancer* 18: 153–156.

Marx, J. L. 1979. "The Annual Pap Smear: An Idea Whose Time Has Gone?" *Science* 205: 177–178.

Mason, T. J., and F. W. McKay. 1969. *U.S. Cancer Mortality by County, 1950–1969.* Department of Health, Education and Welfare Publication No. NI–74–615. Washington, D.C.: U.S. Government Printing Office.

McCall, G. J., and J. L. Simmons. 1969. *Issues in Participant Observation: A Text and Reader.* Reading, Mass.: Addison-Wesley.

McCurtis, J. W. 1979. "Social Contact Factors in the Diffusion of Cervical Cytology Among Mexican-Americans in Los Angeles County, California." *Social Science and Medicine* 13A: 807–811.

McKeown, T. 1976. *The Role of Medicine: Dream, Mirage, or Nemesis?* London: Nuffield Provincial Hospitals Trust.

Mechanic, D. 1968. *Medical Sociology.* New York: Free Press.

Mehan, H. 1979. *Learning Lessons, Social Organization in the Classroom.* Cambridge: Harvard University Press.

———. 1983. "The Role of Language and the Language of Role in Institutional Decision-Making." *Language In Society* 12: 187–211.

Mehan, H., and H. Wood. 1975. *The Reality of Ethnomethodology.* New York: John Wiley.

Mitchell, J. 1974. *Psychoanalysis and Feminism.* New York: Pantheon.

Murphy, K. 1983. "Who's Fueling the Flames of Rising Health Costs?" *Private Practice* (May): 15–20.

Navarro, V. 1976. *Medicine Under Capitalism.* New York: Prodist.

———. 1981. "The Influence of Social Class Structure on the American Health Sector." *The Sociology of Health and Illness,* edited by P. Conrad and R. Kern, 233–243. New York: St. Martin's Press.

Novak, E. R., *et al.* 1970. *Novak's Textbook of Gynecology,* (8th ed.). Baltimore: Williams and Wilkins.

———. 1975. *Novak's Textbook of Gynecology,* (9th ed.). Baltimore: Williams and Wilkins.

OB, GYN News 1983a. "Ca Screen Efficacy Varies by Lesion Sight." *OB, GYN News* 18 (15–31 May): 20.

OB, GYN News 1983b. "Routine Pap Advised Regardless of Patients' Presenting Complaints." *OB, GYN News* 17 (15–31 Oct.): 51.

OB, GYN News 1983c. "Declining Economic Prospects Increasing Physicians Stress." *OB, GYN News* 18 (15–30 Nov.): 9.

Parsons, T. 1951. *The Social System.* New York: Free Press.

Pellegrino, E. 1979. "Toward a Reconstruction of Medical Morality: The Primacy of the Art of Profession and the Fact of Illness." *The Journal of Medicine and Philosophy* 4: 44–45.

Pogrebin, L. C. 1983. *Family Politics.* New York: McGraw-Hill Book Company.

Prather, J., and L. Fidell. 1975. "Sex Differences in the Content and Style of Medical Advertisements." *Social Science and Medicine* 9: 23–26.

Richardson, L. W. 1981. *The Dynamics of Sex and Gender.* Boston: Houghton Mifflin Company.

Richart, R. M. 1980. "Current Concepts in Obstetrics and Gynecology: The Patient With an Abnormal Pap Smear—Screening Techniques and Management." *The New England Journal of Medicine* 302: 332–334.

Riessman, C. K. 1983. "Women and Medicalization." *Social Policy* 14: 3–18.

Robb, D. M. 1951. *The Harper History of Painting.* New York: Harper and Brothers.

Rothman, B. K. 1982. *In Labor: Women and Power in The Birth Place.* New York: W. W. Norton and Company.

Ruzek, S. B. 1978. *The Women's Health Movement.* New York: Praeger.

Sacks, H. 1966. "The Search for Help: No One to Turn To." Ph.D. Diss., University of California, Berkeley.

———. 1968. Unpublished lectures at the University of California, Los Angeles, and University of California, Irvine.

Sacks, H., E. Schegloff, and G. Jefferson. 1974. "A Simplist Systematics for the Organization of Turn-Taking in Conversation." *Language* 50: 696–735.

Sall, S., *et al.* 1968. "Impact of a Cytologic Screening Program on a Gynecologic Malignancy Service." *Cancer* 22: 1120–1125.

Schegloff, E. 1968. "Sequencing in Conversational Openings." *American Anthropologist* 70: 1075–1095.

Schegloff, E., and H. Sacks. 1973. "Openings Up Closings." *Semiotica* 8: 289–327.

Schiefelbein, S. 1980. "The Female Patient: Heeded? Hustled? Healed?" *Saturday Review* 7: 12–16.

Schutz, A. 1962. *Collected Papers I: The Problem of Social Reality.* The Hague: Martinus Nijhoff.

Schwartz, H., and J. Jacobs. 1979. *Qualitative Sociology: A Method to the Madness.* New York: The Free Press.

Scully, D. 1980. *Men Who Control Women's Health.* Boston: Houghton Mifflin.

Scully, D., and P. Bart. 1973. "A Funny Thing Happened On the Way to the Orifice: Women in Gynecological Textbooks." *American Journal of Sociology* 78: 1045–1050.

Searle, J. 1969. *Speech Acts.* London: Cambridge University Press.

Shulman, J., *et al.* 1974. "The Papanicolaou Smear: An Insensitive Case-Finding Procedure." *American Journal of Obstetrics and Gynecology* 120: 446–451.

Shuy, R. W. 1970. "Teacher Training and Urban Language Problems." In *Teaching Standard English in the Inner City,* edited by R. W. Fasold and R. W. Shuy, 120–139. Arlington, Va.: Center for Applied Linguistics.

———. 1976. "The Medical Interview: Problems in Communication." *Primary Care* 3 (September): 3.

———. 1983. "Three Types of Interference to an Effective Exchange of Information in the Medical Interview." *The Social Organization of Doctor-Patient Communication,* edited by S. Fisher and

A. D. Todd, 189–202. Washington, D.C.: Center for Applied Linguistics.

Sidel, V. W., and R. Sidel. 1981. "Health Care and Medical Care in the United States." In *The Sociology of Health and Illness,* edited by P. Conrad and R. Kern, 203–220. New York: St. Martin's Press.

Sloan, D. 1978. "The Emotional and Psychosexual Aspects of Hysterectomy." *The American Journal of Obstetrics and Gynecology* 131 (July): 598–605.

Spletter, M. 1983. "How Important Is a Pap Test?" *Parade Magazine* (4 Sept.): 10.

Starr, P. 1982. *The Social Transformation of American Medicine.* New York: Basic Books.

Stevens, R. 1966. *Medical Practice in Modern England: The Impact of Specialization and State Medicine.* New Haven: Yale University Press.

Strelnick, H. 1980. "Bakke-ing Up the Wrong Tree." *Health/PAC Bulletin* 11: 3.

Strong, P. M. 1979. *The Ceremonial Order of the Clinic.* London: Routledge and Kegan Paul.

Susser, M. 1980. "Prevention and Cost Containment." *Bulletin New York Academy of Medicine* 56: 45–52.

Taylor, R. C. R. 1982. "The Politics of Prevention." *Social Policy* (Summer): 32–41.

Terris, M., M.D. 1980. "Preventative Services and Medical Care: The Costs and Benefits of Basic Change." *Bulletin New York Academy of Medicine* 56: 180–189.

Thomasma, D. C. 1983. "Beyond Medical Paternalism and Patient Autonomy: A Model of Physician Conscience for the Physician-Patient Relationship." *Annals of Internal Medicine* 98: 243–248.

Thompson, J. D., M.D., and H. W. Birch, M.D. 1981. "Indications for Hysterectomy." *Clinical Obstetrics and Gynecology* 24: 1245–1258.

Thorne, B., and N. Henley, eds. 1975. *Language and Sex: Difference and Dominance.* Rowley, Mass.: Newbury House.

Timonen, S., *et al.* 1974. "Cervical Screening." *The Lancet* 1 (March): 401–402.

Todd, A. D. 1983a. "A Diagnosis of Doctor-Patient Discourse in the Prescription of Contraception." *The Social Organization of Doctor-Patient Communication,* edited by S. Fisher and A. D. Todd, 159–187. Washington, D.C.: The Center for Applied Linguistics.

Todd, A. D. 1983b. "Women's Bodies as Diseased and Deviant: Historical and Contemporary Issues." 83–95. In *Research in Law Deviance and Social Control.* Edited by S. Spitzer and R. Simon. Greenwich, Ct.: JAI Press.

United States Congress, House Subcommittee on Oversight and Investigations of the Committee on Interstate and Foreign Commerce. 94th Congress, 2nd session, 1976. *Cost and Quality of Health Care: Unnecessary Surgery.*

United States Congress, House Subcommittee on Oversight and Investigations of the Committee on Interstate and Foreign Commerce. 95th Congress, 1st session, 1977. *Quality of Surgical Care: Hearing, April 25, 29, May 2, 9, on Cost and Quality of Health Care,* Serial 95–32.

U.S. Department of Health, Education, and Welfare. 1975. Public Health Service, National Center for Health Statistics. *Characteristics of Females Ever Having a Pap Smear and Interval Since Last Pap Smear, United States, 1973.* Monthly Vital Statistics Report, Health Interview Survey, Provisional Data (HRA) 76–1120, Vol. 24, No. 7 (Suppl., Oct.).

U.S. National Center for Health Statistics. 1970. *Vital and Health Statistics* ser. 2, no. 39. Rockville, Md.: Department of Health, Education, and Welfare Publication.

U.S. National Center for Health Statistics. 1976. "Surgical Operations in Short-stay Hospitals, US, 1973." *Vital and Health Statistics* ser. 13, no. 24. Rockville, Md.: Department of Health, Education, and Welfare Publication.

Virginia Department of Health. 1977. "Uterine Cancer and the Pap Test." *Virginia Health Bulletin* 29, ser. 2, no. 3. Richmond: State Department of Health.

Waitzkin, H. B. 1983. *The Second Sickness: Contradictions of Capitalist Health Care.* New York: The Free Press.

Waitzkin, H. B., and J. D. Stoeckle. 1976. "Information Control and the Micropolitics of Health Care: Summary of an Ongoing Research Project." *Social Science and Medicine* 10: 263–276.

Waitzkin, H. B., and B. Waterman. 1974. *The Exploitation of Illness in Capitalist Society.* Indianapolis: Bobbs-Merrill.

Walton, L. A., *et al.* 1979. "Factors Influencing the Occurence of Advanced Cervical Carcinoma." *Southern Medical Journal* 72: 808–811.

Weaver, J. L., and S. D. Garnet. 1983. "Sexism and Racism in the American Health Care Industry: A Comparative Analysis." In *Women and Health: the Politics of Sex in Medicine,* edited by E. Fee, 79–104. Farmingdale, N.Y.: Baywood Publishing Co.

Wertz, R. W., and D. C. Wertz. 1977. *Lying In: A History of Childbirth in America.* New York: Free Press.

West, C. 1983. "'Ask me no questions . . .' An Analysis of Queries and Replies in Physician-Patient Dialogue." In *The Social Organization of Doctor-Patient Communication,* edited by S. Fisher and A. D. Todd, 75–106. Washington, D.C.: The Center for Applied Linguistics.

————. 1984. *Routine Complications: Troubles With Talk Between Doctors and Patients.* Bloomington: Indiana University Press.

White, K. L. 1975. "Prevention as a National Health Goal." *Preventative Medicine* 4: 247–251.

Wittgenstein, L. 1953. *Philosophical Investigations.* London: Basil, Blackwell & Mott.

Zimmerman, D. H., and M. Pollner. 1970. "The Everyday World as a Phenomenon." In *Understanding Everyday Life,* edited by J. C. Douglas, 80–104. Chicago: Aldine Publishing Co.

Zimmerman, D. H., and C. West. 1975. "Sex Roles, Interruptions, and Silences in Conversation." In *Language and Sex: Difference and Dominance,* edited by B. Thorne and N. Henley, 105–129. Rowley, Mass.: Newbury House.

Zola, I. K. 1972. "Medicine As an Institution of Social Control." *Sociological Review. New Series* 20: 487–504.

Index